PAUL VALÉRY AND THE VOICE OF DESIRE

THE EUROPEAN HUMANITIES RESEARCH CENTRE

UNIVERSITY OF OXFORD

The European Humanities Research Centre of the University of Oxford organizes a range of academic activities, including conferences and workshops, and publishes scholarly works under its own imprint, LEGENDA. Within Oxford, the EHRC bridges, at the research level, the main humanities faculties: Modern Languages, English, Modern History, Literae Humaniores, Music and Theology. The Centre stimulates interdisciplinary research collaboration throughout these subject areas and provides an Oxford base for advanced researchers in the humanities.

The Centre's publications programme focuses on making available the results of advanced research in medieval and modern languages and related interdisciplinary areas. An Editorial Board, whose members are drawn from across the British university system, covers the principal European languages. Titles include works on French, German, Italian, Portuguese, Russian and Spanish literature. In addition, the EHRC co-publishes with the Society for French Studies, the British Comparative Literature Association and the Modern Humanities Research Association. The Centre also publishes *Oxford German Studies* and *Film Studies*, and has launched a Special Lecture Series under the LEGENDA imprint.

Enquiries about the Centre's publishing activities should be addressed to:
Professor Malcolm Bowie, Director

Further information:
Kareni Bannister, Senior Publications Officer
European Humanities Research Centre
University of Oxford
47 Wellington Square, Oxford OX1 2JF
enquiries@ehrc.ox.ac.uk
www.ehrc.ox.ac.uk

LEGENDA

European Humanities Research Centre
University of Oxford

Paul Valéry and the Voice of Desire

KIRSTEEN ANDERSON

LEGENDA

European Humanities Research Centre
University of Oxford
2000

Published by the
European Humanities Research Centre
of the University of Oxford
47 Wellington Square
Oxford OX1 2JF

LEGENDA is the publications imprint of the
European Humanities Research Centre

ISBN 1 900755 40 8

First published 2000

British Library Cataloguing in Publication Data
A CIP catalogue record for this book is available from the British Library

LEGENDA series designed by Cox Design Partnership, Witney, Oxon
Printed in Great Britain by
Information Press
Eynsham
Oxford OX8 1JJ

Copy-Editor: Dr Bonnie Blackburn

CONTENTS

ACKNOWLEDGEMENTS

I should like to thank Christine Crow for her enthusiasm and encouragement at each stage of the writing of this book; Mme Florence de Lussy of the Bibliothèque Nationale in Paris for the kind welcome which she extended to me as a beginner in Valéry studies; my family and friends, particularly Suzy Marshall, for their support and interest; and Catherine Byfield, whose patience, efficiency, and good humour were invaluable in preparing the manuscript for publication. I should like to express my gratitude to the School of Modern Languages, Queen Mary, University of London, for its generous support in funding this publication.

ABBREVIATIONS

Throughout this book, roman capitals followed by arabic numerals refer respectively to volume and page of the facsimile edition of Valéry's *Cahiers*, 29 vols. (Paris: CNRS, 1957–61). For the sake of clarity, I have italicized where Valéry underlines for emphasis in his *Cahiers* entries; double underlines are shown in italic underline.

OI, OII refer to Paul Valéry, *Œuvres*, ed. J. Hytier (Bibliothèque de la Pléiade; Paris: Gallimard, vol. 1, 1975; vol. 2, 1970).

AJFS   *Australian Journal of French Studies*
BEV   *Bulletin des études valéryennes* (Centre d'Etudes Valéryennes, Université Paul Valéry, Montpellier)
CAIEF *Cahiers de l'Association Internationale des Etudes Françaises*
EM   *Entretiens sur Paul Valéry*: Actes du colloque de Montpellier des 16 et 17 oct. 1971: textes recueillis par Daniel Moutote (Paris: Presses Universitaires de France, 1972)
ENC   *Entretiens sur Paul Valéry*: Décades du Centre Culturel International de Cérisy-la-Salle, du 2 au 11 sept. 1965, sous la direction de E. Noulet-Carner (Paris: Mouton, 1968)
FMLS   *Forum for Modern Language Studies*
FS   *French Studies*
MLN   *Modern Language Notes*
MLR   *Modern Languages Review*
PVC   *Paul Valéry contemporain*: colloque organisé en nov. 1971 par le Centre National de la Recherche Scientifique et le Centre de Philologie et de Littératures Romanes de l'Université des Sciences Humaines de Strasbourg: textes rassemblés et présentés par Monique Parent et Jean Levaillant (Paris: Klincksieck, 1974)
RHLF   *Revue d'histoire littéraire de la France*
YFS   *Yale French Studies*

FOR ENID, WHOSE PRESENCE MADE THIS BOOK POSSIBLE

La forme, c'est à dire — la *Voix*,
qui est l'*unité*. (XII. 806)

INTRODUCTION

Peut-être, ce que le travail littéraire ou artistique a de plus remarquable, c'est d'être un travail grandement indéterminé. On est tellement libre que la plus laborieuse partie de la tâche est de se la prescrire telle et telle — de créer le problème bien plus que de le résoudre. (V, 142)

The present study attempts to account for the power and persistence of voice as theme, image, and informing preoccupation throughout much of Paul Valéry's writing career. This complex notion draws on the literal sense of the voice understood physiologically as one of our primary modes of expression, but also embraces figurative or meta-phorical levels of meaning which relate to the imaginative capacity of consciousness. Voice may, indeed, be interpreted as the innermost aspect and fundamental principle of Valéry's creative theory and practice. My focus, then, traces its central and synthesizing function amidst the diffuse, multi-directional energy of a creative output spanning over fifty years. I make no claim to exclusiveness or exhaust-iveness in my exploration of voice: many other fertile directions might have been selected and have already formed the object of valuable studies. Critical approaches focusing on Valéry's activity as a poet continue to investigate his highly distinctive poetic theory and practice in the context of contemporary concerns; linguistic studies situate his sustained analysis of language in the framework of more recent psycholinguistic and sociolinguistic inquiry; a certain interest in the 'psycho-genèse' of his work reads its development in relation to biographical and psychoanalytic hypotheses; the *approche génétique* examines the detail and variations of different stages of manuscript development; socio-cultural and philosophical readings attempt to situate Valéry's *recherche* in the context of his own actuality and of the contemporary moment.[1]

Voice, as such, is never systematically theorized in Valéry's writings. It has a wide range of applications in his work; the common de-nominator in all of these is an acute sensitivity to acoustic phenomena, to the realm of sound. It is a commonplace of Valéry studies to evoke the central role of 'le regard' and the predominance of the visual faculty in his imaginative response. More remains to be said about a correspondingly powerful impetus in his creative consciousness, namely its phonic or acoustic dimension. The tension between auditory and visual responses to, or metaphorizations of, reality lends itself to conceptualization along a number of lines, as I shall indicate in more detail at a later stage. In this context the value of an exploration of voice lies in helping to loosen further certain over-rigid polarizations which, until relatively recently, have tended to characterize approaches to Valéry's work. I see the present study as contributing to an important shift which has become apparent over the last two decades in the field of Valéry criticism: the defensively purist 'intellectual' *persona* so much in evidence in an earlier phase of interpretation has relaxed its hold and allowed the emergence of a 'suffering' Valéry to be acknowledged. Voice gives expression, in some measure, to the more intimate, vulnerable, or secret self. This book has evolved over many years, during which a number of significant works have accorded space and recognition to voice as part of their wider concern.[2] My own account places voice at the centre of the discussion as deserving sustained attention in its own right.

Literature survives precisely because it is capable of an infinity of resurrections through its contact with each new reader. Valéry emphasized, in particular, the value of texts which resist the mind's attempt to understand in the sense of reductively extracting a meaning; 'un grand écrivain, un grand individu', he suggests, 'c'est celui qui vous résiste (en esprit)' (I, 203). My account of voice has matured over a considerable period of time for this very reason: it bears witness to a coming to terms with the essential irreducibility of the creative process. The voice of the desiring intelligence, both captivating and frustrating, expresses the mystery and uniqueness of Valéry's contribution as a writer. A partial explanation of why he appears difficult, resistant to critical theorizing, unpopular in terms of current literary and theoretical vogues may be that his voice is not easy to understand; is even, in a sense, duplicitous. He speaks, whether consciously or unconsciously, with a double tongue: on the one hand as a representative of the currently unfashionable High Modernism, austere and Olympian; yet also as a mere mortal, a man whose life, experience, and own unrelenting self-scrutiny oblige him to confront the *lacunae* and inadequacies which underpin his wisdom. Voice as a thread through the labyrinthine complexities of the creative mind may offer a certain illusory potential as guiding ideal or guarantee of coherence in the fertile flux of artistic process; but I relinquish very willingly any fantasy that the pursuit of its elusive and enchanting trace leads to answers or resolutions. Much more exhilarating is the thought that Valéry continues to excite, intimidate, baffle, and challenge after many years of acquaintanceship. Voice, if it could be pinned down, should in theory provide the key to unlock the mystery that is Valéry, to enable us to find what lies behind a multi-faceted inquiry which functions, perhaps, as a kind of bluff or defence to throw the reader off the trail. Yet the more one pursues voice, the clearer it becomes that what it stands for is a kind of unrepresent-ability, a black hole or vanishing point, site of those innermost mysteries that defy explanation.

Why voice, why Valéry, why voice and Valéry in the contemporary critical climate are questions which invite some attention. It might seem that both hover rather precariously on the margins of literary critical concerns, dominated as these are by apparently more momen-tous issues of ideology, gender, and postmodern problematizations. Valéry's own renowned intellectual insularity does not help. He willingly admitted to this attitude: 'Je n'aime pas les idées des autres, et c'est pour ne pas faire des miennes les idées des autres que je ne les ai pas publiées' (X, 163). Yet no mind exists without a context, and both Valéry and voice lead directly to a confrontation with a crucial aspect of contemporary inquiry, the question of subjectivity and its status. Whether the angle of approach is literary, philosophical, psychoanalytic, or linguistic, the same governing awareness of the need to assess the nature or very possibility of an entity or position once referred to as a subject predominates. These various fields of inquiry register the impact of the loss of an assured ground or 'origin' resulting from the 'death of God'; each, in its own distinctive manner, demonstrates how the human quest for meaning or understanding has been transferred from a more strictly theological framework to an interrogation of the process by which meaning is produced. Voice, in this context, may be read as referring to an aspect of linguistic inquiry which is not reducible to the parameters of theory; it is the overspill of a contemporary Western interrogation into the processes and power of language within the difficult, resistant realms of the creative consciousness. It may, indeed, represent a lingering trace, barely admissible in an era which shuns the burden of responsibility which subjectivity implies, of humanist preoccupations which, however easy to dismiss, remain difficult to assume.

A determining characteristic of the modern Western consciousness is its alienated nature. The removal of a unifying perspective which a transcendent dimension once ensured has uncovered the split or fissured foundations on which a culture has based its imaginative productions. The mind–body dichotomy which has marked the West since the Christian era, at least, has developed more specific cultural forms which translate, in a range of idioms, the same fundamental awareness of a damagingly divided state. The identification of an unconscious mind operating in tension with the conscious level which Freudian insight conceptualized finds its counterpart in contemporary genderings of the subject position where 'masculine' and 'feminine' vie with each other for recognition and validity; and, in the broader sweep of contemporary conceptions of creativity, the imagination, unseated from its Baudelairean supremacy as 'la reine des facultés', finds itself obliged to restate its allegiance in terms either of a scopic economy deriving from logic, definition, and order or of an unformulated, abject dimension which exists as its dependent, repressed underside or margin. It is within the context of the perceived pain and risk of a divided state of consciousness, whether on a personal or cultural level, that Valéry's pursuit of the voice of a subject in search of itself can be located. This quest is not, therefore, as disconnected from broader contemporary concerns as might initially appear to be the case.

Philosophy touches on this sensitive area in various ways: Husserl's phenomenology and Derrida's dwelling in/on difference continue to situate voice within a perspective deriving from a view of transcendence as self-presence; voice retains its links with its divine associations however much God as origin may have disappeared or is denied. Psychoanalysis, the 'talking cure', evokes the crucial though elusive juncture of speech and *soma*, of word made flesh, in a sequence of theorizations which leave the essential mysteries mercifully intact. Linguistic theory describes and contains current performance yet, simultaneously, finds itself challenged from within by the discovery of a semiotic 'otherness' which subverts while also sustaining the symbolic authority of such performance. An energy within language which is hard to define in the critical vocabulary currently available draws attention to the continuing relevance of the process through which human subjectivity is engendered. Similarly literature, at present struggling to retain something of its specificity beneath the weight of competing critical perspectives, negotiates a passage between the Scylla of narrative theories which affirm unquestioningly the death of the subject in the wake of God; and the Charybdis of gender studies where questions of quality are elided beneath the debate on difference. Interestingly, however, both these approaches retain the hypothesis of subjectivity as reference point: whether absent, dead, or hovering imminently in the space opened up between competing paradigms of desire, the voice of the human subject continues to exert its fascination: as obscure object of inquiry, as utopian vanishing point, as theoretical construction. My reading of Valéry connects his concern with voice to these various fields of contemporary inquiry: to psychoanalysis, in a variety of modes (Freud, Jung, Klein, Lacan); to feminist interpretations of gender and its implications for shifting paradigms of the imagination (Irigaray, Kristeva); and to autobiographical theory in so far as it can offer insights into the changing status of subjectivity in the modern and postmodern era.

It is significant that autobiographical studies have come to the fore over recent years perhaps as evidence of a continuing though displaced concern with issues once associated with traditional humanist preoccupations. A certain empirical honesty urges us, as contemporary readers, to lend our attention to the trace of the autobiographical voice as all that remains as evidence of the irrefutable activity of consciousness. Perhaps even a kind of nostalgia finds expression this way as a culture attempts to heal itself of the sterile effects and implications of an over-investment in forms of thought reliant on structure and function. The entirety of Valéry's *recherche* constitutes a part of an archive documenting a moment in a developing European consciousness, that historical instant during which sustaining structures—moral, ideological, aesthetic—are subjected to intense questioning and the very sense of what human agency implies comes under a degree of scrutiny which dissolves its object. My reading of voice in Valéry can be interpreted as a genealogy of the human subject, as the resurrection of one of those subjugated knowledges whose presence, however problematic, Foucault welcomes as proof of the energy of resistance to authoritative discourses within a culture. Autobiographical concerns occupy a key position in Valéry's work; and voice, in this context, acquires considerable significance in so far as its scope enables him to develop an alternative to traditional autobiographical strategies. He conceives of poetic or creative activity as a means of redefining, even restructuring, the self according to certain formal considerations which belong within his understanding of voice as substance and concept. In his highly distinctive interpretation of the autobiographical mode, Valéry's voice lends its weight as experimental authority to the attempt currently undertaken by a range of disciplines at overcoming the harmful divisions embodied in Western cultural practices.

At the heart of his conception of creativity lies his attraction to form as stimulant to an almost physical level of appetite and as appeal to his appreciation of abstraction. Form replenishes his senses, nourishes his imagination, engages his intellect. In approaching his account of the voice in terms of a psychology of creativity traced through form, conscious and less conscious aspects come into play. The rationally dictated qualities of control, analysis, and disciplined labour cooperate with the less definable dimensions deriving from bodily promptings and intuited imagery. Both aesthetic and psycho-analytical theories offer ways of appreciating the nature and purpose of formal considerations in the genesis of works of art; my account draws on some of their insights where I have found these helpful. Yet it seems to me that Valéry's project stands in its own right as valid in terms of its own intentions and achievements. I once entertained the fantasy or folly of attempting a psychoanalysis of Valéry as though, in this way, some sense could be made to emerge from a corpus whose meaning consistently eluded me. I have settled instead for a different kind of listening to the voice of his creative potential, one which acknowledges the illumination afforded by several psychoanalytically based approaches without subscribing fully to any single theoretical position. This respects the spirit of Valéry's dislike of systematizing closure and certainly represents less of a life-consuming risk to myself as critic. Art lives with or without analysis. It speaks of the same depth and complexity of experience but with an intensity and richness that cannot be translated and reduced to explanatory accounts of motive and meaning without a grave distortion of its symbolic resonance.

Valéry's autobiography, disguised beneath a formalizing vocabulary, embodies the voice of what I shall refer to as his serpent self; a voice which is, quite literally, informed and transformed by a structural awareness of an entire dimension of experience which cannot be encompassed adequately within the parameters of the lucid Cartesian intelligence with which he was for so long identified. That he was able to grant as much space as he did to the radical otherness that being human implies is evidence of the courage required to acknowledge the inherently paradoxical nature of subjectivity. He experienced selfhood, or being a self, as a state of self-division, conflict, and even torment. There was little comfort to be found in exploring the inner depths: 'Il faut entrer en soi-même armé jusqu'aux dents' (XI, 253). The prime texts for analysis in my study of the ego-poetical self are thus those poems which capture precisely this sense of struggle within the creative subject: *La Pythie*, *Fragments du Narcisse*, *Ebauche d'un serpent*. My reading of his confession aims to come closer to understanding an obsession, to explore without simplistically explaining an almost magical possession: that shape and substance of the serpent *ouroboros* whose meanderings throughout his writings as theme, image, structure, and theory come to dictate the genesis of the writing self; and to trace its function in integrating conflicting energies or aspects of that self.

It is no accident that Valéry adopted this animal emblem as totem self, representative of his most urgent intentions and desires, since its significance as a symbol of integration has long been recognized in many cultures. The serpent in Valéry's poetic theory and practice serves, then, as a literal embodiment of desiring and desirable form; it functions in both his creative and critical texts as an incarnation of voice as substance and structure, that ideal object which encourages the creative resources of the mind to release their own inherent capacity for growth and integration. This symbolic and even homeopathic value of *ouroboros* is intuited as much as consciously acknowledged: a degree of disguising or denial of its chthonic resonances is achieved by a process of abstraction or distancing through the use of theoretical terminology. Yet the song of the serpent self which expresses a continuous preoccupation with a hidden level of self-creative activity rooted in the body as physicality is no less powerful for remaining partially unconscious. *Ouroboros* has been equated, traditionally, in Valéry studies with the inherently self-destructive tendencies of analytic self-consciousness; the serpent devouring its own tail represents the impasse encountered by a type of mental process which, unable to conceive of modes of intelligence reaching beyond the compass of its own purely rational functioning, turns against itself in a frustrated paralysing gesture of negatively directed energy. Yet the complementary symbolic resource of the serpent, according to many cultural interpretations, is as stimulus to healing;

Aesculapius, his staff entwined by a snake, emblematizes his restorative power for the Western medical tradition (V, 11). In tracing the shifting connotations of voice in Valéry's work the harmonizing or integrative potential of the serpent's presence emerges as an active force within the poet's sensibility in its guise as counterpoint to the rational; as the feared yet simultaneously desirable secret sister or shadow haunting the sun-flooded yet curiously sterile landscapes of Apollonian clarity. The serpent draws its strength from the earth, from the physical realm; its symbolic status embraces instinct as much as the refinements of consciousness. And voice, for Valéry, derives from the material, physiological reality of the body in equal measure to its intellectual implications. The autobiographical voice of the serpent self helps to anchor his intelligence in its sensory home or corporeal ground.

The body has become an increasingly central focus for contemporary critical inquiry where it may, initially, have seemed attractive for its apparently empirical and irrefutable reality; as substitute ground standing in for a lost God it offered a measure of consolation to a nostalgic consciousness. Something of this quality of sheer presence lends material density to Valéry's speculations around the voice. Yet, as with so many objects of its scrutiny, twentieth-century thought has tended to transform the body, driving it over the horizon to serve as yet another elusive vanishing point. The 'real' body, dissolving beneath the various veils projected onto it as fantasy body, textual body, gendered body, can no longer be located in this process of cultural transubstantiation. Valéry's own interrogation of the body's suggestive potential proposes a range of contexts in which it may be conceptualized: physiological, psychological, auric, spiritual, or imaginary. Voice has its part to play in relation to each of these, connecting body and textuality as the incarnation of subjectivity in/as écriture.

I suggested earlier that Valéry's writings can be read as charting the adventures of the human spirit on its increasingly difficult passage through a period of transition towards new, emergent shapings of reason and experience. The relevance of his formal autobiography lies in its status as mirror or model offering, as a focus for reflection, a methodology of consciousness caught in the labour of experiment and redefinition. The most moving part of this account remains, for me, the Cahiers. Many analogies for these daily notations of the mind's journey suggest themselves—laboratory, alchemical retort, unconscious of the published œuvre—all evoking a space and a time in which the self observes and modifies itself. They form, I believe, the part of his textual trace which Valéry considered the most representative and valuable. These provisional registerings of experience and reflection, whose scope enables a continuous process of self-reading and self-correction, constitute the very material of his poetry. *Poésie*, for Valéry, describes a practice of conscious transformation of the self through creative meditation and its transcription as *écriture*. It is in this sense that his poetic voice is profoundly autobiographical. He did not, however, consider himself primarily a poet in the more widely accepted sense of the term; and my approach is not, accordingly, a study of his poetry as such. A wide choice of interpretations of this aspect of his work already offers a range of intelligent readings; my intention is to remain rather with those parts of his writings which have brought me closer to his most urgent concerns. The voice of a searching, desiring self which is not afraid to admit to the pain and doubt of a life fully lived exerts its fascination well beyond the ambit of his published poems.[3]

Chapter 1, *Voicing the Divide*, explores the concept of an acoustic sensibility and relates voice to Valéry's views on the linguistic aspect of the functioning of consciousness, to poetic theory and aesthetics. Voice acquires significance as creative energy, diction, internal language, and communicative medium. It lies at the heart of the process by which the body becomes articulate and desire translates itself into poetry. Its principal role in the context of poetic theory is as a metaphorical indicator of the balance to be achieved in an ideal interaction of body and mind, content and form, being and knowledge. The body is envisaged here as the cooperation of consciousness and sensibility in a totalized mode of being; and poetry refers, in part, to a psycho-physiological process of transformation whereby the self accedes to creativity. The Kristevan model of the semiotic and symbolic dimensions of poetic language lends theoretical resonance to this phase of the evolution and applications of voice.

Chapter 2, *Imagining Form*, approaches the Valéryan *œuvre* as 'une écriture du désir', the trace left by the desiring subject in its quest for some form of absolute, whether of experience or of knowledge. The chapter reveals the creative potential of the image in the history of the self by exploring certain recurrent networks of image and theme in which voice occupies a pivotal position in the poet's affective landscape. Particularly significant are its associations with form as dynamic expression of the capacity of the imagination to replenish its resources by drawing on a fantasy of completeness, accomplishment.

The archaeology of the voice developed here also initiates an exploration of the problematic of subject and other, whether that otherness evokes a human or transcendent dimension; Valéry's meditations on love and his interest in mysticism draw on a shared dynamic of emotional response and imagery.

Chapter 3, *Integrating the Feminine*, marks a 'retour aux origines', drawing on a number of psychoanalytic approaches to develop further the significance of voice, particularly in its associations with a thematic of darkness, solitude, liquidity, and a feminine presence. A close reading of three seminal texts—*Rêve. Rapport de mer*; *Poésie*; *Fragments du Narcisse*—attributes the fundamental import of phonic or acoustic phenomena in Valéry's creative consciousness to pre-natal and early infant experience. Envisaged within the framework of Freudian and Lacanian hypotheses concerning the dream world and the imaginary order, voice comes to represent a moment of unitive perfection and acquires an almost absolute status as that lost object of desire which, once sensed or intuited, is then projected as the goal of all subsequent creative activity. Writing constructs a future in and through which the pursuit of the self as the m/other functions recuperatively.

Extending the contrast between the auditory dimension and the visual, generally acknowledged as the dominant mode of the Western cultural imaginary, the realm of voice can be theorized in terms of a feminine imaginary which defines itself against those tendencies in Valéry's creative consciousness which work towards definition, control, and separateness. Irigaray's vision of 'le féminin' as the hitherto non-existent, repressed margin on which a patriarchal specular economy is grounded, can account, in some measure, for the unease which his writings reveal towards that entire realm of experience to which voice refers. The voice which breaks through in the semiotic disruptions of texts such as *La Pythie* and *Fragments du Narcisse* and in other similar incursions which punctuate Valéry's work, reveals the constant co-presence within the predominantly controlling activity of the psyche of an occluded aspect, that amorphous, abject, or threatening dimension which was associated originally with the earliest feminine other. The implications for male subjectivity of this maternal body as both physical and acoustic container influence powerfully the vicissitudes of a voice whose narrative explores the interdependence of identity and separateness throughout a lifetime.

The final chapter, *The Serpent Self*, pursues the question of subjectivity along more strictly autobiographical lines and examines Valéry's experimentation with some of the difficulties posed by traditional forms of autobiographical discourse. Voice as mnemonic function ensuring continuity within the creative self operates by analogy with its *modus operandi* as a formally self-regenerating structure within the vocal substance. On both levels its vital contribution is to ensure the transformation of successive, punctual moments into a continuous whole. Valéry's conception of the self as fragment, as elusive subject always in process, for which the conventional temporal and narrative frameworks are clearly inappropriate, finds an accommodation in a redrawing of the autobiographical project. The contingent self is disavowed, transcended by a variety of strategies, chief amongst which is its reformulation as a modulated function of the aesthetic sensibility. The essential component here is memory reinterpreted as part of Valéry's analysis of the human organism in terms of the transformation of phases, as the maximizing of the present instant in the spatio-temporal topography of the voice.

The sequence of projected or mythic selves or *personae* which people the Valéryan *œuvre* embodies a progression of aesthetic, or essentially formal, solutions to the frustrations of contingent existence. The autobiographical voice reveals, furthermore, its integrative capacity in so far as it seeks to balance the masculine and feminine aspects of what may be termed a phenomenology of creative intelligence. The mythic reconstruction of selfhood undertaken by Valéry remains incomplete until the alterity within consciousness has been gendered and the encounter with the other conceptualized as feminine. Valéry's personal investment in certain feminine figures—the Parque, the Pythia, Sémiramis, Agathe, Lust—can be interpreted as part of the progressive transformation of the creative psyche along the lines of an alchemical quest. The goal lies in the harmonizing of the masculine and the feminine poles or energies within the contemporary imagination. In the context of Valéry's redistribution of roles within the authorial subjectivity, Jungian thinking on individuation, and, more specifically, on the *anima*, viewed as the masculine psyche's projection of a desired complementarity in feminine guise, offers valuable insights.

Notes to the Introduction

1. These and other approaches are well represented in *Un nouveau regard sur Valéry*; textes réunis par Nicole Celeyrette-Pietri and Brian Stimpson (Paris: Lettres

Modernes, 1995); and in Paul Gifford and Brian Stimpson (eds.), *Reading Paul Valéry: Universe in Mind* (Cambridge: Cambridge University Press, 1999).

2. Christine Crow's *Paul Valéry and the Poetry of Voice* (Cambridge: Cambridge University Press, 1982); Paul Gifford's discussion of the spiritual aspect of Valéry's quest (1989); Brian Stimpson's analysis of the significance of musical theory and practice for Valéry (1984); and, more recently, the studies by Michel Jarrety (1991) and Serge Bourjea (1997) of the status of the creative subject.

3. My account of voice, though it draws on similar material to that of Christine Crow, develops its own emphases distinctively. I focus more closely on the detail of Valéry's concern with form as the theoretical or conceptual underpinning of voice; and, while some overlap is inevitable between two studies with so similar a preoccupation, mine is less centrally concerned with Valéry's poetic practice, more specifically focused on the insights afforded by autobiographical and psychoanalytic theory. For a reading of Valéry's voice as essentially that of a poet see Jean-Michel Maulpoix's 'Major Poems: The Voice of the Subject', in Gifford and Stimpson (eds.), *Reading Paul Valéry*, 170–86.

CHAPTER 1

Voicing the Divide

Tout le corps humain présent, *sous la voix*, et support,
condition d'équilibre de l'*idée*. (OII, 549)

The mysterious, informing presence of voice throughout Valéry's writing allows free rein to the power of fantasy, liberating the power of desire. It is the highly valued term which enables him to avoid saying 'I'. At stake here is not so much a refusal of responsibility for selfhood as a yearning to arrive at a more accurate, less rigid notation of the complexities which selfhood entails. Voice is, to a large extent, synonymous with subjectivity as a process whose functioning, though often beyond the reach of linguistic precision, yet requires naming. By attributing much of the formless and indefinable activity which makes up such a process to this elusive presence, form or concept—for the voice has many guises—Valéry is empowered to explore areas of subjective experience which lie beyond the reach of theoretical resolution. Voice, in the present chapter, refers to the rich ambiguity of the ground from which the creative energy of the sensibility emerges. On the one hand, it registers the conflicts which characterize human consciousness, torn between an intuition of the formless and a yearning for formalization. On the other, it points towards the possibility of transcending alienation of this kind in the more integrated vision which Valéry's aesthetic and, specifically, poetic theory and practice offer.

To create is to give shape and value to the impulses of the inner self, to make available the instinctual potential of the body for expression and communication. In order to achieve some degree of accuracy or perfection of form the creative artist, in whatever field s/he works, strives to achieve as total an awareness of self as possible. For Valéry, poetry was one of the principal means by which such self-exploration was accomplished, although he viewed his activity as verse-maker as rather arbitrary and in no sense as the central aspect of his intellectual endeavour. Words happened to be the medium most immediately accessible to him and, much as he lamented his incapacity to rival the effects of music in the realm of the response of the sensibility, he perceived the risks involved in pursuing a perfectionist attitude with regard to language to its logical conclusion.

His dissatisfaction with language as an instrument of precise communication encouraged him to develop its potential in a different direction. He resisted the temptation of following in the footsteps of Monsieur Teste, who preferred to remain within the intact purity of the potential by preserving through silence a coincidence of thought and word, a perfection of communication with self uncontaminated by the imprecision of language. Instead he developed a mode of expression which makes explicit that which, ideally, might remain implicit. In poetry, understood in its widest sense, and more specifically in his conception of voice, Valéry creates an alternative to silence by working with words in such a way that the intimacy of tone characteristic of the human organism's perception of its own being is not betrayed. This does not imply a poetry of solipsism but serves rather to intensify its communicative potential.

In the interaction of perception and expression which links self and world, awareness is vital. For the poet, such an awareness, deriving partially from the organic self, may be expanded more particularly in the realm of sound, given that the phonic potential of language is a key aspect of his chosen medium. And it is, indeed, the case that acoustic phenomena occupy a primordial position in Valéry's imaginative response to reality. Within the wider framework of his aim to observe the functioning of the mind an important dimension can be identified under the category of acoustic or auditory consciousness. Teste devoted himself to obtaining as lucid a degree of self-consciousness as was humanly possible, claiming that 'nul plus que moi n'a *reculé* devant toute chose. Je voudrais les renvoyer toutes au *théâtre* — et me dépouiller de tout hors le regard' (IV, 248). Valéry himself, in the context of specifically poetic creation, communicates an identical desire for an exhaustive awareness of the activity of consciousness but transposed into terms of sound. The metaphor which he employs to express 'la conscience consciente' is not uniquely visual, as it was for Teste, but embraces an auditory dimension as well:

O pour moi seul, à moi seul, en moi-même, [. . .]
J'attends l'écho de ma grandeur interne. (OI, 149)

The central importance of the human voice is often stressed by Valéry as, for example, when he observes, 'grand désavantage de la poésie, — l'inexistence d'une notation de la *diction*. — Allure, accents [. . .] Car tout poème réduit au texte nu est "*incomplet*" [. . .]. Le poème n'a pas de sens sans SA voix' (XXVI, 807). Such emphasis on the tonal implications appropriate to a given text suggests that there exists for Valéry a certain association of language with the individual qualities of the human voice without which the poem remains flat, unconvincing. The same issue is explored in more detail in an oft-quoted observation from the *Cahiers* where, clarifying the distinctiveness of his own views on the matter in relation to Mallarmé's conception of a kind of autonomous or impersonal voice of language, Valéry affirms the significance of the imprint on language of the poet's labour. 'Mais, *au fait, qui* parle dans un poème?', he asks.

Mallarmé voulait que ce fût le Langage lui-même. Pour moi — ce serait — l'Etre *vivant et pensant* [. . .] — et poussant la conscience de soi à la capture de sa sensibilité — développant les propriétés d'icelle dans leurs implexes — résonance, symétries etc. — sur la *corde* de la *voix*. En somme, le *Langage* issu de la *voix*, plutôt que la *voix* du *Langage*. (XXII, 435–6)[1]

Unlike Mallarmé, for whom a certain impersonality of language animates the text, irrespective to some extent of the control exerted by the creative consciousness, Valéry's vision places voice as substance at the outset of the process; the poet can do no more than build upon the very real possibilities of sound and rhythm and utterance, construct his verbal artefact by integrating and extending the innately resonant capacities of physiological vocal form.

On numerous occasions Valéry shares with his readers his delight in the substance, shape, and power of the voice as a virtually disembodied force, 'évolution d'une énergie libre' (XVI, 363). In his analysis of a song recital he traces the stream of sound describing developments in time and space as it is released from the articulatory organs of the singer:

Dîner à Villa Rosa Marañon. Chanteurs — guitare — ces voix sont comme fluides en charge [. . .]. On sent que l'essentiel ici est le fluide même. [. . .] C'est le 'silence éternel' rendu par l'effort extraordinaire de l'homme seul qui n'a que sa voix pour compagne, et que *la durée de sa voix*. [. . .] Ce chant me fait penser *Poésie* — Pour moi — *la voix*. [. . .] celui qui va chanter — ouvrir le robinet [. . .] se penche [. . .]. — Onde portante ou porteuse et modulations [. . .]. Le temps — onde porteuse. Le mouvement d'un poème. (XVI, 360–1)

It is during this extended moment that the voice, a force seeking embodiment or re-absorption within the receiving sensibility, reveals certain of its distinctive characteristics. Perceived in its individuality, as 'une voix [. . .] qui est timbre, action, substitution, enchantement, et vivante arabesque' (OII, 1524) it acquires a potency that is hard to rival. In one of his finest prose poems Valéry describes with delight the marvellous materiality of the voice as vibration of energy:

Piano et Chant

La voix vibrante se marie étrangement à la voix abstraite du piano [. . .]. La chambre vibre. Les murs chantent. La substance de l'air attaquée par une fraîche et forte gorge, entièrement émue par ces milliers de chocs cristallins [. . .] devient le lieu de transformations admirables [. . .]. Je frémis. Je sens une force inconnue. [. . .] Toutes mes puissances se trouvent sur la terre. Elles se sentent lourdes et maladroites. Et la parole a honte. (OI, 1722)

He conceives of it as an utterance dictated by the organism in its totality, physiological, emotional, intellectual, and spiritual, evoking it in a letter to Pierre Louÿs concerning La Jeune Parque as 'une espèce de "voix du sang" (en amitié de l'esprit) qui m'est chère plus que tout' (OI, 1624). The body's expressive potential is manifold, with mental and physical dimensions inextricably interwoven. It is clear that the most primitive promptings of voice can be discerned 'du côté du corps', deep within the body's substance, always a source of mystery and therefore stimulus to analysis for Valéry.[2]

In the present chapter, essentially three main aspects or moments in the evolution and application of voice may be distinguished. There is voice as the sounding of the body whether as consubstantial with its rhythms or as phonic substance—this is the ground, the fundamental material; then voice as the acoustic accompaniment to self-consciousness, equivalent to inner language, guaranteeing a sense of self and forming the basis of identity; and finally, voice as possessing metaphorical force within Valéry's poetic theory and practice, where its function is to synthesize the functioning of body and mind in language. Such a supreme moment of presentness to self, where bodily existence has been appropriately articulated in language, and the precise sense in which his conception of poetry as a 'psychesthétique' thus affirmed, is pre-eminently a unitive experience. The significance of voice in its metaphorical capacity as expressive of unity or integration, though approached here in the specific context of poetic theory, acquires greater depth and spiritual significance in later chapters, where it contributes powerfully to the vision of a new form of subjectivity deriving from greater harmony within the desiring imagination.

Certain features of the Kristevan view of poetic language as drawing on both semiotic and symbolic determinations provide a supporting context for this exploration of voice. Her view of subjectivity as process rather than structure, and of the evolving nature of the linguistically marked subject, sheds further light on the Valéryan understanding of voice as both pre-linguistic utterance and, also, as the means of marking the various stages in the realization of the subject in and through language. Much of Valéry's speculation on the topic of voice throughout the *Cahiers* can be paralleled with the materialist account of linguistic practice as both system and transgression, a product of the social space in which enunciation takes place and of the drive-governed origins of sound-production, which Kristeva offers.[3]

Valéry's particular appreciation of the close interdependence of physiological process and aesthetic product enables him to develop a theory and practice of poetry as a mode of transubstantiated language which ensures that the emotions, thoughts, and reactions of 'le poète à l'état pur' are not misrepresented when transposed into words by 'le poète réel' (VI, 717). A similar awareness of the possibility of inscribing the physiological in language, as a difference within the text, is termed 'rejection' by Kristeva, who sees this as a disruptive dimension characteristic of the mobile, unfixed, subversive writing subject, 'le sujet-en-procès'. Her analysis focuses on the tension generated by the confrontation of the thrust towards meaning embodied in language with whatever it is that resists intelligibility. Throughout Valéry's writing a certain struggle is at work between his obedience to the constraints of language, indeed his respect for, and one might even say his imprisonment within, the structures of a formal literary register; and against this, a freer, more fluid, searching style such as is employed in his 'prose poétique' and which hints at a greater awareness of the dissolved, uncontrolled aspects of the sensibility.[4]

This dimension of his work, capturing the elusive mobility and extralinguistic qualities of the rejected semiotic, fulfils a valuable role in preventing the symbolic realm from becoming impossibly rigid and regulated. It acts as a kind of safety valve ensuring that the transgressive energies, which are a precondition of the symbolic, find an appropriate, since controlled, outlet. Indeed, Kristeva's understanding of artistic practices, and notably poetic language, views them as a deliberately resumed functioning of the semiotic *chora* within the signifying structures of language, an intentional semiotic breach of the symbolic. Transposing this oppositional model to the field of Valéryan poetics, a somewhat similar tension emerges from the range of connotations of the term 'voice'. At one end of the spectrum it refers to the deepest level of expressive prompting or gesture within the psycho-physiological system, a pre-verbal realm which can only be evoked with considerable imprecision; at the other end of the span of possible meanings voice defines also a highly perfected mode of poetic language.

Valéry's poetic and, more broadly, aesthetic theory, perhaps more properly termed an 'esthésique', grants a primordial place to those creative forms and activities which retain the semiotic resonance of the voice within its symbolic functioning, thus allowing the sensibility access to its fullest expressive capacity.[5] An acute sensation of life deprives the individual of words; and the question therefore arises as to what form of language can provide a more satisfactory and subtle articulation of the organism's reality. Valéry hints at an answer in noting a specific temporal characteristic as one of the primary features of the body: 'Cette chose si mienne [. . .] est la plus instante [. . .] qui soit [. . .]. *Elle n'a point de passé*. Ce mot n'a point de sens pour elle, qui est le présent même' (OI, 927). If a mode of language is created where a lingering within the present moment of sensation can be maintained, then the organism may be considered to have acquired a more appropriate expressive outlet. Just such a linguistic mode can operate through voice, for 'Le lyrisme est le genre de poésie qui suppose la voix en action, la voix directement issue de, ou provoquée par les choses que l'on voit ou sent comme *présentes*' (VII, 181). During the initial phases of creative self-consciousness the acoustic capacity of the mind lends itself to exploration and analysis in precisely such terms. Valéry's sensitivity to the auditory dimension of consciousness leads him to explore sound as, in some measure, constitutive of consciousness itself and of a sense of identity. The inner voice is perceived as offering a temporal space in which the emergent poetic subjectivity encounters itself, comes to know itself. His preoccupation with the phenomenon of voice translates his interest in a process: it is the coming into being of the self as producer and product of the voice, the creation of selfhood, of *ego poeta*, as well as of poetry which fascinates him.

Poetic creativity in his view transcends the narrowly linguistic sphere and embraces the possibility of a creation or re-creation of the self accomplished by means of the rigorous interaction of critically handled language and the living potential of selfhood that poetic craftsmanship implies. For Valéry, then, to explore the origins of the word as the core of consciousness and sensibility is really to penetrate deep into the primal strata of a self-knowledge which, perfected over a lifetime, may contribute to the formation, understood literally as the recasting in an aesthetic form, of a mythic or ideally reconstructed self. The capacity of the self to renew itself in this fashion, in a kind of aesthetic parthenogenesis, derives from a particular awareness of the primordial significance of form. At an unconscious level, Valéry's creativeness finds expression as much in the reshaping of his own personality as a productive being, as in the creation of the art object; and this process begins with a perception and modelling of identity in sound. Clearly the very concept of personality itself is problematic since Valéry disavowed much of the interest and value of what is normally understood by this term. Yet through the application of creative will to the literal transformation of the vital substance of his sensibility, he evolves a poetically developed *imago* which, as aesthetic form, can be interpreted as integrating different dimensions of experience.

Drawing the threads of this introductory section together, it emerges that voice, in each of its applications within this chapter—as phonic substance produced by the organism, as linguistically derived current generative of identity, and as aesthetic imperative—captures something of the unfigurable nature of subjectivity as a ceaseless and infinitely complex process. As such, it remains, to a certain extent, consubstantial with the body in so far as it articulates levels of subject-ivity involving semiotic rhythm, drives, and pre-linguistic awareness. As it grows out of the body and takes on linguistic form, it obviously differentiates itself from the body yet without ever being entirely distinguishable from it.

Voice, in its first application, emerges from the human organism. The paradoxical intimacy yet strangeness which characterizes the way in which the self perceives its own physical presence is a source of frequent wonder in Valéry's work. In an extract from the *Journal d'Emma*, significantly entitled *Eléments physiques*, the niece of Monsieur Teste describes her sense of unfamiliarity with what is after all closest to her:

Je me regarde au bain, je me dis: mon corps est-il à moi? [. . .] Mon corps, ma terre! Comment peut-on penser à toi, chose la plus intime et la plus étrangère? [. . .] Après tout, ce que j'appelle *mon corps*, c'est le fruit d'une quantité de découvertes! A-t-on jamais fini de s'explorer? [. . .] Pourquoi ne ferait-on pas le journal de son corps? Oserai-je écrire 'mon corps'? [. . .] Non pas mon corps, celui des médecins, mais celui que je me connais. Je ne sais rien au-delà de lui. Il est ma science, et je crois bien la limite de toute science. (OII, 428–9)

Bodily existence can be apprehended, in part, Valéry suggests, by training one's acoustic sensitivity. He tries to penetrate beneath or beyond the barrier imposed by language in order to detect the very pulsation of being, described in the following lines as the product of a thirst for perception of the self as sound: 'comme nul son n'arrête ce désir de son, à la limite du suspens de moi-même, — jusqu'au timbre de mon sang et à l'animation de ma propre durée' (OII, 1390). This evocation of what may be termed the 'sounding' of the organism recalls the Parque caught in a similar moment of physiological self-awareness:

> [. . .] Mais toute à moi, maîtresse de mes chairs,
> Durcissant d'un frisson leur étrange étendue,
> Et dans mes doux liens, à mon sang suspendue. (OI, 97)

Valéry aims to integrate as approximate a rendering as possible of these sounds which are consubstantial with the organism into the complex scope of his conception of voice; poetry for him commences with the attempt to capture and subsequently recreate in words the sensation of sheer existence which precedes verbal formulation and which cannot, perhaps, be translated in its reality.[6] This primal level of self-perception shares certain characteristics with the area of pre-Oedipal experience which Kristeva terms semiotic, evoking as it does a level of organic activity which is inaccessible to language, pre-symbolic.[7] Valéry develops this individual capacity for physiological self-awareness further in positing it as a form of dialogue: 'Chacun, à tel moment ou tel autre, est engagé dans un *tête-à-tête* avec son organisme. Rien ni personne entre eux: [. . .] il faut se rendre au corps qui parle en son langage du corps' (OI, 340). Although he employs a descriptive terminology firmly rooted in the syntax of accepted linguistic usage in analysing this moment of pre-linguistic self-consciousness, he is none the less attempting to deal with an area of experience not easily conveyed according to the rationally coherent structures of linguistic convention.

In the first of the three prose poems which form *ABC* (OI, 1725–7) he evokes a similar sense of pre-articulate awareness as the body is envisaged as a participant in an exchange reflecting the inter-dependence of 'être' and 'connaître', the cooperation of being and knowledge. From the start the reader is immersed in a 'mono-dialogue' between consciousness and pure physicality. The body is presented in its most primitive state by the voice of consciousness observing its partner deep in slumber: 'Animal profondément en-dormi; tiède et tranquille masse mystérieusement isolée' (OI, 1725). Consciousness is quick to acknowledge the degree to which they are mutually dependent: 'arche close de vie qui transportes vers le jour mon histoire et mes chances, tu m'ignores, tu me conserves, tu es ma permanence inexprimable' (OI, 1725). Masked by a phrasing typical of the Valéryan view of the incommensurability of the mental and physical orders of experience lies a grasp of the linguistic implications of this moment which takes us closer to a Kristevan perception of the pre-symbolic subject caught between a phase of drive-dominated, pre-linguistic existence and its entry into a position guaranteed within linguistic representation. Sonority is used on two levels in this text in an attempt to recreate the polyphonic nature of the functioning of being. On the one hand it is the sounding of the organism addressed as an alien element by its witness, consciousness: 'Quel mal tu me fais avec le bruit de ton souffle! Je me sens trop étroitement le captif du suspens de ton soupir. Au travers de ce masque abandonné tu exhales le murmure de l'existence stationnaire. J'écoute ma fragilité' (OI, 1725). Equally it constitutes the more elaborate form of address, the language of dialogue, between conscious and unreflective existence, between the 'moi' and the 'toi' who are the *personae* in this scenario.[8]

Yet the nature of this discourse is problematic and the conventional linguistic structures which Valéry employs seem inappropriate in ex-pressing the body and its functioning, as the following passage from *Réflexions simples sur le corps* makes clear: 'Chacun appelle cet objet *Mon-Corps*; mais nous ne lui donnons aucun nom *en nous-mêmes*: c'est-à-dire *en lui* [. . .] Il n'y a pas de nom pour désigner le sentiment que nous avons d'une substance de notre présence' (OII, 926–7). This groping towards an adequate formalization of the sensation of some dimension of organic function suggests parallels with the characterization of the semiotic in the Kristevan model. She aligns it with the primary processes of Freudian analysis, conceiving it as a distinctive mark, trace, or imprint which embodies the condensing and displacement of energies within the body. More specifically, Kristeva employs the term *chora* to identify a non-expressive totality formed by the drives and their stases. At this stage, she argues, there is no linguistic articulation since the *chora* precedes figuration; the closest parallel is to view it as analogous to vocal or kinetic rhythm.

If further proof were needed of the extent to which *La Jeune Parque* integrates an awareness of the physiological dimension, as Valéry claimed (XVIII, 533), the reader has only to consult the numerous passages where he analyses the nature of poetry in terms of a physiological state for which the organism has no means of articulate expression:

On est devant l'ineffable comme des enfants qui ne savent pas encore parler. [. . .] Il n'y a pas de paroles pour certains états, de même que le cheval n'a pas de mains pour tenir une plume — [. . .] Alors ce sont des organes dont ce n'est pas la fonction qui sont obligés de recevoir ces efforts impuissants *d'expression, d'expulsion.* (VII, 785)

The creative act, a reorganization of the disorder of the sensibility, alleviates while simultaneously maintaining the sensation of the ineffable. There can never be a complete resolution of the tension since poetry can never do more than approximate to this wordless state. Yet, although there may be no adequate conceptual terminology to express the body in its intimacy, the way in which words work in poetry can come closer to an accurate rendering of the body's reality. 'La Poésie', as Valéry notes, 'est l'essai de représenter par les moyens du langage articulé, ces *choses* ou cette *chose*, que tentent obscurément d'exprimer les cris, les larmes, silences, les caresses, les baisers, les soupirs etc, et que semblent vouloir exprimer les objets dans ce qu'ils ont d'apparence de vie' (VIII, 846). The Parque can rely on a bodily effusion to express the anguish which oppresses her while at the same time giving voice, through the poet, to her emotions:

> Je n'implorerai plus que tes faibles clartés,
> Longtemps sur mon visage envieuse de fondre,
> Très imminente larme [. . .] (OI, 104)

A total poetry of mind and body can evolve only if the voice as expression of life incorporates an understanding of this inexpressible realm. The point of departure for the creation of voice in this sense is discussed by Valéry in *Poésie et pensée abstraite* where he makes clear that, in his activity as poet, he discards those mental constructs which do not correspond to any living basis. Poetry for him is the endeavour to capture in language the sense of astonishment registered by consciousness when faced with the sheer vitality of existence, that most fundamental level of emotional awareness captured in the exclamation: 'C'est ma vie même qui s'étonne' (OI, 1319). It is not a question of intellect but of highly trained attentiveness to the preconceptual phase where the stirrings of mind and body are closely intertwined: 'La poésie n'a pas à exposer des idées. Les idées (au sens ordinaire du mot) sont des expressions, ou formules. La poésie n'est pas à ce *moment*. Elle est au point antérieur — où les choses mêmes sont comme grosses d'idées' (VII, 97). Similarly, Kristeva, in evoking the kinetic, functional stage of the semiotic, emphasizes that this phase precedes the establishment of the sign; it is not therefore cognitive in the sense of being assumed by an already constituted subject. Her view of literary practice as embodying both 'genotext', the level of textual creativity at which meaning is engendered outside linguistic structuration, and 'phenotext', the punctual presentation of meaning in words, refers to a somewhat similar balancing of awareness within the creative subject as Valéry evokes here.

It is important, however, for the poet to be able to distinguish at this stage between life as substance, vital flow, and life as poetically transformed material. At its most basic level poetry is akin to the body described as 'le sentiment que nous avons d'une substance de notre présence' (OI, 927) and, indeed, Valéry uses the term 'poésie' in one application to refer to a process of ceaseless transformation of one state of being into another: 'La poésie toute nue n'est autre chose que le sentiment se démontrant à soi-même' (VI, 717). But the poet at this stage, envisaged as little more than 'un vivant groupe de transformations', is identified as 'le poète *à l'état pur* — tel qu'on ne doit l'obtenir et le considérer que dans un laboratoire' (VI, 717); in this state of virtual coincidence with his own unelaborated sensibility he lacks the necessary 'recul' from the functioning of his body without which little of aesthetic value can be accomplished for 'Le poète réel, utilisable — doit comporter un artiste, et le langage est son théâtre' (VI, 717).

Valéry's recognition here of poetry as spanning a range of

applications, from pre-linguistic voice to the refined formulations of poetic language, is echoed in Kristeva's account of the significance of the voice in the unfolding of the subject. Voice articulates, in the widest sense of this term, a continuum which connects the infant with the maternal body. Before entry into the symbolic through 'castration', the subject is fused with the mother in a *jouissance* which does not differentiate between subject and other, infant and mother— their organs, voices, and articulations exist in an unmediated, blended state. Language learning represents the necessity for separation from the semiotic *chora* and the maternal body: the linguistic sign can thus be conceived as the voice that is projected from the agitated body or *chora* on to the facing *imago* or object. Voice is therefore associated both with the fused subjectivity of pre-linguistic existence and with the subject's existence as a positioned entity, differentiated from its objects, individually located in the symbolic.

Moving now to the second application of voice—as acoustic accompaniment to consciousness—its relevance to the structuring of identity emerges as highly significant. Valéry distinguishes two types of creative sensibility, the one tending to conceive of the work of art in terms of visual form, the other laying stress on this formal dimension in its auditory aspect. Under the heading 'Ecrivains' he differentiates, therefore, between 'ceux qui voient *leur* forme — croient la voir, et ceux qui l'entendent. Ceci fait 2 catégories et il ne faut jamais les confondre' (XIII, 53). While clearly not insensitive to the visual dimension, he himself would seem to be equally attuned to the latter category; and it is around the phenomenon of inner language that the nascent moment of formal self-awareness can best be discerned.

To remain for as long as possible within the realm of pure potentiality is a characteristic feature of his temperament and is repro-duced in several of the figures who people his work. Monsieur Teste, 'le démon même de la possibilité' (OII, 14), immediately springs to mind. The unwillingness to commit impulse to outer form is, in part, simply a manifestation of a recurrent aspect of his thought. Yet there is also a more positive value to be attached to lingering within the domain of the pre-verbal. During this psychological pause the rela-tionship between inner word and consciousness can be examined in greater detail: 'Si [la parole intérieure] m'apprend quelque chose de neuf, si je me semble inédit en deçà, mieux connu, plus nombreux, au–delà, — cet organe lie ma conscience à ce qui n'est pas elle — Il fait de la conscience avec autre chose' (III, 698). The inner word contributes to the very formation of consciousness by drawing out into the light of awareness different areas of the self in order to present them to the integrating potential of consciousness. The time factor is essential here for it is only when the creative consciousness can observe and regulate its own process that the gradual acquisition of knowledge of the self becomes possible. It is in this context that Valéry talks of 'la poésie' as 'la *limite* à laquelle arrive la parole intérieure longtemps contenue, peu à peu assouplie, articulée parfaitement, possédée dans tout son groupe [. . .], et d'autre part la limite de la pensée même devenue libre avec les mots, à force — d'un exercice croissant' (IV, 204).

However, to identify the source of the instinct towards verbalization with 'la parole intérieure' would be misleading. Valéry senses that, even at the level of this inner word, he has not succeeded in tapping the point of origin: 'je ne sais quoi met dans notre bouche muette les paroles qui constatent, qui rendent *présent* et *existant* ce je ne sais quoi qui était en suspension dans je ne sais quoi' (VIII, 98); its presence only becomes manifest when it has already moved away from the state of pure virtuality in which it might truly be conceived as the origin. Valéry's persistent preoccupation with this inexplicable upsurge of the sensibility reveals how important he felt it to be not only as the seed from which all future linguistic and therefore also poetic growth develops, but equally as playing a significant part in his conception of the formation and functioning of 'le Moi'.[9] By its very nature consciousness is process and unless there is a means of ordering its ceaseless transformatory potential, it remains chaotic and meaningless. Internal language, referred to by Valéry as 'le langage intérieur' or 'le discours intérieur', is characterized by the way in which it imitates directly each shift within consciousness but exercises no discrimination and barely seeks to distinguish itself from the flux of its constituent elements. He describes it as 'l'éternel brouillon [. . .], *impur*, en prise directe sur le *fonctionnement* mental. Ce langage intérieur, *désordonné* en tant qu'il est fait de tous les éléments réflexes psychiques, qu'il est *non-choix* et contient les *choix*, le tout-venant, "l'esprit" désordre, qui contient l'ordre comme un cas particulier' (XXIII, 106). Just as the mind contains the potential for organization and thus resists the natural tendency towards ever greater disorder, so internal language is shown to possess an inclination towards the imposition, or at least the recognition, of structure or form. This process of organization is closely associated with the formation of identity for Valéry and is, to a very great extent, sound-dependent.

His descriptions of the internal language of the mind avoid categorizing the phenomena observed in any over-systematic way. In this sense they share an awareness of meaning-production as lying beyond the scope of a science of linguistics with Kristevan 'sémanalyse' which emphasizes language as a signifying practice drawing on play, pleasure, desire, and the formlessness of the pre-Oedipal moment, as much as on the social contract. Valéry experiences considerable difficulty in defining with any clarity the actual nature of the inner word or voice. This alien and mysterious entity is evoked as 'une excitation q[uelcon]q[ue] toujours intérieure jouant, volant, tâtonnant dans une attente' (X, 547); impressions of movement, interiority and imminence characterize but fail to identify the phenomenon. His unwillingness to disguise these elusive aspects of 'linguistic' activity within the human organism behind the apparently precise terminology of psycholinguistic theory should not be allowed to detract from the very real import of the force identified here.[10] His references to 'la voix ou la parole intérieure' share certain features of the *chora* as mobile and provisional articulation formed by movements and their ephemeral stases. In so far as it precedes figuration and specularization, and can only be recognized as rupture and articulation of rhythms, it can never be given axiomatic form. Many of Valéry's claims for inner language relate to a somewhat similar intuition of the psychosomatic activity which both generates and distinguishes itself from verbal articulation.[11] He notes, for example, that '*Ma pensée* est le langage de celui — qui — parle — en — moi = *Moi me parle en moi*. Ce langage est mêlé du langage ordinaire et de sensations et d'images. Parmi ces sensations, des *sensations caractéristiques d'intériorité, affectivité*' (XVIII, 56). Such a language is virtually indistinguishable from the products of the sensibility or, in Kristevan terminology, from the semiotic, yet already contains traces of symbolic structure.

The earliest stage at which 'la parole intérieure' is encountered is within the acoustic space of the psyche. It is produced in the interval between the two poles which mark the boundaries of an area within auditory consciousness in which a cycle of emission and reception can occur: 'La parole intérieure [. . .] m'apparaît comme production, passage dans le *vide*. Courant de déplacement. [. . .] Emettre et ouir étant pôles. L'audition de moi par moi' (XIII, 113–14). Valéry emphasizes the degree to which this internal linguistic exchange guarantees to the subject its status as conscious being: 'si je m'entends et intérieurement, je produis pour me recevoir, et je ne suis que par ma production et je ne me connais que par ma réception' (IV, 730). He refutes the notion of consciousness as a homogeneous entity conferring on the individual a secure sense of identity, for 'La conscience [. . .] est une *division*, un passage à l'hétérogène' (VII, 328). Having established its heterogeneity, and that there can be no direct access to it since 'n[ou]s ne pouvons que représenter [ses] propriétés' (IX, 490), he faces the problem of trying to determine the nature of the participants in this internal exchange: 'Chercher à trouver en moi ce qui me résiste; ce qui me parle, qui m'éclaire, qui m'épouvante' (VIII, 98). There is a very real sense of division here, perhaps even of conflict, as one dimension of consciousness strives to assert its autonomy in the face of a foreign presence: 'Et non me confondre. C'est moi et ce n'est pas moi' (VIII, 98). Kristeva, highlighting the extent to which the human subject is constituted in language as plural or heterogeneous, points to a similar state of division inevitable within subjectivity in terms of 'negativity'. The processes by which the semiotic generates the subject, mainly drives, charges, and stases, also undermine the unity which is being engendered since, as Freudian thinking suggests, these drives involve a destructive or aggressive dimension.

The development towards an acknowledgement of the self as divided, fragmented, heterogeneous is the source of the tragedy and yet also the richness inherent in the destinies of such figures as Narcisse, the Parque, and the Pythian priestess. The annexing force which the poet detects within his own consciousness is identified with a voice: 'Vie intérieure — [. . .] C'est de trouver "en soi" quelque chose d'étranger, comme une voix, comme une présence. Quelqu'un attend et quelqu'*autre* lui parle' (VIII, 98). The invasion of her being which the Pythie dramatizes in the powerful terms of her monologue expands this same critical instant of sensing the otherness and extraneity of which the self is capable. It is as though the symbolic order, the assured and safely regulated structures of syntax which contain the potential for expression within conventionally agreed limits, suddenly found itself confronted with the disruptive presence of a quite other element.

Perhaps in an attempt to remedy a bewildering loss of all sense of self in a plethora of potential selves, Valéry devises a graphic repre-

sentation of the relationships operating between the various presences
at work within the heterogeneous space entitled 'le moi'. The figure
to emerge here, a hieroglyphic representation of the circuit of auditory consciousness, may be interpreted as a seminal form or acoustic
imago in the quest for a poetically reincarnated self which Valéry
pursues throughout his life. Bearing in mind his observation, noted
earlier, concerning the tendency of certain creative sensibilities to lend
weight to either the visual or the acoustic aspect in their approach, it
is intriguing that the following characterization unites both of these:
'L'*homme* communique avec *soi* d'une manière un peu différente de
celle dont il communique avec les autres,' he begins. 'Mais, en moi,
qui parle à qui? qui voit et quoi est vu? [. . .] Qui est le plus mien, le
plus moi de ces deux? Il se parle et il s'entend' (V, 78). Sight and sound
coexist in the theatre of self-reflection:

Il faudrait nommer et concevoir ces 2 pôles que j'ai appelés Homme et Soi
— entre lesquels tremble l'arc et s'accomplit cette fantastique consommation
[. . .]. Mon positif et mon négatif. [. . .] De sorte que: le moi est pluralité.
Au mot: moi, correspond cette dualité, cette bouche *et* cette oreille, cette
figure, forme, et cette extériorité de cette forme (V, 78)

This strange being, 'l'hiéroglyphe du Langage intérieur' (XXIV, 145),
illustrating the exponential operation of self-awareness as it occurs
within consciousness, lends concrete form to an abstraction, embodying as it does the critical interval from which voice emerges and
which lies at the heart of the Valéryan conception of poetry. It is from
this split or *Spaltung* within subjectivity that life as vocal vibration,
as articulated intelligence, derives its energy and very possibility.
The imaginative concretization of the space-time of consciousness as
'bouche-oreille' can be interpreted as the fundamental emblem of
Valéry's authorial subjectivity. The interval that both connects and
separates the mouth and the ear of the inner, acoustic space allows
the present instant to be experienced to its maximum before the
intactness of that moment is transferred to the act of expression; it
is analogous to the alchemical retort in which the nascent poetic
sensibility is developed.

A similar traversing of a critical interval/break is discussed by
Kristeva in terms of the thetic phase, a precise transitional moment
at which the threshold between the heterogeneous realms of the
semiotic and the symbolic is situated. Passage through this phase is
essential if the subject is to take up a position within representation,

without which the acquisition of identity remains impossible. All enunciation, that is in the symbolic order, requires an identification whereby the subject separates from his image and his objects, and comes to occupy a position within the realm of signification, distinguishing it from the semiotic governed by drives and their articulations. The thetic break, like the pivotal space-time interval of Valéry's 'bouche-oreille', gives birth to the subject as speaker of a shared language; perhaps something very close to this crossing of the divide between the unformed and the formed as a precondition of propositionality is caught in Valéry's observation that 'la *voix* poétique doit pouvoir se substituer presque insensiblement à la voix intérieure de source' (XXII, 789).

It is in focusing on the third aspect of voice, its role within Valéry's poetic theory, that its potential for integrating otherwise divided or conflicting dimensions of experience comes fully into play. Many of the central features of his poetic theory and practice, understood as a deliberately calculated manipulation of the listener's sensibility, are implicitly or explicitly voice-related. They derive, in other words, from a recognition of the elusive nature of psycho-physiological functioning combined with the attempt to articulate this awareness theoretically in terms of aesthetic form. The governing insight and ambition underlying this conception of poetry as a *psychesthésique* is to promote or generate a unitive experience or integrated form within the sensibility of poet and listener.

Part of Valéry's aim as poet was to bring about a greater degree of psycho-physiological unity in both the creative and the recipient sensibilities. The experiential space opened up by poetry in which this can be accomplished embodies a moment or mood hovering between sensation of life and awareness of that sensation. By reintegrating awareness within the sensual drama of bodily reality, maintaining it there in permanent oscillatory equilibrium, so that neither dimension achieves predominance over the other, poetic language holds the listener-reader in a state of intensified psycho-physiological self-presence.[12] Such a state is clearly simulated: 'Poésie [. . .] correspondance entre l'être et le connaître, mais correspondance simulée — Le connaître employé à faire pressentir l'être — mais ce n'est qu'un *effet*' (IV, 811). However, the artificial nature of the experience in no way diminishes its value since, during this necessarily brief moment, the privileged individual participates in 'un mode extrême d'être'

(XXIV, 22) where the dichotomies typical of everyday existence are temporarily resolved.[13]

On several occasions Valéry has recourse to the image of 'le pendule poétique' to permit a sufficiently subtle description of the functioning of this operation within the recipient organism. The pendulum is not merely a mechanical, illustrative device but a highly sensitive piece of registering apparatus which describes 'le mouvement de votre âme, ou de votre attention, lorsqu'elle est assujettie à la poésie, toute soumise et docile aux impulsions successives du langage des dieux' (OI, 1373). Above all it is a 'pendule vivant' (OI, 1374) which relies on the existence within the living being of two poles between which its trajectory is effected: 'Notre pendule poétique va de notre sensation vers quelque idée ou vers quelque sentiment, et revient vers quelque souvenir de la sensation et vers l'action virtuelle qui reproduirait cette sensation. Or, ce qui est sensation est essentiellement *présent*. Il n'y a pas d'autre définition du présent que la sensation même' (OI, 1332). The value of poetic language is that it preserves, in the sensibility of the reader, by constantly reactivating it, the oscillation of the pendulum between the two points variously termed 'fond et forme, sens et son, absence et présence, pensée et voix' (OI, 1332–3): all equally arbitrary terms referring to the complementary dimensions of 'la sensibilité intellectuelle'.[14] If the Valéryan field of poetic creativity is approached thus as 'une étude précise et organique' (OI, 428) it comes as no surprise that certain key aspects of his poetics involve an awareness of the interdependence of the psycho-physiological and the aesthetic. One clear instance of the convergence of these two levels is in his understanding of the self-regenerative evolution of 'l'infini esthétique' described in terms which are virtually synonymous with his descriptions of the cyclical nature of organic functioning. Referring to the rhythms characteristic of the body, he notes how 'Tout l'organisme n'a d'emploi qu'à la reconstitution de son sang [. . .]. Mais ce sang [. . .] n'a d'autre emploi que de reverser à l'appareil qui le régénère ce qui est nécessaire à cet appareil pour qu'il fonctionne. *Le corps fait du sang qui fait du corps qui fait du sang*' (OI, 924). Precisely the same 'phoenix' effect is created by the infinitely self-renewing potential of poetic form, for 'le poème ne meurt pas pour avoir vécu: il est fait expressément pour renaître de ses cendres et redevenir indéfiniment ce qu'il vient d'être. La poésie se reconnaît à cette propriété qu'elle tend à se faire reproduire dans sa forme: elle nous excite à la reconstituer identiquement' (OI, 1331).

Change and continuity, renewal and reiteration: these are fundamental principles of *bios* as it is experienced, as consciousness attempts
to understand it and as poetry seeks to embody it. In the process of
reshaping energetic impulse into aesthetic form, the critical element
is time.[15] Time in this instance is determined by the body and its
states; it is, on the one hand, curiously static, given that it is a
gathering into the instantaneity of the present of a wide range of
possible transformations of conscious, sensitive existence. On the
other hand, the fact that time here is dependent on precisely these
processes of organic metamorphosis lends it, simultaneously, a dynamic dimension.[16] Approaching it from the static angle initially, one's
attention is drawn to the numerous passages in the *Cahiers* devoted to
the study of the present. Valéry defines it less as a point of transition
in a linear development from past to future than in spatial terms as a
'Domaine de la Présence. Edifice de la Présence. Sorte de Corps
solide' (XIV, 592) within which the same relations of reciprocity
characteristic of 'le monde à part' or poetic universe can be detected:
'C'est une forme qui a la propriété de coïncider avec elle-même'
(XIV, 592). It is as though the usual processes of change which
characterize organic existence had been temporarily arrested in order
to form an intensely actual moment in the life of the organism.

Valéry evokes his ideal in this respect when he observes how vital
it is to 'construire un *temps* qui convienne à l'être vivant et sentant'
(XVI, 176). A reconstructed time of this sort, derived from the body,
becomes almost synonymous with form: 'J'ai songé à une forme qui
représenterait ce que n[ou]s nommons Présent', he notes; and then
indicates how form is the all-important concept taking precedence
over 'time' which is contained within the wider notion: 'Cette *forme*
définie et adoptée, plus de temps — Rien hors d'elle — mais elle
contiendrait ce que n[ou]s percevons comme temps' (XVII, 458). He
defines more accurately the phenomenon so conveniently but im-
precisely referred to in this way: 'et qui est sensations d'impression ou
d'action, et sensations de certaines limites et de certaines gênes'
(XVII, 458), specifying that undifferentiated sensation is not sufficient
in this respect and that a particular quality of sensation is necessary:
'La sensation essentielle peut se nommer *dilatation* ou *écart* — Cet
écart est *intérieur* au *présent*' (XVII, 458). The experience communicated by poetry, the temporal mood which constitutes that 'other
world' of poetic awareness, a time dependent on intensity and
deriving from desire, is a deviation from the purely functional

processes of the body: 'Cet état est un *écart* c'est-à-dire un *temps polarisé*, et évalué en croissance, ou *dégagement* d'*énergie perçu* comme *accroissement*, et désir' (XVI, 640).

The more dynamic aspect of time as it is embodied in aesthetic form brings us back to the voice. The role of the voice is to embody this form-time in the substance of vocal emission in such a way that it not only brings about a degree of unitive or harmonized awareness within the creative sensibility but equally renders itself capable of embodiment in and transmission through poetic language. It is just such a moment and movement of the voice which is captured in the lyrically abstract language of *Dialogue de l'arbre*, where Lucrèce enquires of Tityre: 'lorsqu'il te vient dans l'âme une ombre de chanson, un désir de créer qui te prend à la gorge, ne sens-tu pas ta voix s'enfler vers le son pur? [. . .] Ah! Tityre, une plante est un chant dont le rythme déploie une forme certaine, et dans l'espace expose un mystère du temps' (OII, 193). The analogy drawn here with the mode of time normally associated with processes of natural growth hints at the nature of the voice as guarantor of continuity within the poetic construct. A poem develops according to '[une] *loi de croissance successive*, ou de *création du temps*, qui compose par pulsions et déductions de la forme, l'état de résonance et *la sensation d'infini esthétique cherchée*' (XIX, 152). In other words, a structure or form is substantialized in the material of language in such a way that total cohesiveness of sound and sense is assured: 'Ceci montre', Valéry continues, 'que chaque chose, en laquelle forme et matière sont liées et *se conservent l'une par l'autre*, a son "temps". La "forme" est alors une intégrale de "temps" — qui absorbe en quelque sorte les âges précédents dans l'actuel' (XIX, 152).

Of interest here is the precise nature of the interaction between past and present instants that contribute to the production of the accomplished form-time. The heightened experience of the present made available through poetry is related to a 'telescopic' effect whereby earlier punctual moments are somehow gathered into an experience of instantaneity. Valéry's prolonged scrutiny throughout the *Cahiers* of the role of memory as fulfilling this connective function indicates that a similar process is at work in providing the means by which diverse instances of the self can be understood as forming a continuous being. In the context of his theorizing on music, he explores it under the heading of *mélos*: 'Mélos,' he observes, 'le contour d'une émotion. Un dessin qui est une génération. Pour que ce dessin soit, il faut entre le simultané et le successif une transmutation possible' (VI, 95).[17] And, as later sections of the argument suggest, it is only when the voice acts as vehicle that access to this curious moment or experience of presentness is possible, as the following remark suggests: '[La mélodie] est *caractérisée par les sensations d'attente et d'écart. Elle n'est possible qu'à cause de l'élongation limitée de l'excursion de la voix concevable*' (XVI, 244).

In an attempt to understand how the effect of continuity which can be perceived in melody is formed within consciousness, Valéry explores this idea further: 'Mélos,' he notes, 'comment définir ce trait divin — cette forme ou ligne d'univers que l'homme peut engendrer et engendre, mais qu'il ne peut concevoir? [. . .] en quoi consiste l'enchaînement du mélos? cf figures, lieux des points cf équilibre des substitutions' (X, 172). The following psycho-physiological explanation of the principle of melody attempts to provide an answer by emphasizing the importance of the liaison between one note or element and the following. Each initial impulse creates 'un état énergético-organico-psychique' (VI, 442) such that the organism is alerted to a different state of being or phase of its functioning. A distance is created between the first and second impulses and a mood of 'attente' instituted, with the result that successive impulses are no longer isolated but interdependent: 'Il se fait un état tel que les notes — ou éléments en seraient l'expression — la représentation — A produit ce qui pourrait le produire, ce qui est capable de A. C'est un phénomène élastique' (VI, 442). This self-propagating structure and effect whereby melody creates itself in a cumulative fashion brings into existence a precise type of temporal awareness. Not only does it organize the sensibility by introducing it to a definite disposition of anticipation — 'La mélodie est une attente organisée' (XII, 705) — but it also initiates a kind of cumulative awareness which Valéry terms 'hérédité': 'Mélos est suite de notes suggérant entr'elles d'autres liaisons [. . .] que celles résultant de la substitution — et qui introduisent une *hérédité*' (XII, 705). The significance of this mode of (self-)generation of a form is not limited to the field of musical and poetic theory. A similar process clearly informs Valéry's highly idiosyncratic autobiographical construction of his own mythopoetic *persona* in the intriguingly symbolic form of the serpent.

In so far as specifically poetic form is concerned, a process of substantialization of space and time is realized in the continuum of the voice, for only if the voice has a memory of itself can it maintain past instances of its emission in the present and so achieve that 'continuité du beau son' (VI, 732) which for Valéry is vital to the successful sustaining of the poetic impulse. According to his definition, then, voice possesses a means of self-recognition, almost a form of consciousness of itself, which enables it to project itself into the future: 'La *voix se prévoit*. La suite des émissions est une forme. Comment se fait la liaison?' — and the parallels with his inquiry into melody are apparent — 'cette *perception* — *création* [ajout marginal: 'Forme'] = *Quantum percipio tantum facio*' (XXVIII, 867). The effect of this propensity for self-recognition within the substance of the voice is to activate an echo effect within the auditory consciousness of the poet. He becomes sensitized to a certain quality of the vocal substance as it wells up in him and thereafter attempts to imitate this quality. Thus Valéry envisages 'la Voix' as a 'forme ou formule d'accommodation — de liaison entre *émission* et *réception* (dans le même système-individu). (L'inspiration est l'état optimum de cette liaison, pendant lequel *on* ne sait si le désir ou le don *mène*). Echange. Création par l'*oreille-complète*' (XX, 225).[18]

The propagation within the voice of a structure containing within itself a kind of coding which permits a constant imitation and subsequent reiteration of its own formal nature is defined in terms which suggest that it produces the generative effect which characterized the functioning of melody: 'la *voix communique* une *imitation de sa condition d'émission* [. . .] — le *modelé* — la *dimension* 3 du discours [. . .] c['est]-à-d[ire] ce qui permet ses syllabes ou mots successifs de former un *simultané*, — *condition* de la *compréhension*' (XXIX, 76). The voice as substance, phonic form, or aesthetic imperative derives its being, gains structure and continuity from its capacity to produce and reproduce itself as an integrated, totalizing, affective gestalt uniting past and present in a synthesizing instant in which its effectiveness and conviction is to be found. It is on this basis that much of Valéry's 'théorie des effets' depends.

Interesting parallels can be drawn here between Valéry's preoccupation with the voice as expressive form making bodily time manifest in the matter of language and Kristeva's thinking on poetic language and fetishism. It is possible to read Valéry's reiterated concern with structures such as the poetic universe or the present instant as it is encapsulated in the vocal substance as a form of fetishization. Artistic practice necessitates a reinvestment of the maternal *chora* so that it may challenge the symbolic order. Poetic activity, understood as a semiotic undermining of the symbolic, operates by dismantling the symbolic and then establishing an object (a poem or work of art) as a substitute or fetish which replaces the symbolic order under attack. The object selected may be either the body or the apparatuses eroticized during vocal utterance or the very materiality of language as the predominant object of pleasure.[19] The voice serves as a containing object, giving shape to time and emotion. This fantasized object has the additional value of redeeming its primary materials by recasting them in a purified, aesthetic form safely distanced from any possible associations with the maternal body. The analysis of *La Pythie* which concludes this chapter provides more precise exploration of these themes through the focus of textual commentary.

Poetic power is energy tapped within the poet, transmuted, given consistency, shape, and purpose according to the requirements of his art. It is primary voice remodelled as transubstantiated voice before being communicated to a recipient sensibility. When it deploys its full range it activates a similarly intense experience of the present in the physical being of the listener. It acts as a vibratory bridge drawing two independent organisms into a state of sympathetic union; the poet reveals his skill in assessing this interchange with subtlety: '[la voix] est aussi un moyen qui rend sensible avec telle approximation, l'accommodation immédiate de l'être — à la distance où se trouve l'Autre, au volume dans lequel il faut l'atteindre, — à la profondeur intérieure qu'on veut toucher en lui — à l'effet qu'on veut en obtenir' (VII, 6). This finely tuned device acts as a kind of litmus test in so far as it is equally revealing of the state of both the sensibilities involved, for '[la voix] peint aussi celui qui étant dans tel état veut modifier un autre' (VII, 6). It is the dialectic nature of the communicative potential of the poetic voice that permits a fuller appreciation of his poetic theory and practice as based on the exploitation of the range of effects available to the experienced musician of the nervous system.

The communicative power of the voice is not limited to the simple expression of an emotion or idea but assumes the far greater responsibility of recreating in the listener-reader an awareness of her/his own vital potential: 'L'objet du poète étant de substituer une vie à une vie à l'occasion d'une idée ou sens' (VI, 755). Just as the value of the poetic experience for the creator lies in the knowledge of the self acquired through his interaction with language, so the poem communicates to the listener the possibility of a similar exploration, for 'Le poète fait aux autres hommes un présent non extérieur, mais il leur donne un autre usage de leurs pouvoirs, une nouvelle distribution de leurs ressources' (VII, 71). Language is communicative action and the effectiveness of poetry lies in the peculiarly concentrated nature of the instrument employed. Valéry's choice of the title *Charmes* for the anthology containing those poems which he still considered worthy of publication as a mature poet is revealing in this respect, for the derivation of the Latin *carmen* embraces not only the dimension of song but evokes, too, the casting of a spell through the incantatory magic of the word.[20] The language of poetry as union of 'fond' and 'forme' produces a state of being which prolongs the initial sense of magic, of miraculous revelation—'La poésie cherche sa voie par éléments, — *"prolongements analytiques"* — *Elle procède par éléments qui conservent l'état chantant et se récupèrent. L'état fournit ce qui le justifie, l'alimente, le perpétue. Echange réciproque d'énergie contre matière*' (XVI, 229)—a state conditioned by the energy from which it is generated and which it, in turn, serves to stimulate.

Only when access to this resonant domain or separate universe has been made available through voice, understood in all its senses, can the poet claim to have come close to that perfection of expression which characterizes 'la poésie absolue'. 'Il s'agit pour nous', he observes in this context, 'de tirer [du langage commun] une Voix pure, idéale, capable de communiquer sans faiblesses, sans effort apparent, sans faute contre l'oreille et sans rompre la sphère instantanée de l'univers poétique, une idée de quelque *moi* merveilleusement supérieur à Moi' (OI, 1339). The conception of a separate 'universe' possessing its own structures of formal interaction is a recognizable feature of Valéry's work. It recurs in various guises throughout his writings and, when placed in the context of the typically Valéryan opposition of 'l'arbitraire' and 'le nécessaire' as constituent dimensions of any work of art, it acquires more specific relevance to his poetic theory and practice (XXII, 631).[21] Referring to that 'monde à part' created by 'le Beau et la résonance', Valéry identifies the value of the 'separate universe' in the fact that, paradoxically, despite its apparent 'uselessness', it imposes an aesthetic order on the instability of the sensitive response of the organism and thereby creates its own necessity: 'Quant à la sensibilité — le *beau* lui impose une *stabilité* qui n'est pas *probable* dans son comportement. Inutilité [ajout marginal: Improbable]. *Le beau ne peut pas être*, et *ne pas être autre*' (XXVIII, 308). In so far as poetry is concerned, the text achieves its fullest effect by transporting the listener-reader into a self-referential universe with its own structures and formal relationships:

'L'ouvrage [doit] *tenir* de soi-même en vertu de sa structure — et non par ses ressemblances et attaches extérieures. Même pas davantage par l'excitation directe des passions propres de la vie' (XXI, 478).[22]

Two embodiments of the self-referential 'universe' may be distinguished in the context of voice. One, which has already been discussed, is internal to the substance of vocal utterance, to the voice as a self-reproducing form capable of transmitting itself into the future—'la voix poétique est celle qui institue échange égal entre toutes les propriétés d'une voix' (XVIII, 754) thus leading to '[la] création de l'état de *rebondissement*, de restitution élastique' (XI, 492). The other universe is the effect of the voice in this mode when it is fully operative in the language of poetry, for, as Valéry explains, '[la poésie] est aussi la faculté humaine de faire des "autres mondes", exercée, disciplinée, contrainte aux limites de la voix, du langage, de ces organes, et profitant d'ailleurs de leur pouvoir d'emmagasiner l'excitation, de l'élever par résonnance' (VI, 449).

It is when the voice has been raised in this way to a level that Valéry equates with song that it achieves its maximum communicative effectiveness; the singing state, which is virtually synonymous with the poetic universe, is the means by which the energy resource identified earlier as origin of the poetic impulse is transferred into the receiving organism.[23] In clarifying how this transmission is accomplished, he refers to an imitative response on the part of the receiving sensibility which enables the creative artist to communicate the aesthetic gestalt or form which has emerged from his own sensibility to another being. Once again form can be seen to be the generative current at work within Valéry's conception of poetic communication: 'Le *fonctionnement* d'un ouvrage est celui de sa *forme*. La *forme* est *Ce* qui imprime à un système sensitivo-psychique, par voie sensorielle, des excitations dont la nature, le dispositif, les intensités *ont été produits* par les actes d'un système' (XXI, 829). And it is voice which reveals itself as holding the key to exactly how this yoking of two systems comes about: 'Le système de la voix et de l'ouïe se conjugue avec un système de l'ouïe et de la voix dans l'autre — et en celui-ci, l'ouïe imprimée par la voix d'autrui doit émouvoir sa propre voix mais ne le peut que par l'intermédiaire central, par images, idées, émotions... Le ton — L'attitude vocale — l'énergie donnée' (VII, 7). A truly physical reaction to a vocal stimulus is invited, provoked in the listener-reader whose body is not allowed to remain unmoved by this vocalized intention expressing vitality. The success of the poet's endeavour to communicate the poetic universe requires that two sources of psycho-physiological energy enter a state of quite literal correspondence. The listener-reader is stepping into a simulated world whose existence depends on his participation in the artifice involved in its creation. Only when the voice in its manifestation as a form embodying a unitive state of being is able to convey the impression, however illusory, of its own naturalness and of the necessity of the domain to which it grants access will it succeed in convincing the recipient sensibility of the need for involvement:

La forme, c['est]-à-d[ire] — la *Voix*, qui est l'*unité*. [. . .] Ce n'est pas la conti-nuité, mais la présence soutenue et telle que chaque membre est à sa place fonctionnelle. Alors s'impose à l'autre l'acte tien. Et ce tien peut être fabri-qué, artificiellement monté. Si ce travail est bien fait, l'autre en est saisi et lui obéit. L'autre est le fournisseur de la force et toi agis par relais. (XII, 806)

Notre 'Style' c'est notre voix, altérée par notre travail, complétée. (X, 498)

It is in *La Pythie*, a poem enacting the process by which the body becomes articulate, that many of the aspects of voice which have been explored thus far converge. It evokes the bodily participation of an individual subjectivity in the birth of a voice and invites the listener to experience with a certain measure of corporeal empathy or ident-ification the pain and elation which such a process involves.[24] It is a poem about finding the voice, allowing the breath to breathe through the living body, to assume its true resonance and emerge as harmonious vibration. Its stanzas speak indirectly of the arousing of *kundalini*, the feminine energy associated with cosmic vibration in Eastern thought, as the awakened chakras bring the self into being in terms of transmuted sound. It is also, perhaps, the poem which resonates most profoundly, and at all levels, with the challenges and complexities posed by the Valéryan subjectivity in the formulation of its desire.

For Valéry the act of articulation is one of the least negligible of the wide range of factors involved in the production of a poem. Many of his *Cahiers* analyses emphasize how a narrowly exegetical approach to the poetic text is incapable of providing an adequate account of the initial stages of expression or of how these are incorporated into the 'finished product'. Only the empirical experience of the poet can teach the importance of direct contact with the physical sensation of the reciprocal action between 'audition' and 'articulation' within the creative sensibility which initiates the formation of poetic discourse (XXIII, 197). Whether he is referring to the poet creating a vocal gestalt or to the listener lending his voice to the re-enactment of the text—and the predicament of the Pythie remains sufficiently ambiguous to permit both these interpretations—the power of the breath is shown to be primordial in the production of the voice of poetry.[25] Perhaps the form which is ultimately born of and in this text, 'cette langue prophétique et parée', may be read as that perfected register of language which transcends the immediate language of the sensibility—'voix de ma substance (primitive). Sensibilité du sensible même' (XXVIII, 343)—in so far as it has required selection, effort, and commitment on the part of the poet. Voice as integrity or truth to self, the basis of an authentic affirmation of identity, can only emerge when mind and body have laboured, quite literally, towards the shaping of a new form, an aesthetically transformed self. An inevitability, almost a sense of obligation, becomes apparent in the relationship between creator and language. The poet, in determining the authenticity of his creation, must heed the only reliable gauge of integrity which he possesses, namely the inner standard of the voice: '*Langage vrai*', Valéry remarks, 'est celui dont nous reconnaissons tous les termes comme nôtres, c['est]-à-d[ire] comme si n[ou]s les avions créés pour nos besoins et par eux. Ils sont de notre voix' (XXIII, 526).

Once the products of the sensibility are in harmony with the standard of self-judgement imposed, a sense of conviction may inhabit the work. Yet for this to come about a delicate sensitization of poet and listener is required since 'il faut pour la poésie une organisation de l'individu des plus délicates quant au montage, s'il doit atteindre le pur et le vrai de cette production' (XXII, 213). It is not easy to decide what marks such purity but it is a highly significant act of self-definition in relation to language since it communicates to the listener the intrinsic worth of the creative consciousness.[26] The optimum state being striven for is one in which the artist's critical capacity is integrated so totally that it becomes instinctive. To a certain extent he must learn simply to trust the words that rise up unbidden:

Et, comme viennent les larmes aux yeux de l'ému, ainsi les paroles divines et *plus qu'exactes* du poète — Comme viennent les larmes d'un point de la vie plus *profond* que toute liberté et que toute maîtrise des actions, ainsi viennent ces discours, langage qui n'obéit pas à la pensée dégagée, et qui se précipite avant. (XX, 678)

It is from this obedience to promptings more powerful, sure, and revealing than those of will or consciousness that the drama of the Pythie derives its force. The voice to which she submits possesses a wisdom drawn from the depths that renders it incontrovertible in its evidence and efficacy.

The more deliberately a poet learns to handle his phonic sensibility the more possible it becomes to talk of the poetic voice as a consciously exploited imposition of style. The question then arises as to how the distance is bridged between the conscious and unconscious levels in the creative process; and Valéry's observations in this regard allow a considerable margin of ambiguity since the idea of the poet surrendering passively to forces outside his control clearly held limited appeal for one who prized the value and virtue of lucidity. The essential point here is choice; and the extent to which an active or passive attitude is predominant within the creative consciousness when the expressive impulse demands formalization is a question of will in relation to aesthetic considerations: 'La *forme* est une acquisition — par *adjonction*', Valéry observes in the context of the balance to be reached: 'J'ajoute, — ou plutôt: il *s'ajoute* — à une diversité ce qu'il faut de *moi* (*actes virtuels* et *images* visuelles ou tactiles qui s'ajustent) pour engendrer une *Unité* — à répétition. [. . .] *Relations Forme — Volonté*. Recherche d'un accord entre [. . .] *faire* et *produire*' (XXVIII, 648). Something of this problematic is worked out within the tension and struggle of subjectivity in process, on trial, that the creative agony of the Pythie recounts.[27] In order that the voice is not purely an unconscious encoding but rather a cooperation of conscious and less conscious aspects of the self, a degree of personality regulates or asserts its presence in relation to the impetus of language at work within the sensibility, the semiotic realm.

This is a poem about birth, about the moment of separation between an unmediated relation of the subject to its own reality as semiotic, still absorbed in the impulses and flow of the pre-verbal state, and a new mediate *rapport* in which the subject, no longer fused with its own process, acquires the capacity to see itself as a distinct entity in the world of objects which has been created in and through the process of detachment from the semiotic *chora*. *La Pythie* depicts the coming into existence of subjectivity as distinctiveness; that Valéry elects to trace the emergence of subject status through the metaphor of feminine consciousness is significant both with regard to the feminine as an important dimension of his own creative self (the focus of a later chapter) and in the context of psychoanalytic theory where the maternal body may function as a symbolic container. Separation from the mother's body is a prerequisite of the subject taking up a position in the symbolic order and thereby acquiring an identity. Dependence on the mother is severed and transferred into a symbolic relation to an Other; this otherness as radical difference may be envisaged as death. The Pythie encounters the horror of such a void in the course of her prolonged agony which is both a death and a birth as the earlier merged self is succeeded by the autonomous being developed in the time of the text. Semiotic motility, the realm of drive, rhythm, impulse, is transformed in order to remove it from the maternal or auto-erotic enclosure. By introducing the mark of separation, or thetic break, and so affirming the signifier/signified relation, meaning is permitted to emerge. From the vessel of the Pythie's female depths a voice emerges that is clearly distinct from the spasmodic articulations of the initial phase of her anguish, as the typography of the final stanza itself makes clear.[28]

Perhaps, then, it is legitimate to read this disruptive text as an enactment of negativity, an embodiment of what Kristeva terms rejection and which she identifies as symptomatic of the modernist poem: the torment of the 'hysterical feminine' subject gives voice to the semiotic sensibility struggling, in Valéry's creative consciousness, against the rigidly controlling structures of the syntax of the symbolic order, the formalistic rituals of the French poetic tradition, the austere lucidity of patriarchal rationalism. Although the body of the priestess is torn by the force working through her, the containing structures of linguistic convention do not fragment despite the power of the on-slaught; the precarious thetic, though challenged, survives.[29] This ambivalence translates the paradoxical yearning noted earlier as an aspect of Valéryan creativity torn between the logical and the emotional, the language of conservatism and the voice of experiment. The practice of the artist in Kristevan theory is a deliberate mani-pulation of the disruptive potential of the semiotic. In order to protect the self from drive attacks directed against the thetic and so as not to succumb to the risk of psychosis, the artist/subject uses fantasies to articulate semiotic energies, thus creating what is termed a 'second degree thetic', in other words a resumption of the functioning characteristic of the semiotic *chora* within the signifying device of language.

Nor is it so hard to sense why this exploration of the internal dynamics of subjectivity is connoted feminine in Valéry's poem. For one as acutely conscious of the apparent value of control as Valéry, to acknowledge the power of the unconscious is difficult and dangerous. Disguised by being attributed to the Other, the feminine, it can, to a certain extent, be disavowed or at least distanced. Reading his own autobiography in the mirror of his writings, Valéry, the arch-rationalist, is spared a certain degree of anxiety since full confrontation with the self has been mitigated by the disguise of gender exchange.[30] Analogously, if the idea that much of the repressed dimension of Western culture may be connoted 'feminine' is accepted, then clearly the unconscious in this text will bear those features.[31] A further aspect of Kristeva's exploration of the psychoanalytic status of the mother argues that the symbolic is founded on her expulsion or rejection. In other words, before the 'beginning' of the symbolic, the drives move towards 'abjecting' the maternal body. When the symbolic is successfully in place, abjection continues to function as a kind of background support for the symbolic and its attendant ego; the abject can therefore be read as the undesirable face or dark side of narcissism. The female body, the formless and unstructured voice, the chaotic power of disruptive drives—all evoke, in the Valéryan text, the threatening reality of the abject as the ambiguous, that which defies boundaries, disturbs identity, system, and order.

A brief assessment of the form of *La Pythie* as text reveals a clear containing structure, a symbolic womb formed by syntactic parameters. Within a framework provided by the introductory stanzas (1–3) and those which conclude the poem (22–3), all recited by an unidentified 'narrator', it is the voice of the priestess herself which predominates in the main part as she explores different states of her sensibility, whether past or present, joyful or harrowing. Like the Parque and Narcisse before her she desires to make sense of a conflict which divides her by externalizing the relationship between her relatively uncomplicated physical nature and the awakening to a painful, yet fuller mode of existence exemplified by the intercalation of language with all that it implies. The poem as textual site incorporating both genotextual and phenotextual dimensions constitutes a lingering within the experiential space lying between the poles of 'être' and 'connaître' which was earlier identified as the poetic instant par excellence. The experience evoked is a journey in and through both the body and the voice; the Pythie as prophetess represents the incarnate feminine and embodies, in a sense, the fetish alluded to earlier for, as Valéry suggests, 'la Poésie [. . .] est la divinisation de la Voix' (OI, 597). Her testing, 'procès' and 'épreuve', is realized in the progression which takes her from the confusion, violence, and pre-verbal promptings to which her physical self is exposed—and body here may be read as the *chora*, a receptacle which is nourishing, maternal though deprived of unity, or identity—to the creation of the more structured voice of poetic discourse which emerges at the end of the poem.

The body throughout serves as the site or space in which the dramatic encounter between semiotic and symbolic takes place. In referring to herself as 'ce corps de mort' (stanza 9) the priestess evokes an awareness of a stage identified by Kristevan theory in which the subject, as both semiotically and symbolically determined, is both generated and negated, where its unity asserts itself against and is attacked by the charges and stases that produce it. Such an experience resembles death because the process of coming into being as subject or as text demands an acknowledgement of the reality of the death drive. The Pythie struggles to resist the thrusting upon her of a total awareness of life and self, a synthesis of the physiological and psycho-logical dimensions which has been shown above to be the goal of Valéry's conception of the poet's task: 'de nous donner la sensation de l'union intime entre la parole et l'esprit' (OI, 1333), between body and consciousness. She responds to the enactment of the thetic phase with all the ambivalence which subjective positioning implies.

Bodily awareness is obviously central to *La Pythie*; Valéry refers at one point to a 'poème sur l'animalité' (IX, 918). It is perhaps the most vivid and harrowing depiction that he provides of how physically demanding a process the creation of poetry is. A remark from the *Cahiers* seems particularly apt in this respect: 'Inspiration est la cause inconnue de la création ou production par le "mouvement" — la puissance/violence des pensées qui veulent se faire jour, engendrerait la "forme" la plus énergique, "Forme Vive"' (XII, 463). Rather than considering inspiration in the traditional sense, the reference to the birth of form here may be viewed as an account of the thetic phase which marks the separation from the semiotic or maternal *chora* and initiates the emergence of meaning. Valéry captures in this text the precise instance of emergence of the form that embodies the sense of the poem. It is the moment of insemination of form by meaning, of the semiotic by the thetic impulse. The ambivalence of the reaction of the priestess to the invasion of semiotically governed drives and fantasies which threaten the fragile hold of the symbolic is conveyed by the terms of stanza 21, simultaneously derogatory and admiring:

> Ah! brise les portes vivantes!
> Fais craquer les vains scellements,
> Epais troupeau des épouvantes,
> Hérissé d'étincellements!
> Surgis des étables funèbres
> Où te nourrissaient mes ténèbres
> De leur fabuleuse foison!
> Bondis, de rêves trop repue
> O horde épineuse et crépue,
> Et viens fumer dans l'or, Toison! (OI, 135)

The first five stanzas depict the invasion of her body by a force similar to the rhythmic impulse which Valéry identifies in the following passage as a contributory factor in the process of poetic creation: 'je fus tout à coup *saisi* par un rythme qui s'imposait à moi, et qui me donna bientôt l'impression d'un fonctionnement étranger. Comme si quelqu'un se servait de ma *machine à vivre* [. . .] la sensation d'étrangeté dont j'ai parlé se fit presque pénible, presque inquiétante' (OI, 1322).[32] In the third stanza the Pythie gives vent to the pain which such an invasion of one's being can produce:

> — Ah! maudite!... Quels maux je souffre!
> Toute ma nature est un gouffre!
> Hélas! Entr'ouverte aux esprits,
> J'ai perdu mon propre mystère!...
> Une Intelligence adultère
> Exerce un corps qu'elle a compris! (OI, 131)

In both instances, be it Valéry's account of a personal experience or the transposition of this into the poetic text, it is the foreign and divisive nature of the force in question which is emphasized.[33]

The panic which the priestess communicates recalls the horror aroused by the prospect of an invasion of the self which the drama of Narcisse conveys. Both describe the experience in terms of an influx of sound and, in both poems, the upsurge of anxiety recounted may be read as transcribing the effect of the subject's enforced encounter with the realm of a hitherto repressed 'abject'. Thus in the fourth stanza the Pythie recoils from the assault of which she is the victim, desiring, like Narcisse, to maintain her purity and intactness. The violent and disrupted nature of the language which conveys the agonizing experience of the priestess as she is raped into awareness suggests parallels with a view of the *chora* as a space of rupture and articulation against which discourse defines itself:

> Qui me parle, à ma place meme?
> Quel écho me répond: Tu mens!
> Qui m'illumine?... Qui blasphème?
> Et qui, de ces mots écumants,
> Dont les éclats hachent ma langue,
> La fait brandir une harangue
> Brisant la bave et les cheveux
> Que mâche et trame le désordre
> D'une bouche qui veut se mordre
> Et se reprendre ses aveux? (OI, 131)

Her voice is no longer her own; an anonymous vocal force has usurped her powers of articulation, shaping them in order to grant an outlet to an aspect of her own subjectivity which is as yet unfamiliar to her. Such a phase of misrecognition or 'méconnaissance' necessarily precedes the moment of recognition within the creative conscious-ness, marked by the completed voice which confirms the authenticity of the poet's production. To move through the self's alienation from self is a prerequisite of the ultimate reunion that is only approximated to in the perfection of a fully conscious and fully embodied know-ledge of self in language; and only achieved in death.

Her body is transformed, becoming simply a vessel serving some unknown purpose, as she observes with bitter indignation:

> Qu'ai-je donc fait qui me condamne
> Pure, à ces rites odieux?
> Une sombre carcasse d'âne
> Eût bien servi de ruche aux dieux! (OI, 133)[34]

and throughout the poem the spatialization of the inner depths of the organism, recalling the *chora* as a kinetically and vocally characterized space, renders very vividly the idea that it is the human body as container, field, and sounding-board which is the scene of this drama of voice. In the opening stanza, the image of 'les flancs mugissants' suggests the resonant capacity of the body, a theme which is devel-oped further as the priestess listens to the usurping voices within her (stanza 5), or reproaches the force which has violated her, employing an analogy with the realm of sound:

> Mais une vierge consacrée,
> Une conque neuve et nacrée
> Ne doit à la divinité
> Que sacrifice et que silence,
> Et cette intime violence
> Que se fait la virginité! (OI, 133)

During a moment of nostalgia in which she recalls the original harmony of her untouched body in terms reminiscent of those used by the Parque in similar mood, she leads the listener-reader through an exploration of those inner spaces:

> Mon cher corps... Forme préférée
> Fraîcheur par qui ne fut jamais
> Aphrodite désaltérée,
> Intacte nuit, tendres sommets,
> Et vos partages indicibles
> D'une argile en îles sensibles,
> Douce matière de mon sort. (OI, 132)

She hints at a further dimension which the body possesses: its absorbent capacity, which she emphasizes as she breathes in the vastness of the universe:

> [. . .] soulevée à mes narines,
> Ouverte aux distances marines,
> Les mains pleines de seins vivants,
> Entre mes bras aux belles anses
> Mon abîme a bu les immenses
> Profondeurs qu'apportent les vents! (OI, 133)

Like her sister the Parque, her awareness of her psychological state and of the tensions which it causes can only be expressed, in the literal sense of the term, in tears. The description of the physiological process of the rising wave of emotion, symbolizing the upheaval of the sensibility inherent in any creative process, where the pain associated with birth is akin to a kind of death, provides a further opportunity to highlight the internal dimension of the body and its role as source:

> O formidablement gravie,
> Et sur d'effrayants échelons,
> Je sens dans l'arbre de ma vie
> La mort monter de mes talons!
> Le long de ma ligne frileuse
> Le doigt mouillé de la fileuse
> Trace une atroce volonté!

> Et par sanglots grimpe la crise
> Jusque dans ma nuque où se brise
> Une cime de volupté! (OI, 135)

This intense moment of mingled pain and pleasure is, again, not unlike that discussed by Kristeva in relation to the irruption of drives within the speaking subject. When these invade the realm of the signifier they shift the metonymy of desire so that a *jouissance* normally invested in the object/the other turns back on the auto-erotic body ('mon cher corps'). Language holds an ambiguous position in this process: it functions as a defensive construction, attempting to limit the influx of semiotic forces, yet also betrays the death drive underlying it.

A passage from the *Cahiers* reveals how Valéry envisaged the organism as a sounding-board whose potential should be developed in life and poetry:

La poésie, peut-être, c'est toute l'âme, — toute la parole, tout le dictionnaire possible de l'être, tout l'être en tant qu'appels, réponses, actes, émotions, considérés comme un instrument. Telle est la Lyre, et non autre chose. Parcourir d'autorité, avec liberté totale [. . .] ce registre, clavier universel, aux cordes innombrables — Mais chaque fois il faut créer la corde — Montage de la lyre. (VII, 425)

The Pythie views her body in a similar fashion as she considers the modulations of the organism which she must inevitably face:

> Hélas, ô roses, toute lyre
> Contient la modulation!
> Un soir, de mon triste délire
> Parut la constellation!
> Le temple se change dans l'antre,
> Et l'ouragan des songes entre
> Au même ciel qui fut si beau! (OI, 133)[34]

The lyre of her sensitive being changes in its function; the image of the temple, originally the form traced by the priest attending a prophetic ceremony, and which recurs in *Fragments du Narcisse* and *La Jeune Parque* in the same equation with the body, possesses associations of symmetry, balance, and harmony. Imminent, by way of contrast, is the horror attendant upon the descent into the depths, cavernous, dark, chaotic, where the outrage which will ultimately lead to the emergence of unsuspected dimensions of the priestess's being will take place.

As the poem develops towards its climax (stanzas 18–21) the focus on the physicality of the creative process becomes even closer. It is in this context that Valéry's observation of how 'L'inspiration est peut-être une participation *particulière* du "corps" au labeur de l'esprit' (VII, 905) acquires full significance. With the opening lines of stanza 19 the process of labour which will eventually lead to the birth of the voice begins: 'Entends, mon âme, entends ces fleuves!'; and the terms used by the Pythie to describe this moment are very close to those which Valéry employs in a theoretical discussion concerning the nature of 'inspiration': '[Le poète] n'agit pas sur ce poème dont il n'est pas la source. Il peut être tout étranger à ce qui découle au travers de lui. Cette conséquence inévitable me fait songer à [. . .] la possession diabolique' (OI, 1377).[35]

The questions now posed by the bewildered victim: am I the origin of this force ('Est-ce mon sang?') or simply the vehicle for an anonymous impulse ('Sont-ce les neuves / Rumeurs des ondes sans merci?') lie at the heart of the poem's ambiguity.[36] The identity of the 'Puissance Créatrice' is never revealed for the simple reason that even the consciousness of the poet is incapable of apportioning precise responsibility to one or other of the multiplicity of tendencies at work within him during a period of creativity. Whatever the exact nature of the dichotomy, the priestess senses that the tensions within herself, even though they may not be identifiable, are on the verge of achieving some form of resolution as she calls out:

> Frappez, frappez, dans une roche,
> Abattez l'heure la plus proche...
> Mes deux natures vont s'unir! (OI, 135)

It is to a unity of a similar sort that Valéry refers in observing that 'Il y a rythme quand la connaissance participe au fonctionnement de l'être — quand nos actes sont liés par des sensations au domaine psychique — Il n'y a pas division' (VII, 488). In giving birth to the rhythmic language of poetry the priestess will facilitate in herself a greater harmony of being.[37]

The moment of birth and the rupturing of the body by the long-contained forces of creation are depicted in stanza 21 with a painful degree of physiological realism. The closest that Valéry comes to defining the exact nature of these forces is as 'une qualité spéciale, une sorte *d'énergie* individuelle propre au poète' (OI, 1377) which wells up within him on occasions of inestimable value, those 'instants [qui] nous trahissent des profondeurs où le meilleur de nous-mêmes réside'

(OI, 1377), and which casts an illuminating beam on his inmost self.
This force or energy, the dynamism of the semiotic *chora*, which
introduces the self to a hitherto unknown state of psycho-sensory
awareness, is hailed as contributing to that ultimate 'Illumination,
largesse' in the closing lines of the poem because of the precious and,
perhaps, unwarranted privilege which it bestows; and because it is an
essential component of symbolic discourse.

In the final two stanzas the idea of unity predominates. It is by
voicing her inner turmoil that the priestess achieves a degree of
catharsis:

> Mais enfin le ciel se déclare!
> L'oreille du pontif hilare
> S'aventure dans le futur:
> Une attente sainte la penche,
> Car une voix nouvelle et blanche
> Echappe de ce corps impur. (OI, 136)

She has exorcized the demon which inhabited her, demonstrating the
therapeutic value of expressing emotion in language ('Parler n'est-ce
pas se mettre / En équilibre?' (III, 772)). The agony of the creative
process is over and a sense of calm prevails now that a measure of
integration has been accomplished.[38]

It is not entirely clear to whom the statement made in the final lines
of the poem should be attributed. It may be read as the utterance of
the newly born voice testing its powers for the first time, revelling in
the sense of autonomy achieved now that it has been liberated from
the organism. The voice of poetry addresses itself, pointing to the self-
referential nature of all poetic language:

> Honneur des Hommes, Saint LANGAGE,
> Discours prophétique et paré,
> Belles chaînes en qui s'engage
> Le dieu dans la chair égaré,
> Illumination, largesse!
> Voici parler une Sagesse
> Et sonner cette auguste Voix
> Qui se connaît quand elle sonne
> N'être plus la voix de personne
> Tant que des ondes et des bois! (OI, 136)

The thetic phase has brought about the production of the object; in
positing the imaged ego, the ego as distinct from the maternal *chora* by

its assumption in the symbolic order governed by language, the world of objects as separate and signifiable is also posited. Thus the sign, bearer of meaning, can emerge. The priestess, by submitting herself to the radical fissuring of her being, conceiving of her own status as subject by her distance from unmediated selfhood, has passed through the stage of the specularization of the ego, portrayed in this text auditively in terms of the self as echo. The language of perfected poetic discourse, the connoted mimetic object which simultaneously transgresses and maintains thetic unicity, is the fetish object which reveals itself at the close of the poem, 'Honneur des Hommes, Saint LANGAGE'. This self-referential voice unites *chora* and symbolic order in its power of synthesizing resonance: 'La Poésie n'est pas la pensée; elle est la divinisation de la Voix' (OI, 597).

Notes to Chapter 1

1. For an interesting exploration of the mimetic virtue of language in the Mallarmean/Valéryan version of cratylism, see Gérard Genette, 'Valéry and the Poetics of Language', in Josué V. Harari (ed.), *Textual Strategies: Perspectives in Post-Structuralist Criticism* (Ithaca, NY: Cornell University Press, 1979), 359–73, and Robert Pickering, 'Valéry et le cratylisme', in Régine Pietra (ed.), *Valéry: la philosophie, les arts, le langage* (Grenoble: Université des Sciences Sociales, 1989).

2. 'Poésie — Langage immédiat de ma réalité. Voix de ma substance (primitive). Sensibilité du sensible même. (Expressions qui êtes la chose exprimée)' (XXVIII, 343).

3. The principal texts by Kristeva referred to in the following pages are *Séméiotiké: recherches pour une sémanalyse* (Paris: Seuil, 1969) and *La Révolution du langage poétique: l'avant-garde à la fin du XIXᵉ siècle. Lautréamont et Mallarmé* (Paris: Seuil, 1974). For critical assistance, see also John Lechte, *Julia Kristeva* (London: Routledge, 1990) and *The Kristeva Reader*, ed. Toril Moi (Oxford: Blackwell, 1986).

4. Rejection describes all that is repressed or kept at bay in the operation of the symbolic; in other words, the drive-centred activity of the body, its semiotic dimension, although rejected by the symbolic, remains present in, and an integral part of, its functioning (Lechte, *Julia Kristeva*, 135–6). Stephen Romer explores the 'euphoric' nature of Valéry's prose poetry in 'Esprit, Attente pure, éternel suspens...: Valéry's Prose Poetry', in Gifford and Stimpson (eds.), *Reading Paul Valéry*, 121–37.

5. 'Esthésique [. . .] j'y mettrais tout ce qui se rapporte à l'étude des sensations; mais plus particulièrement s'y placeraient les travaux qui ont pour objet les excitations et les réactions sensibles *qui n'ont pas de rôle physiologique uniforme et bien défini*. Ce sont, en effet, les modifications sensorielles dont l'être vivant peut se passer, et dont l'ensemble (qui contient à titre de *raretés*, les sensations indispensables ou utilisables) est notre trésor. C'est en lui que réside notre richesse. Tout le luxe de nos arts est puisé dans ces ressources infinies' (OI, 1311). See also Brian

Stimpson's 'An Aesthetics of the Subject: Music and the Visual Arts', in Gifford and Stimpson (eds.), *Reading Paul Valéry*, 219–35.

6. A feeling referred to elsewhere as 'la sensation panique d'*Etre*. Car *Etre* [. . .] — ce n'est qu'une sensation' (XXVII, 482). For a range of contemporary readings of the relationship between mind, body, and *écriture* in Valéry's writings see *Corps et écriture*: Actes du Colloque de Sète, *BEV* numéro spécial, 65–6 (1994). See too Michel Jarrety's *Valéry devant la littérature: mesure de la limite* (Paris: P.U.F., 1991) for a reading of Valéry's attitude to language which distinguishes between *énonciation* or *parole vive*—the living act of utterance which characterizes the subject of speech—and *énoncé*, expression dictated by linguistic convention and so incapable of adequately articulating the subject's desire. He interprets voice in Valéry as subversion of language since voice as *énonciation* of singularity stands in opposition to the *énoncé* of system and code.

7. In presenting a theory of the processes which constitute language and which are thus centred on the speaking subject, Kristeva posits a human subject always involved in both the semiotic and the symbolic as modalities by which meaning is produced. Before the final positioning of subjectivity is accomplished through the acquisition of identity in the symbolic order, subjectivity as a process, rather than as a position or structure, is operative at the level of pre-Oedipal drives. She refers to this level, the semiotic, as a 'psychosomatic modality of the signifying process; it precedes meaning; it is not a symbolic modality but rather one which articulates a continuum deriving from the body's drives and rhythms' (*The Kristeva Reader*, 93); this view of subjectivity assumes the Freudian notion of the unconscious in so far as theories of drives and primary processes connect linguistic signifiers to psychosomatic functioning.

8. 'Poème-scène. Celui ou celle qui se considère le corps. Poème — monologue — dialogue. Poème — discours' (XII, 875).

9. Valéry's interest in the psycho-physiological bases of sound-production permits a 'rapprochement' to be made with the area of linguistic science which covers this, namely, phonostylistics. His interest in this field may have been aroused, and was certainly encouraged, by Michel Bréal's *La Sémantique*, which he reviewed in the *Mercure de France* in 1898 (OII, 1448–54). He was probably aware, therefore, of the work being carried out at the 'Laboratoire de Phonétique expérimentale' founded in 1897 at the Collège de France, mainly on the initiative of Gaston Paris and Bréal himself. It is worth noting, in this respect, that the earliest *Cahiers* references to the field of internal language occur around 1897, which would suggest that Bréal's work was, indeed, a seminal influence on Valéry's thought, as Jürgen Schmidt-Radefeldt indicates in 'Valéry et les sciences du langage', *Poétique* 31 (1977), 368–85. Equally interesting, as Valéry's reference here to 'la parole intérieure' in association with the concept of difference suggests, is the possibility of shared ground connecting his thinking in this area with that of Jacques Derrida. In elaborating his opposition to traditional Western modes of thought as essentially phonocentric, Derrida explores the phenomenology of consciousness in relation to the production of meaning. He contests the primacy of the voice as the medium of the subject's auto-affection on the grounds that the units of sound which convey meaning in speech display their dependence on differentiation as much as do the units of meaning in written language; it seems, therefore, perverse to prioritize speech as in some sense closer to the instant of

origin, or coincidence of desire and expression. Derrida's deconstructive reversal suggests that, instead of basing a theory on idealized speech—in particular, the circuit of hearing oneself speak, where meanings seem to be made immediately present by the spoken word—language can be seen, rather, as a play of differences, a proliferation of traces and repetitions which give rise to meaning. Chapters 2 and 4 explore the parallels in the thought of Valéry and Derrida further, with particular reference to the voice as origin and to the question of temporal difference as constitutive of identity.

10. For a more linguistically based analysis of Valéry's reflections on language see Schmidt-Radefeldt, *Paul Valéry linguiste dans les Cahiers* (Paris: Klincksieck, 1970). Jarrety offers valuable comment on the nature of the inner word and language, suggesting that they are already contaminated in so far as they draw on conventional language (p. 26). He distinguishes, too, between source and origin: 'La source relève de l'Etre, point mystérieux d'un continuel départ dont le mystère est celui d'un secret commencement, quand l'origine relève de la constante mobilité de la pensée' (p. 131).

11. He focuses, for example, on the critical instant when the inner word crosses the threshold between a state of imminence and of articulated existence: 'Comment est-elle *entendue?* — Comment *écrire* rationnellement cette différence singulière? La parole ext[érieure] ne diffère de la secrète que par des fonctions qui s'associent et se coordonnent à elle — l'alourdissant de leur inertie et de leurs résistances passives, mais l'assujetissant à leur monde plus ardu et solide — plus lié' (III, 483).

12. He notes, for example, that '[les vers] sont pour me rendre plus présent à moi-même, plus entièrement livré à moi-même, dépensé devant moi inutilement, me succédant à moi-même, et toutes choses et sensations n'ont plus d'autres valeurs' (OI, 1449); and, similarly, 'le désir du poète, si le poète vise au plus haut de son art, ne peut être que d'introduire quelque âme étrangère à la divine durée de sa vie harmonique, pendant laquelle se composent et se mesurent toutes les formes et durant laquelle s'échangent les *répons* de toutes ses puissances sensitives et rythmiques' (OI, 1378).

13. The illusory sensation of a state of perfect correspondence is described more specifically in terms of how language affects the body: 'La Poésie préside aux rapports du langage avec le corps en tant que les mouvements et les variations de l'énergie produite/dégagée par ce "corps" par l'excitation verbale, entre en échange réciproque avec les sensations auditives, les significations, les images. Ce qui est poétique c'est qui [*sic*] provoque l'état d'échange réciproque — avec [. . .] illusion [. . .] d'*expression exacte* créant la chose ou sentiment dont elle semble issue ou être expression' (XI, 562). And the overcoming of dualities is emphasized in the following remark: 'Comprendre la poésie, c'est avoir surmonté ce préjugé, qui ne doit pas être excessivement ancien, qui se rattache à l'opposition naïve et non immémoriale entre l'âme et le corps, et à l'exaltation de la "pensée" même niaise aux dépens de l'existence et de l'action corporelles même admirables de justesse et d'élégance' (XI, 230).

14. 'Si la poésie agit véritablement sur quelqu'un, ce n'est point en le divisant dans sa nature [. . .]. La poésie doit s'étendre à tout l'être; elle excite son organisation musculaire par les rythmes, délivre ou déchaîne ses facultés verbales dont elle exalte le jeu total, elle l'ordonne en profondeur, car elle vise à provoquer l'unité' (OI, 1374–5).

15. 'Rôle du "temps"', Valéry observes with regard to poetry: 'Ce temps est, en réalité, *énergie*' (XIX, 147).
16. 'Le temps *vrai* est une réciprocité — un va-et-vient — un cycle — un échange — un écart. Je veux dire que tous ces mots se disputent pour entrer dans une définition impossible. Car si je veux représenter mon état et le changement il faut bien que ce qui se conserve se substitue — et que ce qui se substitue se conserve en quelque manière. Il faut que ce qui change demeure et que ce qui demeure change' (XVI, 249).
17. For a full discussion of *mélos* in relation to Valéry's writing on music see Brian Stimpson, *Paul Valéry and Music* (Cambridge: Cambridge University Press, 1984); and for a situating of *mélos* in the context of a specifically Valéryan redefinition of autobiography, see below, Ch. 4.
18. At times he seems to suggest that memory at work within the vocal substance provides the voice with such a degree of autonomy that the poet can, in some sense, renounce a consciously interventionist role and allow self-propagation in sound to conduct the creative process. Referring, for example, to a poet's necessarily acute sensitivity to sound, he observes how 'un bruit réel entendu par cette oreille est gros de mélodies et d'harmonies. Un mot fait un poème, et même un espace de poèmes, par ondes circulaires. [. . .] L'invention, effet de sursaturation' (VI, 442).
19. Poetic text and fetish are not, however, identical: the poetic function is distinguished from the fetish mechanism by the fact that the former retains a signification; it is not a substitute but a sign (*The Kristeva Reader*, 113–17).
20. Valéry reveals his regret at the passing of an age when words still possessed such magical force in observing that 'la "Science" a tué la Parole' (XXII, 693); and comments on poetry as 'une tradition des temps où la parole comptait' (XXI, 308) contemplating 'toute une archéologie des valeurs de la parole: Incantation — *pouvoir*' (XXI, 308).
21. By studying these evocations of different 'domains' of experience it is possible to discern certain constants in the description of such distinct realms independent of the angle from which the idea is approached. Often Valéry describes how a self-sufficient 'universe' is created from the sense of a perfect harmony of being which is the result of physical activity. So, in depicting the movements of a dancer (and texts such as *Degas Danse Dessin* (OII, 1163–1240), *Philosophie de la danse* (OI, 1390–1403), and *L'Ame et la danse* (OII, 148–76) come to mind), what matters is the sensation of encountering a new and rarely attainable experience of the self in relation to time and space. Formal variations are the key to a different reality. In this respect, one of Valéry's most successful evocations of a world of liberty in transformatory powers, sharing strong parallels with the world of dream, must surely be his re-creation of 'la danse des Méduses' through the suppleness of his lyrical handling of language (OII, 1173). Or again, rejoicing in the feeling of complete harmony with himself which he experiences while swimming, he defines a 'universe' of reciprocal action and reaction where forms and forces engender a mode of autonomous existence: 'Par [l'eau], je suis l'homme que je veux être. Mon corps devient l'instrument direct de l'esprit, et cependant l'auteur de toutes ses idées' (OI, 1091). Similarly, in describing the effect of 'l'émotion poétique' within the sensibility, he notes that '[les] choses et [les] êtres connus — ou plutôt les idées qui les représentent — changent en

quelque sorte de valeur. [. . .] ils se trouvent [. . .] *musicalisés* [. . .] et comme harmoniquement correspondants. L'univers poétique ainsi défini présente de grandes analogies avec ce que nous pouvons supposer de l'univers du rêve' (OI, 1320–1). See also Susan Kozel, 'Athikté's Voice: Listening to the Voice of the Dancer in Paul Valéry's *L'Ame et la Danse*', *Dance Research Journal* 27 (1995), 16–24.

22. These observations belong to what is, perhaps, the best exposition of the defining characteristics of the 'poetic universe', specifically in its relation to the sensibility, to be found: a passage where Valéry analyses the language of *La Jeune Parque* as particularly representative of his conception of 'le monde à part'. That he devotes so much attention to the idea, and with regard to the poem that can perhaps be said to have possessed the greatest autobiographical value for him, is proof of the vital import of the rare state of enchantment which is described in the following lines: 'J[eune] P[arque]. Du vrai de la Poésie qui se trouve en observant ce que chacun y cherche. [. . .] Moi — ce fut *l'enchantement* et l'édification de *l'état* d'*enchantement* ce qui excluait quantité de sujets et d'expressions, dès l'origine; les maximes, les plaidoyers, les relations directes avec le réel — et les interventions personnelles' (XXI, 478). Already one defining feature of this rarefied realm, its isolated nature, has been made apparent. Valéry then defines it more precisely: 'Tout me semblait devoir être *transporté* afin de constituer cet *état rare* — dont les produits ne s'échangeaient qu'entre eux, aussi séparé de l'état ordinaire que celui qu'engendre la musique, par l'exclusion des bruits et similitudes des bruits' (XXI, 478).

23. 'Poésie — Le principe de la Voix — c['est]-à-d[ire] la Voix chantante — comme condition — est pour tempérer les descriptions etc pour paralyser les choses non vibrantes; ou obliger à trouver d'abord cette vibration sine qua non. Mais tout ce qui vibre n'est pas bon — D'ailleurs ne pas se méprendre: ce que j'appelle vibration, n'est que l'obligation imposée par le *texte* même à la voix du lecteur, et *indépendamment du sens*, de sonner, de s'entendre elle-même, de remarquer des relations et des enchaînements et des contrastes, soit dans les timbres, soit dans l'articulation des mots' (VII, 125).

24. The degree to which physical participation plays a part in the composition of poetry emerges from Valéry's admission that he found himself performing a sort of muscular 'mimique' while engaged in the process of creation: 'Je me surprends esquisser (*faire sans faire*) un *pas de deux* en cherchant le verbe d'un vers de *La Cantate du Narcisse "dans mon esprit"* à partir d'une image qui me sert de première matière' (XXI, 749). The energy of the body's creative, semiotic mobility is inseparable from the process of mental productiveness.

25. 'Poésie — phonétique. Tout ce qui est parole est sujet aux conditions de la vie respiratoire. La périodicité, à période limitée variable, de la respiration est une condition de liaison. [. . .] Oxygène et action verbale sont liés. [. . .] Le cycle respiratoire assujettit la voix. Sa période (variable entre limites) est donc la première condition à considérer dans l'art de la voix' (XIX, 471).

26. 'Lit[térature]. Chacun n'ayant que son être auprès de soi pour en tirer ce qu'il offre aux autres en échange de la valeur qu'ils peuvent lui donner, il se définit soi-même par ce qu'il choisit ou qu'il exploite dans ses ressources, dans son expérience et dans ses possibles, et qu'il met en forme, et en lumière au regard des tiers. Ce choix révèle bien des choses' (XXII, 534).

27. Kristeva's characterization of emerging subjectivity as 'le sujet en procès' exploits both these senses of the term 'procès' in French.

28. For a fuller discussion of the poem's final stanza — its strangely alien quality and the question of gender in relation to langage — see Ch. 4, pp. 158–60 and 184–5. Interestingly, too, as Florence de Lussy observes, it is during the genesis of *La Pythie* that Valéry conceives of the overall vision for his collection *Charmes*, suggesting that both poem and *recueil* are dealing in some way with the emergence of a restructured poetic subjectivity (*'Charmes', d'après les manuscrits de Paul Valéry: histoire d'une métamorphose*, 2 vols. (Lettres modernes; Paris: Minard, 1990, 1996), i. 261).

29. In relation to the genesis and composition of *La Pythie*, de Lussy registers Valéry's interest, as a young man, in the phenomenon of madness and quotes from a letter to Breton (1916) where Valéry mentions one particular 'démente', a very beautiful woman, 'une Cassandre à hurler sur les bastions de Troie' (p. 166). She also cites Valéry's admiration for a particular stanza from Hugo's poem 'Lumière' whose thematics and structure clearly reinforce Valéry's own conviction: 'rester maître de soi en refusant les idoles, faux dieux et Pythonisses' (p. 165).

30. In support of my reading of the Pythia's voice and experience as auto-biographical, it is of interest to note that the genesis of the *Charmes* manuscripts reveals an undercurrent or recurrent presence of an unidentified voice which breaks through into written form as the poet is at work. Discussing the way in which *Equinoxe* and *Au Platane* originate in the same 'texte matriciel', de Lussy reveals how, gradually, then more substantially, an entire stanza of *La Pythie* emerges: 'Qui me parle à ma place même?' (Cah. Ch. II, 20^v), pp. 237–9.

31. Chapters 3 and 4 develop this idea in more depth with reference to the work of Luce Irigaray and C. G. Jung.

32. Numerous remarks in the *Cahiers* indicate the extent to which Valéry envisaged rhythm as central to poetry and how closely it relates to the body (XV, 127). He is careful none the less to distinguish between rhythm *per se* and rhythm employed for poetic purposes: 'Le rythme, comme problème *poétique*,' he notes, 'revient à donner à des éléments *conscients* [. . .] une forme d'automatisme. [. . .] C'est pourquoi il faut se garder d'assimiler à la légère le rythme purement auditif avec le rythme dans le langage' (XIV, 795).

33. 'Toutefois nos souvenirs de rêves nous enseignent [. . .] que notre conscience peut être envahie [. . .] par la production d'une *existence*, dont les objets et les êtres nous paraissent les mêmes que ceux qui sont dans la veille; mais leurs significations, leurs relations et leurs modes de variation et de substitution sont tout autres et nous représentent [. . .] les fluctuations immédiates de notre sensibilité générale, non contrôlée par les sensibilités de nos sens *spécialisés*. C'est à peu près de même que l'*état poétique* s'installe [. . .] en nous' (OI, 1321).

34. Modulation for Valéry embraces not only tonal shifts but also the range of psycho-physiological potential available to any human organism and represents for him the most truly poetic subject matter: 'Je ne sais rien de plus véri-tablement poétique à concevoir que cette modulation extraordinaire qui fait parcourir à un être, dans l'espace de quelques heures, les degrés inconnus de toute sa puissance nerveuse et spirituelle' (OI, 816).

35. When he claims that 'le poète [. . .] change le lecteur en "inspiré"' (OI, 1321) by means of 'une forme exceptionnelle d'excitation' (OI, 1337) he is, in effect,

defining the central ambiguity of *La Pythie*. For it is both poet and listener who undergo this experience; this is the secret of the communicative power so essential to Valéry's understanding of the poet's art: 'L'inspiration, mais c'est au lecteur qu'elle appartient [. . .], comme il appartient au poète [. . .] de faire ce qu'il faut pour qu'on ne puisse attribuer qu'aux dieux un ouvrage trop parfait, ou trop émouvant pour sortir des mains incertaines d'un homme' (OI, 1378).

36. It is interesting to note the recurrence of the term 'waves' in Kristeva's definition of semiotic drives as 'waves of attacks against stases, which are themselves constituted by these charges' (*The Kristeva Reader*, 95).

37. 'Si la poésie agit véritablement sur quelqu'un, ce n'est point en le divisant dans sa nature [. . .]. La poésie doit s'étendre à tout l'être; elle excite son organisation musculaire par les rythmes, délivre ou déchaîne ses facultés verbales dont elle exalte le jeu total, elle l'ordonne en profondeur, car elle vise à provoquer ou à reproduire l'unité et l'harmonie de la personne vivante' (OI, 1374–5).

38. 'Poésie est formation par le corps et l'esprit en union créatrice de ce qui convient à cette union et l'excite ou la renforce. Est poétique tout ce qui provoque, restitue, cet état *unitif*' (XI, 289).

CHAPTER 2

Imagining Form

Nous sommes par nature condamnés à vivre dans l'imaginaire
et ce qui ne peut être complété. Et c'est vivre. (V, 11)

Any attempt to understand how creative desire inseminates the poetic
sensibility leads inevitably, in Valéry's case, to a closer study of the
origins of form in the auditive imagination. The previous chapter
offered an assessment of the range of meanings which the term 'voice'
possesses for Valéry. The present one focuses on the process by which
the initial stimulus to creativity within the poet's acoustic consciousness takes on form, acquires a structure, through the images which are
selected to embody the promptings of desire. The central preoccupation of this chapter is not, then, uniquely voice but the desiring
imagination as capable of giving aesthetic form to the insights derived
from the poet's acute sensitivity to reality encountered, in large
measure, in terms of sound. In examining a network of images
recurrent throughout Valéry's published work and the *Cahiers*, it
becomes clear that the auditive imagination functions at each stage of
the creative process: as initial prompting impulse, as the means by
which formalizing patterns provide embodiment for such impulses
in terms of certain textual dynamics and imagery, and as generative
of the goal, albeit fantasy or ideal, of this same creative process.
The discussion will situate Valéry's views on the sources of mental
creativity in the context of contemporary attitudes to the imagination
and the unconscious. Voice, here, has less in common with Freudian
and, more broadly, psychoanalytic approaches; and may be more
readily likened to that elusive level of the subject's activity acknowledged in the framework of the thinking of postmodernity, in terms
of the failure of representation.

The poetic voice is the voice of a desire directed less towards an external force than towards the actively self-transforming capacity of the poetic consciousness. Valéry's 'mystique personnelle' is an appeal or challenge to his own potential for growth and transformation to assist him in creating once again, in relation and resistance to the substance and structure of language, an impression of oneness, harmony, or totality imprinted on the human consciousness since the earliest phase of existence. It involves a self-reflexive voice, enterprise, form: the poet, as Narcissus, depends on his creation to supply the linguistic or textual mirror and echo in which he may trace the process of the self's reconstruction.[1]

The voice here is the intimate instigator of creativity deep within the phonic sensibility of the poet, initiating and sustaining the urge towards expression:

La vraie 'création poétique' se passe dans le complexe de l'être qui a la *voix* pour résolution/motricité — auditivité — Synthèses — [. . .]. Ce qu'il faut pour 'monter' tel vers. [. . .] — Vers 'régulier' c'est-à-dire prévision ou *transmisssion* de forme de proche en proche. [. . .] Cette 'forme' est de l'énergie de cycle d'acte. [. . .] c'est *la voix qui développe le poète*, le modifie, lui est sa *véritable* 'profondeur'. Il se fait une Voix idéale (XXVI, 80)

This primordial impulse or desire stimulates a longing for a form that will be adequate to the fantasy of completeness: 'Il y a dans le fonctionnement de l'être', Valéry confides, 'une *partie* ou une Voix qui représente le *Tout* [. . .] Mais elle *n'est pas le Tout* (qui d'ailleurs n'existe pas)' (XVI, 511). The images released by this imaginary or fantasized state of unity will be explored in more detail later in the chapter. Most immediately significant are those which connect voice with the terminology of divinity.[2] Valéry's inner God-voice, though sharing some features with the psychoanalytic unconscious, alludes also to the power and incontrovertible authority of this energy of desire. His association of inner voice with God bestows recognition on the primordial value of the auditive imagination in shaping subjectivity.

His intuition of a God is primarily as a being conceived of in terms of utterance, of an inner word, but an utterance which predates the categorizing effects of language. Beneath the heading *theta*, in an intensely moving passage entitled *Psaume* which explores the relationship between language, a sense of identity, and certain states of organic existence, he imagines a form of God resembling the semiotic dimension of subjectivity: 'Où est encore le *nom* de Celui qui s'éveille? Qu'est devenu le *nom* de Celui qui est saisi par l'extrême douleur? Comment s'appelle celui qui, cramponné et saisi dans les charpentes de la femme, se foudroie en soi-même et subit son éclair?' (XXI, 870). In other words, what becomes of a sense of individual identity during moments of extreme sensation, whether painful or pleasurable? Moving towards an answer, he observes that 'Au delà, en deça des *noms* sont les *pronoms*, qui sont plus — *vrais* déjà, et plus près de la Source' (XXI, 870). The further one moves from the sophisticated elaboration of articulate language, the closer one draws to the direct articulation of unmediated sensation: 'Et ces mots qui viennent aux amants et aux mères, et qui sont de l'instant, du tout près de la sensation de la vie — quand la chair trop près de la chair balbutie. Pourquoi avoir nommé *Dieu*?' (XXI, 870). The unexpected intrusion of the notion of a deity is developed more fully in terms of voice. Valéry laments the fact that the godhead was named since, in this way, the Pure, the Intact, the Absolute is exposed to the degradation which accompanies existence in, and vulnerability through, language.[3] The definition of 'God' is as 'la Réponse improférable, l'Essentiel essentiellement niable' (XXI, 870). God would appear to represent an apprehension of existence without the mediation and distortion inevitably concomitant upon the intervention of a linguistically structured consciousness, for 'Avec le nom, commence l'Homme. Avant le nom n'est que le Souffle, la rumeur qui doucement consume le dormeur, Le râle du jouir, du mourir, Dans tous ces temps qui sont sans connaissance. Ecoute le son de la Voix, Vierge ou Veuve de mots' (XXI, 871).

A god-voice, or idealized state of uncontaminated utterance, is splendidly explored in a passage revealing Valéry's acute sensitivity to the substance of the voice in precisely such a state of linguistic virginity. He ignores what the voice says in order to perceive more finely the message contained in the sound alone:

'Albe' [. . .] Albe me dit '*Viens-tu?*' *Viens-tu?* Je me sentis participer de deux natures. *Viens-tu?* Mon oreille à regret m'invitait à comprendre, à venir — — Mais ce timbre, cet *u*, cette mélodie de deux notes m'ôtait la force de me rendre et d'obéir. Je demeurai enchanté, dans un monde sonore où ces sons de cristal étaient de la substance ... etc. (XXIII, 110)

Having first envisaged sound in the purity of the Edenic state, he then describes the Fall of the voice into existence:

Albe me dit: *Mais viens donc!* Or la voix n'était plus la même: il y avait en elle de la volonté, de l'impatience, [. . .]. Le son cédait au bruit. Le Reste envahissait l'Eden. Le temps pur se chargeait des nues du souvenir et des devoirs. La compréhension supprimait la substance. La magie, Le Non-sens créant un sens. (XXIII, 110)

If the fall into language in its symbolic function marks loss and deterioration, it seems not improbable that the purest contact with this God would be in terms of the dialogue within consciousness. Indeed Valéry points to the intimacy of the connection between the evocation of a God and the significance which he attributes to 'la voix intérieure' for, within the circuit of internal dialogue, the sense of solitude is effaced by the intuition of the Other. Neither of the two articulating forces need disperse their integrity externally: 'Mystique — Discours du Dieu. *Je ne suis que ton Dieu* — dit cette voix que je ne reconnus pas. Car je connais ma voix intérieure, et celle-ci était intérieure, mais non du tout la *mienne*. Mais que veut dire... *Mienne?*' (XXVIII, 3).[4] Here the question of the 'source' of mental inventivity in relation to the division within auditory consciousness is no longer envisaged in terms of psycholinguistic phenomena but rather as an enigmatic vocal presence stimulating the acoustic imagination of the poet by its attempt virtually to usurp his position: '*Je ne suis que ton Dieu*, dit cette voix, et il n'y a presque rien entre nous. Je te parle à ton oreille intime, dans l'épaisseur même de ton arrière masque, à ta place ordinaire et inexpugnable' (XXVIII, 3).

It is not easy to decide what precise significance Valéry attached to the associated notions of 'Dieu' and 'voix intérieure'. It may well be that his analysis of the unidentified voice within consciousness, both a part and yet not a part of himself, from an apparently spiritual perspective, is an attempt to redefine those mental operations so often referred to by the problematic term 'inspiration'.[5] This does not imply that he attributes the 'origin' to some transcendent being but that he recognizes how valuable for his own spiritual development are those precious, unelicited upsurges of the sensibility. There is nothing strange, therefore, in his borrowing from the vocabulary of spirituality in an evocation of his own creative activity: 'Le Poète: J'attends de moi d'heureuses surprises. *Veni Creator Spiritus...* O Moi, étonne, émerveille, comble Moi! Fais que ma soif se fasse source. Et que mon ouïe intime écoute avec ravissement ma voix intime' (XXIV, 283). The circuit of inner dialogue, a constant accompaniment to consciousness, is the spring from which the dynamic and imagery of the poem as complex, completed vocal form may be drawn. The voice of God is equivalent to the power of creative desire when this is channelled towards the realization of that same desire in language; the inner voice is metamorphosed in its transition from the time and space of the sensibility to the page of the text. Prayer and poetry share certain features and, specifically, the requirement that desiring energy be focused if they are to yield an adequate response: 'Faire prières. Mais inutile encore de dire à Qui? et à fin de quoi. Prière, cette attitude externe-interne. Mais d'abord — externe. Prendre une figure de face et de corps telle qu'un... *Dieu* s'ensuive, et la parole correspondante. Je déchiffrerai cette figure et cette Voix. Car cette Voix doit donner le texte' (XXII, 434). Obedience to the dictates of the unbidden voice is essential (XXIV, 862); to refuse, to ignore the command, to fail to decipher the enigma of the voice would be to betray the very nature and power of the self as creative. The voice of poetry is the voice of the higher self claiming its right to incarnation, beyond the impurities, inadequacies, and accidents of language.[6]

Two contrasting passages in the *Cahiers*, cast in the form of dramatic monologue or dialogue, enact in vivid detail the benefits and risks experienced by the poetic consciousness depending on how it reacts to the intrusion of the god-voice or god-self within the resonant space of its acoustic capacity. The first describes a sense of alienation overcoming the experiencing self in its solitude: 'Drama. (*Intérieur*) *Le Seul* (titre et sujet) Tout à coup, le personnage P se sent autre. Le temps lourd — lui fait pressentir une crise. Il n'est plus celui qu'il vient d'être — étonne les présents — dit n'être pas bien etc.' (XVIII, 884). The intrusive force is then cast in demoniacal guise as a hostile, aggressive vocal energy: 'Seul, il va et vient — Propos etc. Confession (ce qui tient à l'intrigue). Sent venir l'Autre — le Soi démoniaque. Lutte — Une table se renverse. Alors — vient la *Voix*. Injures — Cynique — Impérieuse. Duo entre sa voix ordinaire et la Voix étrangère. Il se blottit, pleure etc. Injonctions épouvantables de la Voix tonnante. Un éclair d'obscurité' (XVIII, 884–5). Whether this hallucinatory scene is read in terms of the return of the repressed occasioned by the mood of 'attente' during which the control exerted by will-power has necessarily been slackened; or whether a conflict similar to the confrontation of the Pythian priestess with the released abject is dramatized here, the voice as dominant presence commanding obedience is undeniable. The mood of profound disturbance, anxiety, and even fear suggests that Valéry is evoking in this extract an autobiographically relevant experience; and that the reader is witness, in this instance, to the sub-text or pre-text, that level of genetic labour from which the text as *écriture* can be born.

In the second account of a somewhat similar moment of creative readiness, the voice striving towards its embodiment in language, though still distinctly alien, inspires wonder, speaks with promise. Again, the scene is set within auditory consciousness as *soma* and *psyche* overhear the strange and beautiful song of Daimon: 'ψ: Et maintenant il se fait entendre. Ecoute — mais c'est une sorte de chant. / φ: Quelle *voix* sans pareille! ψ Ne trouves-tu pas dans ces accents, quelque résonance connue? / φ: Tais-toi' (XXIII, 204). A mood of harmony is evoked, hinting at extremes of beauty or accomplishment. The two witnesses overhear 'le chant du Daimon' composed of 'les vers innombrables *qui n'ont pas encore été faits* et qui seront ou non (qu'importe)! Ils sont et ils ne sont pas' (XXIII, 204); it is a lyric of the purely potential whose value does not depend on any concretization. They note its richness, its unfinishedness, the ceaseless, spontaneous flow of ideas, words, and promptings which combine temporarily before merging into new patterns; this flooding of creative energy, witnessed in its pristine and protean powers, embodies all possibility: 'tous les projets [. . .] et les *commencements*' (XXIII, 204). In the following lines of the scenario Valéry attempts to convey the positive force of silence as an actively creative dimension of the voice of the poetic self: 'φ: Il se tait? Je n'entends plus rien. / ψ: Mais quel silence! Silence non fait de rien, mais bien de tout. *Ecoute* encore plus. / φ: Ce Silence d'une force extraordinaire. Silence plein. / ψ: Toute la force du désir entièrement ressenti. / φ: Viens, ô sorte de dieu! Approche et nous parle! Qui es-tu?' (XXIII, 204). And so, after this prolonged, imaginary dwelling in the cellular sonority of the inventive sensibility, the reader finally hears the voice of the unidentified god: 'Daimôn: Voyez et connaissez le Daimôn de Socrate. [. . .] *Je suis je puis et rien de plus*' (XXIII, 204). The innermost reaches of the creative process are revealed in this intimate confession as the visitation of the voice reveals to the poet's consciousness its generative potential as energy, as vibration, and, ultimately, as meaning.[7]

Whether the ideal of unity or integration into some form of totality which has emerged as a governing mode of the desiring imagination is expressed as the underlying dynamic of a text or in terms of its imagery, its fundamental significance for Valéry is as representative of an absolute towards which his subjectivity tends. To understand more precisely what status this absolute may hold for him leads to a consideration of his thinking on the imagination and its interaction with the reality which it inhabits. Often it is the encounter between the creative sensibility and 'la plénitude du réel' which, reaching deep into the emotional reserves of the poet, provokes a powerful response: 'Il se peut bien, après tout,' Valéry observes, 'que le sentiment en nous soit le réel, la voix réelle, la chose autant qu'elle peut directement être plus qu'être ou être perçue' (V, 33). The order of the real, an incontrovertible level of being which escapes the grid of language, lies beyond the reach of syntax and may only be conceivable as radically and inalienably other.[8] Its strength lies in its utter presence to itself, its irreducibility, representative of a *nec plus ultra* in the experience of reality which makes it valuable as a ground or limit in the world of sensation.[9]

Yet although this elusive level of a degree of absoluteness of contact with reality resists all attempts to contain, comprehend, or otherwise reduce it, its enigmatic nature provokes the human imagination to make such an attempt for, as Valéry comments '*l'imaginaire mord et déchire le réel*' (VIII, 466).[10] It is the arts which, in their various ways, harness the stimulus supplied by this absolute or saturated mode of existence, attempting to transcribe it adequately into equivalent aesthetic form.[11] A kind of dialogue or tension is at work between 'le réel' and 'l'imaginaire', each necessary to the other yet belonging to radically distinct realms of experience. The images in which the auditive imagination cloaks itself may be read as perhaps the closest that the imaginary can come to an equivalence with the real: they embody themselves necessarily in the order of language yet translate, also, the pattern and purpose of that current of absolute reality which provokes the responsive organism. Through Valéry's intense awareness of and response to the world as sound, a network of themes and images enriches the idea of voice through the resonance of patterns embroidered by the poet's imagination. It is not easy nor perhaps desirable to categorize too tightly the extensive range of evocations relating to sound and voice which appear throughout Valéry's writings, sometimes as part of a developing argument and at others, simply as illustrative of thoughts, impressions, emotions. These may, however, be grouped within the scope of the imaginary to indicate how, despite their apparently disparate nature, they not only have in common their role as images developing some aspect of voice but also reveal recurrent preoccupations or tendencies of Valéry's imagination.[12]

It is tempting to try to abstract some meaning from these images which contribute to the developing presence of the voice of the creative self throughout Valéry's work. The following pages balance their argument between the descriptive and the interpretive in exploring an appreciation of his response to auditory phenomena; and serve, too, as a prelude to later chapters which address, from a more strictly psychoanalytical point of view, the reasons which dictate this response. And it is, indeed, in the network of significant images as translating the inner responses of the poetic sensibility that the vital function of form can be convincingly demonstrated. Form, which Valéry refers to as the organic reality of any work of art (XXII, 783), reveals itself as the guiding force which transforms imagined entity into created object or aesthetic unity. Imagination, in his view, is essentially a constructive faculty not to be confused with loose definitions implying inspirational flux or facility. Rather in the way that Baudelaire envisages 'la reine des facultés' as embracing both an analytic and a synthesizing capacity, Valéry views it as comprehending both artistic and scientific inventiveness and, predictably, as simply one amongst a multiplicity of equally important mental functions. Its productive power is prompted by the desire to 'remplir quelque vide — à occuper tout l'espace, à transformer toute la substance qui lui est offerte' (IX, 455); it has, to a certain extent, a compensatory function.[13] The material which it offers is not, according to Valéry, an invention *ab nihilo* but rather a translation or method of noting the outcome of a preceding operation within the mind (XV, 776). Such a view of 'l'idée inventive' as almost always 'une *application*' (XV, 776) robs the creative faculty of some of the pre-eminence accorded it elsewhere and is entirely in keeping with Valéry's intention to view experience in an objective and 'de-transcendentalizing' fashion.[14]

A reading of virtually any Valéryan text reveals how closely he observed the natural world.[15] His imaginative transposition of the detail of a physical landscape into the evocation of the psycho-physiological disposition of the Parque, for example; or his perceptive account of the manner in which Degas transcribes the forms of reality in the creation of his own art, is evidence of his acute sensitivity to the colours, shapes, and substances which furnish the fabric of the universe.[16] As the listener-reader follows the monologue of the Parque, s/he is introduced to a truly cosmic perception of natural reality: the distant, star-patterned sky; the tumultuous sea; the magnificent awakening of natural forces to the call of spring; the delicately observed appearance of dawn with the accompanying emergence of the archipelago of islands; all bear witness to the keenly attentive focus of the observing consciousness for, as Valéry notes, 'les œuvres d'imagination pure doivent se nourrir solidement d'une nourriture invisible, qui est l'observation actuelle. *Car éternel est le détail*' (XV, 776).

Without diminishing the importance of the combinatory activity of the imagination (XVIII, 183), he attaches considerable value to the powerful effect and overwhelming 'reality' of the senses in relation to the imaginative faculty. So, when he poses the question: 'De quoi disposons-nous pour *imaginer* "complètement" [. . .] ce dont nous ne voyons qu'une partie?' (XX, 485), his definition is presented in terms referring to our physical existence: 'c'est-à-dire sur le plan et dans le domaine du *réel-sensible, vue* et *actes*' (XX, 485). In this way he reveals how, for him, the power to imagine is tightly interwoven with the sensory stimulus derived from perception of the surrounding reality:

Le *réel-sensible-présent*, le PLEIN de la perception et de l'action est 'l'absolu'. *Nous ne pouvons pas le dépasser* (d'où la puissance de l'imitation par les arts et la non-vanité de la peinture — c'est nous représenter ce que nous pouvons *faire de mieux* sans le savoir ni vouloir — avec nos *sens*). (XX, 485)

It is rare for Valéry to accord absolute status to any quality or function since to do so implies that no further exploration or transformation is either possible or necessary, and suggests an appreciation of the static or definitive which is quite alien to his thought. Yet it is, perhaps, the intuitive nature of the sense perceptions on which imagination draws that leads him to evoke it in these terms, for he continues: 'Je dirai que ce qui est ainsi est le *Parfait*, quel qu'il soit. *Il sature notre connaissance immédiate*' (XX, 485).[17] It is as 'le grand apologiste de l'Apparence' that Goethe is so highly praised in the essay which Valéry devotes to him.[18] The poems of *Charmes*, in so far as they draw analogies with the processes of the natural world, illustrate the progression within the creative consciousness as it moves from a 'point de départ' in a saturation of the sensory apparatus, through the refining and controlling influence of constraints imposed by language, to achieve a state of poised equilibrium in which the reader detects the tension operating between the impact of lived experience in its raw immediacy and the containing demands of conceptualization and linguistic structure.

The highly empirical nature of Valéry's view of the imagination is strengthened by the emphasis which he places on the type of limits attached to this particular branch of mental activity: 'Imaginer, c'est construire — et la limite de l'imagination est *toujours* la conscience de mon corps en tant qu'édifice, liaisons, libertés — et donc *groupe* d'actes' (VII, 258). A tight link is thus forged between the specific nature of the constructive processes employed by the imagination, and that of the organism viewed functionally as a series of operations and of states in constant transformation. However, a significant distinction is to be made in this respect: whereas the organism can be relied upon, in a state of normal functioning, to conserve certain elements in its process and so ensure a measure of continuity, 'l'imagination poéti-que', in contrast, 'est [. . .] surtout féconde en substitutions gratuites, non enchaînées — ne constituant pas une transformation conser-vative' (XXIX, 398). In the light of this improvisatory freedom of the process of image-production Valéry is led to affirm the supreme value of form as a necessary anchoring technique or productive constraint which the untrammelled imagination requires, for 'elle puise sans compter dans un trésor sans fond — Elle n'épuise pas. C'est pourquoi elle doit (ou se doit de) s'attacher aux *formes*' (XXIX, 398).

As his assessment of Leonardo emphasizes, the pivotal component in any creative undertaking is form; whether the domain in question is philosophy, music, mathematics, architecture or poetry, the creative consciousness addresses the quest for the most comprehensive form by means of which to communicate, as exhaustively and as appropriately as possible, the nature of the creative vision. Valéry's understanding of form suggests that it not only relates to the world of abstract structure but serves also as a kind of analogue of the emotive life. In the previous chapter its role in enabling the voice to (re)produce itself as a recognizable structure sharing qualities with certain forms in the natural world was situated in relation to a temporal dimension. In the present context of the creative resonances of the imagination its interest lies in its positioning on the frontier of conscious and uncon-scious mental activity: on the one hand, deriving its energy and authority from the depths of the organic sensibility yet, equally, pro-jecting itself externally on the texture and shape of a created object.[19]

Valéry's particular conception of the creative power of the imagination views it as generating a primordial or matrix form into or around which the cognitive mind can subsequently develop a more rationally dictated content: 'Un autre mode de l'imagination consiste', he observes, 'dans la division *secrète* entre une forme et une matière, l'une conçue la première et s'imposant à l'esprit comme loi à exemplifier, comme formule d'actes et l'autre fournissant *ensuite* le corps nécessaire à l'existence, à l'exécution, à la représentation, à la réalisation' (VI, 927). A shaping organic impulse is the initiating force which then requires embodiment in the textures and patterns of linguistic form. In a further comment on the relation between inspiring impulse and formal incarnation Valéry indicates unambiguously how the final authority rests with form:

Dans la poésie, c'est l'exercice d'un art formel qui m'a finalement intéressé — J'ai fini par considérer le *contenu*, 'idées', images, comme ... *ne coûtant rien* — et produits 'accidentels' arbitraires [. . .]; mais tenir toujours pour subordonnés à *la figure de la forme*, [. . .] laquelle est la réalité organique de l'ouvrage — et ce qui fait de l'ouvrage une unité de passion et d'action et un moment d'*univers poétique*. (XXII, 783)[20]

Quite how to understand the origin and nature of this commanding form is problematic. Psychoanalytic theory offers a range of hypotheses concerning the connections between the work of art and the unconscious mind. One of the obvious risks incurred by such approaches is that of reducing the power and uniqueness of the created object to an 'explanation' in terms of instinctual drives, neuroses, and sublimation, clearly not a desirable or satisfactory avenue to follow. The other difficulty lies in the need to respect Valéry's particular views concerning the nature of an unconscious zone of mental activity. His curiosity is indubitable: he conceives of the 'inconscient' as a region of immense possibility (IX, 157); as a pre-formal realm outside time and structure (IX, 331); as a part of the complex functioning of the human organism whose nature is distorted by attempts to define it linguistically (IX, 733); and as a psychic mode whose very functioning embodies paradox (X, 157). It is the term 'sub/inconscient' which irritates him (XIV, 57) rather than the concept, whose undoubted value he acknowledges when he explores it according to his own category, 'l'Implexe'. Under this heading he is, in fact, exploring many of the phenomena described by classical Freudian theory although he attempts to differentiate the two rather unconvincingly on the grounds that his 'Implexe' refers to the entire potential contained in the individual being which can, by deliberate manipulation, be encouraged to emerge (XXIII, 398). Shared areas of interest include the notion of a functional or structural 'other' which underpins the activity of consciousness (XVI, 62); the relation of the products of the unconscious mind to sensation, on the one hand, and to the linguistic sign, on the other (XXIII, 317); the symbolism of dreams (XI, 621). The major obstacle for Valéry appears to be his unwillingness to relinquish his belief in the possibility of accounting for the functioning of the human organism in terms of a comprehensive system. Ultimately, he is ambivalent; he recognizes that there is a radically alien dimension of the self's activity—'ce travail inconnu et inconnaissable qui s'opère sans doute dans un "temps" et à une "échelle" où la personnalité n'existe pas' (XIII, 252)—yet speaks also of the ability to harness its power through the integrating activity of artistic creation.[21] When the unconscious can be considered as a resource nourishing the lucidity of the intellect in a cooperation where Apollo and Dionysos hold equal power, he is prepared to grant it a reality.[22]

In conceiving of the imagination as an operation effected outside the full light of consciousness, in what he refers to as an off-stage or 'lateral' zone of activity, Valéry implies some contribution from the 'implexe' or 'inconscient',[23] and touches on an appreciation of certain aspects of the formal component as an essentially unconscious dimension of the creative process.[24] Many aspects of the entire personality contribute to the moulding required in the creation of a work of art (VI, 712); aesthetic form may be interpreted as a recurrent, dominant statement of the self imprinted on and expressed through the chosen medium. Whether or not this concept is conceived of in terms of primal repression, the fundamental significance of form as a projection of selfhood, whether willed or involuntary, onto the shapes and textures of the material world is a vital preoccupation of aesthetic theory which Valéry identifies as a primary element of his approach. Voice, in his imaginative universe, as image, theme or informing awareness is one of the critical shaping forces which give birth to his work and to his very being.[25]

Both aspects of the imagination—its image-producing potential and its capacity to translate organic form into art—come to play a valuable role in the context of the voice. Voice is the vehicle of desire, the bearer of an energy seeking expression in a world which remains far from perfection. Creative desire is an energy which may be experienced physically as the urge to shape reality anew as when love's caress models the body of the beloved with precision of touch and joy; or it may be an inarticulate impulse driving towards some mysterious point of perfectedness intuited beyond the immediate scope of the conscious mind. Whatever its nature, it provokes the very conditions in which its satisfaction may be sought so that the experiencing sensibility is, indeed, only searching for the desired object because it has already been granted a glimpse of its power.[26] Desire, that impulse and energy of life directed towards the objects of its satisfaction, whether real or illusory, stirs the sensibility and prompts its crystallization, in the guise of an image.[27] Gradually, with the vigorous and incontrovertible support of a form that cannot be denied (XXII, 631), and with the participation of memory as the embodiment of form in the body, the image-form is projected into the structures, patterns, resonances of language giving birth to the verbal icon of the poetic text.[28] It is a process such as this which Valéry appears to envisage in 'Conte ou sorte de Poème abstrait' where 'un homme a réussi à *isoler* — au sens des chimistes — l'émotion de "Beauté" — des objets ou compositions de sensations qui la produisent' (XVIII, 417). In a closely controlled manipulation of the desiring self, the focusing power of the creative imagination transforms disorder into order: 'Il a observé en lui-même le désordre délicieux (que provoque le sentiment d'un certain *ordre*), l'infini *intuitif* de désir et de certitude absolue, le rayonnement d'énergie libre dans *tout l'être*. Et il est parvenu à produire ces effets directement sur soi-même par une *concentration* particulière, ou contemplation bien dirigée' (XVIII, 417).

A form of creative meditation or self-attentiveness encourages the structuring tendencies of the sensibility to bear fruit; and from this early stage of aesthetic attunement to the self as source images begin to evolve. Indeed the image can be considered as providing more immediate access to consciousness in so far as it appears to precede verbal formulation, to be capable of its own autonomous statement. It is to the images associated with an auditory awareness, with voice and sound and associated emotions, that Valéry accords considerable importance. He observes, for example: 'L'action vocale [. . .] comme production spontanée de l'énergie, comme abondance, preuve pour soi, signe et chose signifiée quant à la force [. . .] Le seul acte immédiatement sensible [. . .] en quoi par quoi, l'être se croit source, origine et centre personnel de choses' (VII, 99). The magnetism of the voice, its manifestation as physical energy released by the body, suggests that an experience of absolute coincidence between intention and expression, interiority and exteriority can be located in the phonic sign. As argued in an earlier chapter, sound in the context of the circuit of internal language within consciousness was closely associated with identity and the capacity for self-perception. Similarly, Valéry's description of the way in which the action and effects of the voice confirm an impression of presentness to the self, might appear to align him with other thinkers who privilege the present instant as manifest in sound as the origin of self-perception and self-identity.[29]

Yet the very notion of origin is suspect for Valéry; behind each *Ursprung* lies an unseen genealogy which forbids a simplistic identification of beginning with source or origin: 'Il faut remonter à la *source*', he notes, 'qui n'est pas l'*origine*. L'origine est, en tout, *imaginaire*. La *source* est le fait en-deça duquel l'*imaginaire* se propose; *l'eau sourd là. Au-dessous, je ne sais ce qui a lieu?*' (XXIII, 592). It is the imaginative realm that is primary for Valéry as poet and as creative thinker; and it is to the category of fantasy that the image or metaphor of the voice as origin belongs and from which its value to him as an artist derives.[30] He is not deluded by the seductive appearances of the phenomenological reduction, however tempting its promise of a hypothesized Eden contained in the ideality of the vocal sign. He is as sensitive as Derrida to the paradoxes inherent in time–consciousness as his poeticized exploration of Zeno's predicament in *Le Cimetière marin* reveals.[31] It is voice as acoustic stimulus to the emotions, as nourishment of the poetic imagination and as mysterious guide to the formative process that excites him above all:

Poète, attends, — accueille — la *Voix*. Regarde la Voix totale et analyse la Voix. Flux et modulation. Energie et fréquence — Passage de l'émotion à expression. Délivrance — charge. Acte — Construction — Dessin — Comparaison. Bornes et registre. Continu et discontinu. [. . .] Et sur cette voix, bâtir le contenu. . . (Comme tout ceci est hors de ce temps! — qui bafouille!) Comment cette liaison et construction s'organise? Comment la production du discours? [. . .] Potentiels. Images et impulsions. (XVI, 395)

The focus in the remaining part of the chapter shifts to a close commentary on a range of significant networks of images which aim to substantiate the more theoretical claims of the earlier part. As introduction to these 'réseaux imaginatifs' it is worth considering briefly the terms in which Valéry discusses the auditive consciousness since his attention to sound and silence as its key characteristics serve as a prelude to more precise evocations of associated images and themes. The detailed analysis of sound which Valéry conducts throughout his writings approaches this phenomenon from a variety of angles. In a perceptive passage from *Fontaines de mémoire* he describes how poetry should ideally penetrate the listener's consciousness, developing an analogy with sound: 'La Poésie n'a pas besoin d'être annoncée. Elle est un fait, qui est ou n'est pas. Elle doit se produire sans promesses, et s'introduire telle quelle, par soi seule, dans le monde d'un esprit, comme le son pur tout à coup devient. Le son pur tout à coup s'impose et se dilate' (OII, 1366). He reveals here his attentiveness to the very nature of sound and, in a passage from the *Cahiers*, an attempted 'translation' or interpretation indicates the various dimensions which interested him:

Traduction du son — [. . .]

Hauteur	amplitude,	durée,	timbre
↓	↓	↓	↓
position phonique	énergie	stabilité	significatif-particularité
écart anatomique imitabilité		écart de 2 espèce[s]	mimique

[. . .]

(XVIII, 819)

He analyses it from the point of view of physiology, physics, and psychology, since all contribute to a total poetry, assessing not only the demands which sound production places on the organism which creates it, but also the manipulation of the vocal emission which is necessary in order to achieve the desired effect on a listener. He is careful to distinguish between 'le son' and 'le bruit' (XIX, 894), indicating that the former is part of an implicit structure of related sounds whose existence springs to mind as soon as a given sound is heard, whereas the latter does not draw upon any such organization of imminently present or related elements. An interesting comparison between the visual and the sound image suggests why the latter was so important to Valéry as a poet working with the substance of language. He notes how 'L'image d'un effort est un effort. L'image d'un mouvement est un commencement, ou plutôt un montage de mouvement — L'image visuelle *n'est pas* un commencement de vue. L'image sonore, grâce aux mécanismes physiol[ogiques] de production de sons, est un commencement d'exécution et donc de son' (XX, 457). The production of the sound image involves a more gradual process of evolution within the organism, so enabling consciousness to be more aware of its own functioning, an awareness precluded in the case of the visual image by the rapidity with which the act of production is accomplished.

But although both the nature and effect of sound can be analysed in considerable detail, it remains to a certain extent a mystery and one which lies at the heart of the greater enigma posed by the nature of the sensibility as a whole.[32] For the poet, as for the musician, it is experienced largely through the senses and remains beyond the grasp of the analytical procedure of the mind. These two types of creative artist are sensitized to certain non-intellectual properties of the substance with which they work, as the following passage makes clear: 'Pour le musicien-né les *sons* sont plus que des sons, et pour le poète-né les *mots*. Il y a une sensibilité seconde — qui donne à ces éléments une sorte de valeur et une sensation de leurs différences entr'eux, qui les distingue ou les appelle les uns les autres plus que chez les non-sensibilisés' (XXV, 586).[33] Valéry indicates why it is that sound possesses such critical significance for him: 'Il y a donc une espèce de *signes*, non signes au sens des signes de langage, qui excitent des "idées" — des non-soi. Mais qui sont comme *éveilleurs d'états et de possibles*. Tout à coup l'univers des sons [. . .] (qui n'est pas une audition [. . .], mais un implexe devenu dominant) se *prépare*' (XXV, 586). It is in the capacity of sound to awaken states of being which antedate the conceptualization of experience and to grant direct access to the 'sensibilité pure' or unmediated reality of the body that its value to Valéry lies.[34]

The same attentiveness to sound is translated into more continuous pieces of prose and poetic writing where the Valéryan text impresses itself on the reader's mind as embodying and developing the resonance and tonality of the voice. The gently conversational tone of *La Distraite*, for example, leaves the reader awaiting the words to which the poet's plea has alerted her/him through the urgency and directness of the speaking *Je*:

> Daigne, Laure, au retour de la saison des pluies,
> Présence parfumée, épaule qui t'appuies
> Sur ma tendresse lente attentive à tes pas,
> Laure, très beau regard qui ne regarde pas,
> Daigne, tête aux grands yeux qui dans les cieux t'égares,
> Tandis qu'à pas rêveurs, tes pieds voués aux mares
> Trempent aux clairs miroirs dans la boue arrondis,
> Daigne, chère, écouter les choses que tu dis... (OI, 323)

The poem remains suspended as though the voice were stilled, in a state of anticipation similar to the mood evoked in *Les Pas* (OI, 120–1) where, once again, consciousness is attentive to the virtually silent footsteps moving abstractedly within the spaces of the auditory sensibility. And the intimately probing tones of the voice of the various *Psaumes* contained in this same collection (*Mélange*, OI, 318–19; 337; 338) reveal the movements of the mind in their less polished, more immediate form as direct transcription of the inner monologue.[35]

Silence, often presented as either closely associated or interchangeable with voice, is as powerful in the communication of emotional intensity, as articulation itself.[36] Much space throughout the *Cahiers* is devoted to an analysis of its nature and implications. It is seen as distinguishing itself against the context of sound, often in terms of an 'absence' or 'attente du bruit' (VII, 88; XVIII, 359); and as having a vital role to play in the world of hearing (XVII, 306). It acts as a vigorous incitement to speech, provoking a need for sound as a complement or response (IV, 313). Valéry uses it as a painter might those colours which are necessary in providing a backdrop against which contrast and brightness can be affirmed.[37] So, in *Méditation avant pensée*, an evocation of a state of tranquil and unthreatened virtuality where the sensibility is left to enjoy the pleasurable interplay of its own forces, Valéry talks of how 'l'âme jouit de sa lumière sans objet. Son silence est le total de sa parole' (OI, 351).[38] The association of the positive and negative poles of auditory awareness is used by the poet to convey the intensity of an experience or sensation. Thus, in *La Ceinture*, the poet's voice recreates the acute sense of solitude in an image suggesting extreme fragility:

> Cette ceinture vagabonde
> Fait dans le souffle aérien
> Frémir le suprême lien
> De mon silence avec ce monde...
>
> Absent, présent... Je suis bien seul,
> Et sombre, ô suave linceul. (OI, 121)

An association of opposites presents a voice aware of the proximity of its silence where silence hints at the precariousness of existence, the fragility of the organism's connection with life.

I suggested at the start of the chapter that the voice of desire animating Valéry's *écriture* might be fruitfully associated with contemporary postmodern attempts to define the energies which underlie yet simultaneously undermine the representational project. In this sense, the images which Valéry uses to evoke the auditive imagination and, more specifically, voice, may be interpreted as a kind of provisional attempt, which necessarily fails, at formulating in language the creative drive which empowers subjectivity. Perhaps the ambiguity of reference which characterizes the poetic image, still freer than the concept or definition in its polyvalence, can better satisfy the requirement to give expression to an aspect of subjectivity as imaginative process which theoretical discourse has shown itself unable to capture fully.[39]

In the following pages four such attempts at voicing the essentially inexpressible will be traced through four thematic nexuses, each of which, implicitly or explicitly, draws on voice and the acoustic imagination. Taken together they communicate an awareness of a state of separation which provokes a longing to achieve a measure of satisfaction of desire or, even, a degree of unitive experience. An initial grouping—silence, solitude, darkness, and vulnerability—modulates into a thematic of tenderness associated with a feminine presence; a third network involving acute sensitivity to form as simulating equivalence with reality evokes intense psycho-sensual satisfaction; and, finally, poetry, love, mystical awareness, in their call to the Other, speak of the immense appeal of transcending the divisions which mark experience.

The first of these thematic groupings begins by situating the emotional state of solitude very clearly in the context of its equivalent sonorous analogy: 'Solitude — Insonorité. Certains mots (fort nombreux) sont impossibles dans le moi rigoureusement isolé. Ils ont besoin d'une atmosphère, d'une caisse de résonance, d'une collectivité qui les réfléchisse, et *ils ont alors pour _sens_ leur valeur d'action extérieure*. Ils n'existent pas dans *l'insonore de la solitude*' (XX, 480). The state of solitude renders the organism more acutely conscious of the extent to which its existence depends on the surrounding environment for response and recognition. The passage continues in terms similar to those employed in a pivotal stanza of *Le Cimetière marin* (stanza 8): 'Réciproquement, cette "solitude" est l'état dans lequel l'être est réduit à ses seules résonances — c'est-à-dire qu'il n'est entretenu que par sa puissance excitante propre' (XX, 480). The solitary state provides a heightened awareness of the resonant pulsation of life within the body. This sense of solitude is then further developed in connection with darkness and sensations of vulnerability and fear. The nocturnal hours are experienced with an intensity that leaves no aspect of the organism's potential for response untapped. *Poésie perdue* (OII, 656–62), a series of prose poems reflecting on moments of existence which possess profound significance for Valéry, reveals a current of auditory awareness associated with images of this sort. Consciousness distinguishes itself from the substance of darkness and is revealed as engaged in a form of dialogue: 'Divisé de la nuit, divisant nettement ses puissances! / Alors les ténèbres l'illuminent / Le silence lui parle de près' (OII, 656). In this silence, the ear perceives sound acutely: '*L'ouïe*. Entends ce bruit fin qui est continu, et qui est le silence. Ecoute ce qu'on entend lorsque rien ne se fait entendre' (OII, 656). Sound and silence are complementary dimensions of a totality which is the intensity of sense perception absorbed into consciousness; their resonance within auditory awareness is explored in minute detail: 'Mais entends ce sifflement si pur, si seul, si loin, créateur d'espace, comme au plus profond, comme existant solitaire par soi-même' (OII, 657).

Just as the blackness of night threw the white light of consciousness into relief in the previous passage ('Nuit coupée [. . .], mêlée de trop de noir et de lumières trop aiguës [. . .]. / Le réveil de l'esprit bien opposé à la substance de la nuit' (OII, 656)), so, here, an acutely refined sensitivity detects the depths and substantiality of sound more finely when it is perceived against a backdrop of silence. The thin whistle of sound makes space and time more accessible to interpretation: 'Plus rien. Ce rien est immense aux oreilles. / Sifflet encore. Sifflet sinistre, simple, éternel, égal à lui-même; filet éternel du temps, qui se perd dans l'univers de l'ouïe, consubstantiel à l'espace, coulant dans le sens de l'attente infinie, emplissant la sphère croissante du désir d'entendre' (OII, 657).[40] However, night and its accompanying stillness may provoke panic and fear in an organism which is sensed as an excessively fragile object in the face of the unidentified threat contained in darkness. Valéry confides his own sense of dread at the approach of evening in a brief dialogue with himself or an imagined presence:

Autour de nous, bientôt, la profonde unité des ténèbres sera [. . .] / Je sais, en toute certitude, que toutes les terreurs des hommes, et celles des petits enfants, celles des bêtes elles-mêmes, sont en vous à cause de l'heure. Il y a l'âge, l'organisme si frêle, les ténèbres au dehors si rapprochées, les contes et les brutes, les assassins et les esprits... Une personne est bien peu de chose auprès de tant de périls qui émanent d'elle, la nuit venue. Je le ressens comme si j'étais dans votre chair. C'est pourquoi il faut se prendre dans les bras l'un de l'autre, et les paupières fortement fermées, étreindre une chose vivante, et se cacher dans une existence. (OI, 1730–1)

The nocturnal hours are hard to bear alone; and the anxious consciousness reacts by projecting the voice in search of a response which will bring reassurance by confirming the presence of another human being. Speech is an attempt at overcoming the sense of isolated apartness; this attempt, though ultimately disappointed, perhaps because Valéry's conception of the degree of communication attainable belongs to the realm of the ideal, may be read as an aspect of his longing for a state of oneness, for a reunion with a lost totality that the voice as image and theme conveys.

Evidence in the *Cahiers* suggests that, from an early age, Valéry was highly conscious of his own relationship to others in terms of acoustic positioning. An instance of this self-consciousness through the intermediacy of the voice is entered under the rubric *Ego* and, significantly, placed immediately after several pages devoted to 'Freud [et les] psychiâtres': 'Histoire de moi tout enfant qui apprend déjà du La Fontaine. Et tout à coup, de mon petit lit, ma voix s'élève, je mets fin à une discussion entre P[apa] et M[aman]' (XXI, 710). It is striking that the child Valéry is more aware of his own voice and of its power to intervene, to affect others' behaviour than he is of the conversation overheard; the context in which the remark is set, the atmosphere which it evokes, are revealing: darkness, the warm, sheltered space of the bed, the presence of two figures closely related to the speaker emotionally, and the vividness with which the scene is imprinted on his memory, particularly in association with the voice.

A similar nexus of themes is apparent in Valéry's account of his acquaintance with Mallarmé, an intellectual and emotional closeness which must have affected him strongly. Not only was Valéry acutely aware of the quality and timbre of his own voice, as the last remark revealed—and he observes humorously elsewhere that 'le son de ma propre voix m'est assez vite insupportable' (OII, 1601)—but, from the start of his friendship with the older poet, he reveals how attentive he was to 'la voix du maître', a voice which spoke to him intimately both on a personal and on an artistic level.[41] Following his first visit to Vulaines in October 1891, he begins by describing Mallarmé's physical appearance, then continues: 'yeux mi-clos — parole morte — très basse puis soudain grands yeux — et haute phrase avec des aspirations' (OI, 1761). On a later occasion, the importance of voice emerges in his account of his reaction when asked to pronounce a few words at Mallarmé's funeral: 'On m'a forcé de parler. / J'ai bafouillé quelques mots sans suite ni sens, car j'étouffais' (OI, 1763). This markedly physical reaction is itself curiously linked with the very manner of Mallarmé's death as Valéry describes it: 'tandis qu'il causait [. . .], il est tombé mort asphyxié par un spasme subit de la glotte' (OI, 1764). It is hard to avoid reading these admissions along psychoanalytic lines in the light of the connection established in analytic theory between articulation of emotion, unconscious repression of affect, and the hysterical symptom as physical manifestation of trauma in the body.[42] Later Valéry found a way of paying homage to the Master, of sub-limating his emotion in symbolic form in the composition of the penetrating lines of *Psaume sur une voix* (OII, 682). Here the restrained yet gently emphatic tone is created, in part, by the repetition of the key syllable, 'voix', which breaks against the wall of the listener's consciousness with the relentless rhythm of the sea:

> A demi-voix,
> *D'une voix douce et faible disant de grandes choses:*
> *D'importantes, étonnantes, de profondes et justes choses,*
> *D'une voix douce et faible.*

The power of the poem lies in its restraint. The listener senses the breathing of the voice through the crescendo and decrescendo created in sound and rhythm by Valéry; and the unobtrusive and self-effacing temperament of Mallarmé is delicately suggested by the simplicity of the words themselves:

> *Je songe aussi pour finir*
> *Au bruit de soie seul et discret*
> *D'un feu qui se consume en créant toute la chambre,*
> *Et qui se parle.*
> *Ou qui me parle*
> *Presque pour soi.*

In a letter to Gide dated 26 September 1898, Valéry describes his final visit to Mallarmé shortly before the latter's death: 'Le soir avec sa fille, il m'accompagna à la gare de Vulaines, dans des conditions de nuit, de calme et de langage à trois voix, inoubliables' (OI, 1764). The association of voices in darkness, of close affective links, and the per-sistence of the memory all serve to underline the continuity of this particular thematic grouping in Valéry's imaginative response. At the same time, a significant further element is introduced, namely, a specifically feminine presence; and this leads into a second config-uration of images embracing childhood, tenderness, femininity within the compass of the voice.

Often the sound of the voice arouses a feeling of overwhelming tenderness which weakens the whole structure of the sensibility so that it dissolves into tears. Valéry talks, for example, of 'Une voix qui touche aux larmes, aux entrailles; [. . .] qui [. . .] épuise les moyens de la sensibilité' (IV, 587). From a state of tenderness aroused by the voice, the transition back to childhood, effected by memory, is swiftly accomplished: 'La tendresse [. . .]. Cet amollissement, cet adieu universel, ce retirement avec larmes naissantes, cet abandon, cette démission, ce penchement, ce refus — cet état assez voisin du sommeil venant, et qui est comme d'assoupir le réel, — qui est aussi un retour à la très petite enfance. Une faiblesse passionnée, une force pour l'abandon' (VII, 837). This state of abandonment and vulnerability in tenderness links itself in Valéry's consciousness with the faintest suggestion of a feminine presence. A brief passage from *Poésie brute*, a part of his writings which reveals most perfectly the unelaborated state of the sensibility characteristic of the 'poète *à l'état pur*' (VI, 717), expresses this connection somewhat tenuously: 'Douces seraient des lèvres sur les paupières' (OI, 353), going no further than to suggest a sensation of tenderness and of femininity in its delicate tracing of an emotional response. But the association becomes explicit in the dialogue between Faust and Lust, Valéry's most splendid evocation of the desire for harmony with another being. Faust asks of Méphistophélès: 'Peux-tu concevoir que j'aie besoin d'un aimable dévouement auprès de moi, une présence douce et complaisante, et tout près d'être tendre?' (OII, 293); and then moves one stage further: 'Et même... assez tendre. Oui, la tendresse, tout court' (OII, 293). It is Lust herself who reveals an understanding of what lies behind the yearning for so gentle and uncomplicated an emotion. Although, initially, she doubts whether the extremes of purity and intellect sought by Faust can encompass such apparent weakness, it is at a later stage of the play and of her own development, while defending Faust in the face of his uncomprehending disciple, that she emphasizes how he, too, possesses 'sa tendresse... à lui...' (OII, 374); and that without it his humanity would be diminished.[43]

Tenderness, a tranquil and placated emotion and perhaps more often asssociated with the experience which maturity brings, characterizes Faust's reaction to the universe; he revels in the sheer joy of being alive and finds the burden of emotion placed on mind and senses too great to bear: 'Il fait divin, ce soir. Trop bon, trop doux, trop beau, même... La Terre est tendre...' (OII, 318). In savouring this moment of life's splendour, he communicates the intensity of his emotion by means of a simile evoking sound and the effect of dissolution which it provokes in the sensibility: 'Ce moment est d'un si grand prix... Il me possède comme ces accords de sons qui vont plus loin que la limite du désir de l'ouïe, et qui font tout l'être se fondre, se rendre à je ne sais quelle naissance de confusion bienheureuse de ses forces et de ses faiblesses' (OII, 319). Whether it is the child calling out in the darkness towards the voices of his parents or the grown man, profoundly aware of an inner solitude, who turns to a being outside himself in order to communicate the intensity of his emotional burden, the fundamental impulse is the same: the overwhelming desire to transcend the isolation of the individual consciousness by merging it with another existence, that is, to transform monologue into total and sympathetic dialogue.[44]

In a moving passage from the *Cahiers* Valéry confides how powerful an impetus towards an exchange, a sharing, is the sensation of acute solitude: 'Voici cinquante ans que je *tombe*. Affreusement seul' (VIII, 373). As is the case on more than one occasion when he is facing intense emotion, he voices his feelings in Italian, the language which he associated with his childhood and, above all, with his mother. He continues: 'non ho che tu [. . .] *Seul et Seule font Un*. être seul à deux [. . .] O mon cœur, cette solitude qui parle' (VIII, 373), suggesting that a form of dialogue emerges from within the self when all other outlets towards communication are blocked. This exchange may also adopt the guise of a hallucinating conflict of voices within the self (XVIII, 884). To find another responsive being, an 'être résonateur' (VIII, 373), is the aim of his appeal to a woman, to a god, or simply to another voice as manifestation of presence. In this particular passage he evokes the female figures who for so long, in Western cultural symbolism, have represented the perfection of exchange, an ideal of mutual understanding: 'Laure — Béatrice — Comprendre' (VIII, 373). It is the belief that he is understood which matters before all else, and that the burden imposed by a feeling of the extreme isolation of the self within the confines of individual consciousness may be lessened by being shared.

In the third thematic nexus images which evoke a measure of satisfaction within the desiring imagination reveal further highly charged aspects of the auditive consciousness. The images which follow, drawn primarily from the natural world, speak powerfully of the joy which the creative mind experiences when a sense of equivalence with reality has been achieved through its choice of analogies.

Dawn and dusk, like the overture and finale of a symphony to life in its totality, are privileged moments for the Valéryan sensibility. But it is the former, especially, the emergence of light from darkness, and of life and movement from the tranquillity of the nocturnal hours which moves him to song. He shades in delicately the increasing intensity of the dawn light and depicts the gradual structuring process which accompanies each new day: 'A l'aurore. Ce cyprès *offre*. Cette maison dorée apparaît; que *fait*-elle? Elle se _construit_ à *chaque instant*. Ces monts se soulèvent et ces arbres semblent offrir et attendre' (XII, 189). In this state of anticipation, the phenomenal world awakens and attains coherence through sound: 'Sous la lumière naissante, tout chante et les choses divisées de l'ombre désignant la direction du soleil sont unisson' (XII, 189). A progression can be observed from a state of disunity to the harmony or chorus expressive of the unity of the universe with the birth of a new day.[45] Or again, he remarks: 'Chant. Produit naturel du matin' (XXI, 732) and then introduces a further feature of his emotional landscape: 'Oiseaux' (XXI, 732). The place of the bird and its song in Valéry's imaginative response to the surrounding world reflects something of the immensity and uncapturable nature of the universe as it is perceived by the individual consciousness. Often it initiates a meditation on the theme of unity: 'Duos d'oiseaux — Le duo harmonique créé par oiseaux — les parties d'un Tout distribué entre des êtres distincts' (XXIV, 465).[46]

A series of texts from *Poésie perdue* (OII, 656–62) provides a splendid evocation of the interconnected images of light and vitality accompanying the dawn, of the first birds whose cries pierce the sensibility of the listener so causing it to vibrate, and of the tree, that most deeply suggestive of all Valéryan images. In addition to the richness of the poet's imaginative transposition of emotional response through the skilful handling of language which this pattern of images reveals, each of these impressions, or sketches, contributes, implicitly or explicitly, to a guiding symphonic intention, to a steady development towards the statement of a fullness or saturatedness experienced by consciousness in its response to reality and accomplished through the acquisition of form. The various passages which form *Poésie perdue* trace the emergence of consciousness from the depths of sleep to a state of total lucidity. It is significant that as the waking mind gathers its forces for the coming day, it registers sound before all else: '*Reprise.* / Roulement des roues premières. Des revenants laborieux toussent et causent dans la rue probable' (OII, 657). Daylight strengthens and with it the faculty of vision: 'O vie, ô peinture sur ténèbres! / Belle matinée, tu es peinte sur la nuit' (OII, 658). Then sight and sound converge as the dynamism of the movement of birds is compared to the evolution of sound: 'Ces hirondelles se meuvent comme un son meurt. / Si haut vole l'oiseau que le regard s'élève à la source des larmes' (OII, 658).

Many entries in the *Cahiers* reveal the fascination which the movement of birds possessed for Valéry. He envies their liberty of motion, their freedom of expression, and the extent to which intention and action are one.[47] He also betrays his susceptibility to all that speaks of structure, liaison of points in space and of dynamic form. It is the latter which provides a key to an understanding of the association of the image of the bird with the idea of voice. So, when Valéry observes that 'chanter est donner à une voix la *forme* d'une plante croissante — ou de l'activité d'un oiseau dans l'espace' (XIX, 208), the two analogies employed to describe the 'shaped' sound which is song both suggest movement and organic development.[48] Another passage in *Poésie perdue* explores the qualities of birdsong in greater detail: 'Oiseaux premiers. Naissent enfin ces petits cris. Vie et pluralité vivante au plus haut des cieux! / Petits cris d'oiseaux, menus coups de ciseaux, petits bruits de ciseaux dans la paix! Mais quel silence à découdre!' (OII, 657). Here, as elsewhere, the implicit presence of dawn is an important factor in assessing why this particular sound is so vital to the poet. The early morning hours, poised between the more emphatically demarcated zones of night and day, symbolize that most splendid and valuable state of 'réversibilité', of 'pureté dans le non-être', when consciousness maintains itself intact and uncommitted, savouring a period of anticipation prior to action.[49]

One of Valéry's finest evocations of his joy in the song of birds is the text entitled *Oiseaux chanteurs*: 'L'oiseau crie ou chante; et la voix semble être à l'oiseau d'une valeur assez différente de la valeur qu'elle a chez les autres bêtes criantes ou hurlantes. / L'oiseau seul et l'homme ont le chant. / Je ne veux seulement la mélodie, mais encore ce que la mélodie a de libre et qui dépasse le besoin' (OII, 660). Whereas other creatures use the voice to express need, the bird stands apart in this respect, for 'comme il s'élève et se joue dans l'espace, et a pouvoir de choisir *triplement* ses chemins, de tracer entre deux points une infinité de courbes ailées, et comme il prévoit de plus haut et vole où il veut, ainsi l'Oiseau, jusque dans sa voix, est plus libre de ce qui le touche' (OII, 660).[50] It is the freedom from the dictates of necessity which the poet recognizes in the voice of the bird, a voice which sings supremely and above all else about life in its totality:

> C'est la vie, et *non la mort que n[ou]s ne pouvons regarder fixement*. Car il n'y a rien à voir dans celle-ci. Mais celle-là nous offre un spectacle incompréhensible et désespérant — une monotonie, une fatalité, des contradictions, une inutilité, un mélange de puissances et de faiblesses, d'ordre et de hasard. La réaction de l'être — sensibilité et connaissance — devant la 'vie' [. . .] dans l'instant a pour produit expressif un *Monologue*. Et comme l'oiseau chante Amour au Soleil, chante *Oui* par *effet* de *lumière*, l'*Ame* chante Non et Mort devant la Pensée — Somme. (XXVIII, 667)

In the face of life's inexplicable presence, the voice asserts itself triumphantly.[51]

However, the penetrating cry of the bird, provoking an almost reflex response in the poet's sensibility, leads to a level of awareness bordering on the mystical. Often 'l'oiseau' and 'la voix' are linked on an axis of verticality so that references to height and depth describe both the bird's activity in space and the evolution of the voice according to a dynamic of upward or downward development.[52] As Valéry watches birds in flight he notes that part of their fascination lies in the intensely vital quality which their movements communicate.[53] They suggest an extreme of existence beyond the power of expression, that sense of the real which defies language yet stimulates a *jouissance* that is irreplaceable: 'J'écoute l'oiseau invisible dans la structure dorée, sombre, immobile de ce que je vois du parc. J'écoute, j'écoute et [. . .] je ne trouve que l'inexplicable en soi, le bruit, la sensation impénétrable' (XI, 662). The bird sings out in unreflecting joy at the sun's glory as the soul sings its defiance in the face of the incomprehensibility of the absolute. It matters little what form this outburst takes since the act of expression is proof of a desire to utter what cannot be articulated more clearly: '"Mystique" est essentiellement l'inexprimable. Tout ce qui se peut *exprimer* est extra–infra–ultra–*mystique*. Donc, problème de l'expression. Qu'est-ce qu'exprimer? Quoi est exprimable? Expressions limites — Cris — larmes [. . .]. Ces *expressions sont aussi des éliminations énergétiques*' (XXII, 85). Voice, cries, the unburdening of the sensibility in tears are the responses which convey the mind's difficulty in tolerating the unfathomable quality of sheer existence; and this is what Valéry envies in the bird. It possesses an apparent weightlessness and a potential for liberating itself from the burden of existence for '[les] larmes [. . .] sont l'expression de notre impuissance à *exprimer*, c'est-à-dire à nous défaire par la parole de l'oppression de ce que nous sommes' (OII, 183). Thus his reaction to observing the path followed by a bird's flight—'J'envie cette mobilité à un point fou' (V, 631)—evokes a ravishing of the senses similar to his description of the wordlessness of certain moments: '"Ineffable" ne veut plus dire: Impossible à dire ce qui conviendrait à: désastre ineffable, mais engage un sens de ravissement' (XXI, 327).

The image of the tree, a recurrent theme throughout Valéry's writing, completes this thematic nexus.[54] The poetic imagination, as he conceives it, operates as a process of transformation of one image into another. This is particularly clear in his treatment of the tree image where it is not so much an animistic belief which lies behind his conception of this natural form as metamorphosis, but rather the fact that the tree possesses a suggestive dimension which is irresistible to the particular mould of Valéry's creative impulse. The variety of resonances which it awakens within the imagination are described in a brief entry in the *Cahiers*: 'Poète ou devin sous l'Arbre, comme si l'Arbre fût un vivant et un oracle, un conducteur tellurico-atmosphérique — Charge et *flux* de l'*Arbre* — Ceci ferait une belle Poésie — Source — Oracles, par la voix des milliers de feuilles sensibles. Les *Vents*. Et devin pour l'eau profonde, la lumière' (XVII, 730).[55]

One of the texts which explores most richly and attentively the intermingling of the ideas connected with birdsong, voice, and tree is *Arbre*, also in *Poésie perdue*, and which appears in less polished form in the *Cahier* of 1923 (IX, 428). Here the poet contemplates the tree in all its magnificence, voicing his immediate response to the murmur of this living being: 'L'arbre chante comme l'oiseau' (OII, 659). The breeze ruffles the foliage and, as the poet's awareness becomes more finely attuned to this sound, he observes how the wind 'épouse [l'arbre], le change en rumeur qui grandit et s'affaiblit et le change en ruisseau perdu' (OII, 659). Then, in ever closer approximation to the reality of the tree's existence as he senses it intuitively, Valéry observes how: 'Ceci donne pur rêve du ruisseau. / L'arbre rêve d'être ruisseau; / *L'arbre rêve dans l'air d'être une source vive...*' (OII, 659). Yet again, the idea of verticality is introduced, as the source of this living murmur is located high in the atmosphere. The suggestion of liquidity in association with sound, whose full significance will emerge in the third chapter, not only conveys the idea of the nourishment required by the organism of the tree but implies, too, that the tree is transformed to become a spring which replenishes the poet's sensibility.[56]

Gradually a natural form metamorphoses within the poetic imagination as '[l'arbre] de proche en proche, se change en *poésie*, en un vers pur' (OII, 659). It is not enough for the poet simply to observe this living presence; he must, also, identify with its organic processes, espouse its sensuous reality: 'J'analyse et épouse le frissonnement des petites feuilles de l'arbre immense qui vit dans ma fenêtre' (OII, 659). The movement of the tree as it is touched by the breeze finds its analogue in sound as Valéry describes the oscillation of the leaves: 'Reprise maintenant, reprise accélérée. Ce sont sextuples croches, trilles insoutenables. Nous voici à l'extrême de l'aigu' (OII, 660). Sight and sound merge in this synaesthetic appreciation of the vitality of the tree: 'Il y a une combinaison harmonique visible de la vibration affolée de la feuille avec celles de la tigelle' (OII, 660); and finally, sound fades into silence as the wind passes and leaves the tree in peace: 'Un amortissement délicieux achève la crise et la leçon de *poésie*' (OII, 660).

Poetry conjoins the natural processes and the sensory richness of the living world with the creative imagination of the poet. The poem, like the tree, obeys a pattern and pressure of development dictated by a kind of organic imperative: 'J'aime qu'un poème s'élève *tout seul* à la Poésie par la seule vertu de ses forces de développement organique, [. . .] comme une *mélodie naissant de la voix*. Je propose de définir *Mélodie* par *Voix* — et *Voix* par énergie linéaire, issue d'énergie de *volume* [. . .] et en somme, d'une *vie*' (XXII, 141). The voice of the poem, like the tree in its evolution, embodies and communicates the multiplicity of lived experience; both of these virtually interchangeable images refer to a vital energy and to the constant process of growth essential to life itself: 'L'Arbre — quel beau *sujet*! [. . .] L'arbre est le poème de la Croissance — Le Crescendo* [*ajout marginal: 'image de la connaissance'] (XXV, 118). The tree, an element of the natural world, and the voice as substance of the innermost self, embody the mystery and irrefutable challenge of the real. Both call on the resources of formal development to assist them in reaching their maximum deployment as energy. Just as '[l'arbre] *expulse* ses *forces* sous l'*espèce de sa forme*. La forme, élimination périphérique fermée des forces intérieures [. . .] Expansion — Expression' (XXV, 118); so too, the voice, defined as 'une association

Force — forme de forces' (XXVII, 887), gives birth through poetry to that wholeness or completeness of experience, child of fantasy and of the idealizing urge of the imagination: 'L'inflexion, la plénitude, [. . .] le dessin miraculeux de la forme interne à la fois désir et possession, regret, espoir, durée, mouvement et ce qui meut et est mû, avec le plus haut et le plus bas, *arbre gigantesque de la Voix*, arbre sacré, poussé dans la chair, chargé des idées, Poésie même' (VIII, 38).[57]

The path to be followed now in exploring the resonances of acoustic imagery for Valéry leads to the fourth of the thematic nexuses where the predominant characteristic emerges as a desire to achieve a state of unity or perfection in communication capable of transcending earlier moments of solitude and separateness. Valéry's reflections on love, poetry, and mysticism belong within this grouping since all depend, in varying degrees, on an appeal to the other. The imaginative association of love and poetry, both drawing on the entirety of an individual's sensitive potential, both envisaging voice as the closest approximation available to the state of the ineffable, 'l'indéfinissable', both dependent on and communicative of a sense of vitality, highlights their common goal as achieving a state of unity. It is in this context that Valéry conceives of poetic creation as forming part of 'la "mystique" psychesthétique' (XX, 665), involving mind and body at a very intense pitch of psycho-sensory awareness; and that his evocation of a God, whose reality as the voice of imaginative desire opened the chapter, acquires fuller significance.

'Amour' and 'poésie' are, potentially, creative states; referring to the sensibility when it is aroused to a phase of hypersensitivity in love, Valéry observes: 'Au lieu du *faire un enfant* — cela veut faire... ce qui n'a jamais été, — un état de choix, qui s'oppose au cycle vital, et qui soit le chant, l'hymne de la sensibilité' (XXVI, 153). Similarly, he views 'les états poétiques', that is, those 'qui se font finalement achevés en poèmes' (OI, 1319), as departures from the normal cyclical functioning of the organism during which a certain creative potential is satisfied; and he refers to this phase as 'le cycle d'un acte qui a comme soulevé et restitué extérieurement une puissance de poésie' (OI, 1319).[58] His poetic theory emphasizes the element of fabrication or 'poiein' which must succeed this initial, and predominantly spontaneous, phase; and the same is true of his conception of love. It is not an experience to be undergone passively but a privileged opportunity for creation accorded to the individual: 'puisque l'homme a ce pouvoir d'agir l'amour comme il a celui de penser et de modifier les choses du monde selon sa pensée et ses forces — il doit faire quelque chose de l'amour comme il a fait quelque chose de ses autres puissances — et, construit la lyre [. . .], organisé la parole en poèmes et en systèmes' (XXIV, 240). Lover, poet, and musician, all strive to give material form to the desiring energy which lies at the source of every aesthetic enterprise. In the interaction of the elements involved, whether human beings in love, or words in poetry, or the sounds of music, the quality of the unknown enters as in a chemical experiment where the outcome of a particular combination of potentialities cannot be accurately or exhaustively forecast: 'L'homme, à chaque instant, *rencontre l'indéfinissable. Il semble, à chaque instant, qu'il approche de quelque point duquel il est aussitôt comme repoussé. [. . .] Les indéfinissables ne sont pas *objets d'étude* [. . .] mais ils sont *objets de culture* — Comme la puissance des sons et le soin de l'approfondir' (XXIV, 240–1). Just as it is the awareness of a necessarily insuperable state of separateness and an appreciation of its indefinable qualities which give love its value—'C'est à l'indéfinissable de l'amour que commence l'amour supérieur. Qu'il faille deux êtres, [. . .] qu'il y a un abîme entre eux — ou plutôt [. . .] cette impossibilité de rompre la "barrière de potentiel" du moi — de ne pas être le *Seul*' (XXIV, 241–2)—so the value of poetic creation is to be found in what it withholds from the individual's attempt to understand, and therefore to discard as worthless to the mind which thrives on new material: 'La puissance des vers', Valéry observes, 'tient à une harmonie *indéfinissable* entre ce qu'ils *disent* et ce qu'ils *sont*. "Indéfinissable" entre dans la définition. [. . .] L'impossibilité — ou du moins la difficulté, — de définir cette relation, combinée avec l'impossibilité de la nier, constitue l'essence du vers' (VII, 151).

A prose poem from the *Cahiers* gives perfect expression to the fusion of these related states of the sensibility, 'amour' and 'poésie', and demonstrates, too, how Valéry wished to 'donner un sens nouveau à ce qui est Amour, ou Œuvre — Alors l'Amour est une Œuvre — L'Œuvre est acte d'amour' (XXVII, 416). Love is shown to be a truly creative force and, at the same time, to be the object of creative intent:

'Quelle étrange chose que ce qui est bon!' Ce parfum, — cette crème de lait — le tour de ce col; et, de mes mains, la descente par les épaules sur les seins — jusqu'à la formation du solide du torse selon une douceur continue du toucher, et une suite de modulations de forces dans mes doigts, de pressions et de glissements au contact, qui rendent l'âme créatrice de ce qui s'offre à cet acte de place en place et de meilleur en meilleur. Je te fais et refais — Je ne puis abandonner cette action par excellence, perdre ce chant de mes mains. (XX, 710)

This love-song, understood in the most literal sense of the word, could scarcely evoke more succinctly the intertwining of ideas such as 'musique, amour, fabrication' and 'poésie' which blend in the formation of Valéry's distinctive 'esthétique'.

An observation from amongst many which are placed under the rubric *Eros* reveals how close is the connection linking Valéry's conception of love and the principle of a self-perpetuating cycle of 'demande-réponse' at the heart of 'l'infini esthétique': 'Nous aimons ce qui augmente en nous la sensation de vie, ce qui semble la communiquer,' he notes. 'Nous aimons parfois les êtres auxquels nous donnons cette sensation, car les voir vivre par notre fait, nous vivifie en retour' (IX, 460). Just as the success of a poem is determined by the extent to which its presence and action on the reader's sensibility has rendered it indispensable to him, so 'Etre amoureux, c'est avoir pris conscience d'une soif dont la satisfaction est la propriété d'un individu unique determiné en tant qu'il est de plus en plus *inventé* par cette soif même. [. . .] Quand l'accomplissement réexcite, renouvelle, rallume, renforce le besoin, alors il y a cercle et résonance' (IX, 839). Furthermore, a similarity can be detected between the ways in which 'l'infini d'amour' (XXVII, 715) and 'l'infini esthétique' achieve their effect. Both set in motion the harmonics which allow the organism to resonate (VII, 637); and both seek to create a state of enchantment.[59]

In a fragment intended for inclusion in Valéry's final dramatic project, Faust evokes for Lust an ideal vision of existence:

Nous serions [. . .] des harmoniques, intelligents, dans une correspondance immédiate de nos vies sensitives, sans parole, — et nos esprits feraient l'amour l'un avec l'autre comme des corps peuvent le faire. Cet accord harmonique serait plus qu'un accord de pensée; n'est-ce pas là du reste l'accomplissement de la promesse, en quoi consiste la poésie qui n'est après tout que tentative de communion? (OII, 1414)

A virtually mystical intuition of loving communication is transcribed as a form of duet in which musical vocabulary evokes the nuances and subtle shifts of response perceived by one or other of the participants (XII, 301). There are several ways in which this rare and heightened state of the sensibility can be achieved in love, amongst them by activating 'des configurations, des relations singulières des lieux et formes dans le visage qui produisent [. . .] des effets d'*enchantement. de* même, le timbre de la voix' (XVI, 121). Once again the sense of sound and, specifically, the voice are shown to play a vital role: 'Il y a, dans le grand amour, un désir [. . .] de tirer d'un être et du sien des moments et des lueurs — ou comme des *sons* — qu'on suppose implicites, comme des éléments radio-actifs — noyés dans la masse minérale' (XXVI, 153).[60] The extent to which it is 'l'amplitude de vibration' (VII, 637), that is, a total psycho-physiological response of the other person, which is essential in love, just as it is the resonance of words in their totality, and not their purely intellectual connotations, which matters in poetry, emerges from Lust's observation that 'La personne qui t'aime ne t'écoute pas quand tu parles et ne comprend pas ce que tu dis [. . .]; elle s'enchante du timbre de ta voix. Qu'importe le discours? Ceci est de grande signification. Que peut-on/elle dire de plus intéressant que ce que l'on est?' (XXVI, 203). The interdependence of being and awareness and of 'son et sens', without which 'l'infini esthétique' could not operate, is reproduced here in the context of the love which exists between two individuals: 'L'âme amoureuse se meut sur un autre fil que le fil de la seule pensée. Qu'importent les paroles même admirables, quand le chant qui les emprunte est si beau qu'il les réduit à leur sonore fuite?' (XXVI, 203); and the terms employed to describe this state of resonance are identical to those which emphasize the value of the substantiality of poetic language: 'Ton discours, ton récit, ton raisonnement vont à leur fin. Mais ta voix veut en moi, veut encore ta voix!' (XXVI, 203).

The appeal to the Other may also take the form of an appeal to a transcendent being; certain passages in the *Cahiers* express, in tones of naked anguish, an awareness of the emotional and psychological predicament which prompts the need for a faith or, at least, ensures an understanding of the grounds for access to a spiritual reality. In a moving entry dated 1922, a lone voice emerges from the darkness of the night calling from its position of anguished solitude:

Nocturne. O seul. [. . .] J'ai trop souffert dans mon âme [. . .]. Pourquoi n'y a-t-il point de Dieu? [. . .] Personne n'entend ma Voix intérieure. Personne pour me parler directement, pour avoir l'intelligence de mes larmes et la confidence de mon cœur. N'y a-t-il donc point un 'monde' qui toucherait à celui-ci par l'intérieur de l'esprit, qui serait la substance où nos racines plongent et duquel elles tirent l'arbre de l'univers visible? (VIII, 466)

A degree of comprehension through which the personal and extrapersonal dimensions of consciousness might be merged is so desperately desired that the speaking voice draws on the deepest resources of the sensibility to furnish those pivotal images—darkness, trees, voice—which convey the intensity of its emotion most effectively. A passage such as this comes close to an avowal by Valéry of what might, in a broad sense, be termed a religious awareness, although clearly his is not a belief in a traditional or institutionalized form of religion. Throughout the *Cahiers* a thread of mystical awareness expresses his curiosity about this further dimension of the human experience although his attitude is by no means clearcut.[61] By certain features of his own personality he is ready to situate himself in the ranks of the mystics.[62] His deep-rooted longing for the Other and for a dimension transcending the petty bounds of selfhood or contingent consciousness, expresses a need which is characteristic of a mystical yearning. The Other may be sought through sexual relationships; often Valéry evokes the mystical aspect of his sensibility in his reflections on erotic love.[63] Or, again, his response to the material world, to the shapes and textures of the natural environment, betrays a mode of vision which pierces deep beyond the surface reality uncovering 'la *profondeur de l'apparence*' (XII, 190).[64] It is the artist, he argues, who can come closest to the intensity of sense-perception characteristic of a mystical response by developing such a mode of vision to its maximum (X, 836).

Finally, and perhaps most significantly, Valéry's conception of life as the opportunity for constant elaboration of the self, variously referred to as *ascesis*, 'dressage' or progress, seems akin to the mystic's pursuit of an ever more perfected state of existence (IX, 561). His striving to transcend the limits which bind the self within the banality of routine, his will to 'enfreindre incessamment notre définitif' (III, 528) prompt him to evolve an internally focused technique by means of which to strengthen, purify and develop his human potential.[65] This is a highly personal form of mysticism, as he is the first to acknowledge. The fundamental difference which distinguishes him from traditional currents of Western mystical thought is his radical scepticism concerning the proven existence of a God as the being to whom the desiring energy animating the mystic's project is directed. He cannot bring himself to place his rational powers in the service of a faith; in this respect, he condemns the elusiveness of a mode of thought which cannot be submitted to rigorous analysis (VII, 489). He is unswerving in his conviction that much of what he regards as the doubtful power exerted by mystical thought lies in the imprecision and fertile ambiguity of its language (XXV, 228). God, for him, in this context, is synonymous with what is indefinable, that intimate value required by human consciousness in its pursuit of its own perfection (XXVIII, 92); as a conceptual stimulus, belief in a godhead makes available a certain type of energy (XXIX, 868).

The duality of his stance could scarcely be more succinctly summarized than in his own comment: 'Je pense en rationaliste archipur. Je sens en mystique' (VII, 855). Yet it is precisely from this ambivalence that the voice of the self draws nourishment. It is the traditional terminology and associations of the divine that Valéry takes issue with; whilst his understanding of the emotional and psychological dispositions which characterize a mystical approach legitimate the situating of the desiring self within such a framework. On more than one occasion he envisages the possibility of overcoming the separation of the knower from the objects of knowledge, a separation which is a source of pain, by reintegrating the knowing self in the reality of the world of matter.[66] This attempt at a fuller integration may be accomplished by an attunement of the vibration of energy in the individual human sensibility with the cosmic vibration perceptible in the wider world. It is, perhaps, the poet, the artist who approximates most successfully to this accommodation, although whether the union evoked in the following remark from the *Cahiers* refers to an attainable goal or simply to an hypothesized ideal remains, in the final analysis, unimportant:

Je crois que [le véritable principe poétique] est à rechercher dans la Voix et dans l'union *singulière*, exceptionnelle, difficile à prolonger de la voix avec la pensée même. Donner à la Voix en acte une sorte de vie propre, autonome, intime, impersonnelle — c'est-à-dire personnelle-universelle [. . .]. faire de la parole un résonateur de l'esprit c'est-à-dire *du tout perçu et percevant*, subissant et répondant, — tel est le but, le désir, le signe, le commandement. (VII, 71)

Notes to Chapter 2

1. 'Mystique privée, individuelle. Ma littérature fut de moi à moi' (XIV, 722).
2. 'Mystiques et autres valeurs "intérieures" c'est trouver "*en soi*" du nouveau, du "vrai" — un réel *bis*, une suite, des développements, des voix, des vues, [. . .] et jusqu'à des êtres — dont Dieu. Toute une vie seconde, dirait-on. Et tout ceci incertainement, irrégulièrement, et tout ceci dans des rapports non simples avec ce qui se touche et se voit, — avec le rêve aussi, avec le langage, avec les heures — Parfois plus intense, plus pressant que le jour; parfois effacé par lui. Parfois

abondant, parfois rare ou nul. L'individu se segmente à l'infini dans un coin de parc ou de chapelle — jusqu'à ce qu'un accident l'interrompe. Comme fécondé tout à coup par x il entre en développements, s'éloigne dans cette division nouvelle de temps neuf — s'éloigne de l'état d'échange' (XII, 334).

3. '[Pourquoi] avoir exposé aux louanges, aux blasphèmes, Avoir livré aux combinaisons des propositions, Aux images qu'on peut dessiner, aux démonstrations d'existence! Avoir rendu semblable à un être et à une chose La Réponse improférable?' (XXI, 870). See too *Ebauche d'un Serpent* (OI, 138–46) for a poetic enactment of this problematic. Jarrety builds his argument around the opposition at work in Valéry's activity as a writer between a 'pure' and a 'fallen' state of language. His discussion of voice (pp. 109–54) argues its role as expression of authenticity on the part of the *Sujet* or *Moi ontologique* in contrast to linguistic convention which conditions the statements of the *Moi empirique*.

4. The use of the definite article with regard to this 'God' implies that it is a particularized deity, as opposed to the general Godhead of whom the indefinite article is normally used ('de Dieu' rather than 'du Dieu'). The process of appropriation is taken a step further by the use of the possessive adjective, 'ton Dieu'.

5. See e.g. his association of mysticism, internal voice, and literature in the following extract: 'Mystique privée, individuelle. Ma littérature fut de moi à moi; de moi presque à moi; D'un moi en 3 personnes; L'attendant et le recevant, situés *auprès* du 3ème innommable, indéfinissable, Sinaï, nuée, janua coeli, Trinité générale. Attente, — réponse; et l'Inconnu auquel il faut attribuer la répondance. Celui que crée la merveille de la production, *qui n'est pas transformation.* [. . .] Comme si ce fut un autre, qui se servant de la même personne, même bouche intérieure, même voix silencieuse, eût vu et dit ce que le même ne savait' (XIV, 722).

6. 'Par [l'insularité de mon esprit] j'en vins à considérer la littérature — comme une voie d'opposition au "monde" — une mystique de développement interne, de recherches dans l'esprit par le moyen du langage, [aj. marg: exercices spirituels], ayant donc une fin intérieure, une possession du domaine des combinaisons verbales' (XXIV, 405–6).

7. 'La pensée que nous nous percevons est un écho dont la voix originale qui le met en train n'est pas perçue — et n'est pas … une voix. Cet écho est assez étrange. Il transforme cette voix originale et originelle … qui n'est pas une voix à proprement parler. Il en fait *de la parole* et de *l'image*' (XXIII, 760).

8. 'Le réel, *résidu*. L'inépuisable par la connaissance' (XIV, 84). Valéry's conception is perhaps not so far removed from the Lacanian Real as the irreducible foundation or ground of being which lies forever beyond the grasp of human subjectivity.

9. 'Le Réel est ce qui a puissance de *sensation. Sensation* étant *non-expression.* La véritable *chose en soi* et *par soi*. L'individu instantané — et l'étalon d'existence' (XXIV, 409).

10. 'Croyances. Impuissance où nous sommes de ne pas répondre, de supporter le pur réel, — le discontinu, l'informe, le hasard, l'injuste, l'obscur, l'absurde, — et en somme, ce qui n'est pas *conforme* à nous, bon pour nous, fait pour nous' (IX, 436). See Jarrety's rich analysis of the vital role which Valéry attributes to the senses in the context of his discussion of Valéry's attempt to forge a language

which would more adequately express both Subject and reality (pp. 21–64). His suggestion that the Valéryan *imaginaire* serves to prolong contact with 'le réel sensible' confirms my own reading of the function of voice in this respect.

11. An evocation of the effect of Bach on his own sensibility conveys the successful outcome of the creative operation which transforms the real into an aesthetic object without any compromise of the original intuition: '*Miraculeuse Suite en Ré majeur de Bach* — Exemple *adorable* — où j'entends ni mélos, ni pathos, ni rien qui ne soit ... *réel*, qui ne se développe qu'en soi-même, et s'expose sous toutes ses faces *sans me voir*. Intensité de pureté. Nul emprunt au cœur, ni au hasard heureux, ni à moi, ni au passé — Quel Présent! Exemple adorable. Action en soi, qui semble à l'infini de tout objet, pure de tout dessein, volonté isolée, acte pur; m'ignorant et m'éblouissant [. . .] *Ma sensation pourrait* . . . *se passer de moi*' (XIV, 375). The autonomous purity and rigour of the musical structure succeeds in capturing, very precisely, that almost inhuman otherness of the original, irreducible sensory real.

12. The term and concept of 'l'imaginaire' has a varied history within the French tradition and has acquired considerable significance in the context of Jacques Lacan's conception of the Imaginary Order where the ego identifies with an imaginary unity which is illusory since it is not coextensive with the subject. Chapter 3 explores the psychoanalytic understanding of this term in more detail. For the purposes of the present chapter, the contribution of three other major thinkers to the development of 'l'imaginaire' is more immediately relevant. Gaston Bachelard, in his analyses of the phenomenology of the imagination, conceives of it as the faculty of mind that alters and distorts the images provided by perception. This distortion may be creative in the case of the literary imagination but contaminates the effort to acquire scientific knowledge. Knowledge has, therefore, to purify itself of the images supplied so readily by the imagination in order to achieve genuine objectivity. Jean-Paul Sartre, in *L'Imaginaire* (1940), views it as the intentional object of the imagining consciousness. In the context of contemporary feminist philosophy, Luce Irigaray proposes a reading of Western cultural productions in the light of a dominant masculine imaginary based on the repression of the feminine; this concept is developed more fully in Chs. 3 and 4. For a thorough discussion of the Valéryan *imaginaire* as a way of being present to the world and as a defence against abstraction, see Jarrety, pp. 38–54.

13. 'Le moteur de l'imagination est la privation' (VI, 257).

14. It is increasingly acknowledged by contemporary critical thinking in this area that Western philosophy has traditionally neglected the imagination and its products. The privileging of sight as the faculty most likely to ensure a desired objectivity, long recognized as a dominant trend in Western metaphysical speculation, has not, paradoxically, enhanced the status of the image. 'Recourse to imagery [has been] viewed as an inferior form of mental activity by those who deal in abstract ideas; whether or not image-free thinking exists, predominant philosophical attitudes range from distrust to disgust' (Edward Casey, *Imagining: A Phenomenological Study* (Bloomington, IN: Indiana University Press, 1979, p. x)). Valéry's deliberately functional interpretation of the imagination can, I believe, be situated in this context: his is a carefully unenthusiastic, non-ecstatic attitude which seeks to purify this contentious mental capacity of any impure

associations with unconscious promptings. As suggested in Chs. 3 and 4, gender considerations may be relevant in this context: 'masculine' logic, abstraction, and rationality are trusted at the expense of 'feminine' fantasy. However, somewhat ironically, the nature of the images produced can be seen to subvert the controlling, cleansing intention of Valéry as theorist of the imagination. For further discussion of gender relevance to the imaginative faculty, see Christine Battersby, *Gender and Genius: Towards a Feminist Aesthetics* (London: Women's Press, 1989).

15. The work of Walter Ince, Jarrety, and Pickering, listed in the Bibliography, explores the implications of this attentiveness to the sensory qualities of the natural universe in terms of Valéry's intuition of a depth and mystical dimension to reality.

16. *Degas Danse Dessin* (OII, 1193–5).

17. The idea that sensory awareness may be a highly accurate indication of the 'reality' of experience is suggested, for example, in the following remark: 'Il se peut bien, après tout, que le sentiment en nous soit le réel, la voix réelle, la chose autant qu'elle peut directement être plus qu'être ou être perçue. Mais alors, faut-il convenir que le réel est le vague, l'instantané, l'informe, — le sans-valeur! la bête-l'aveugle?' (V, 33).

18. *Discours en l'honneur de Goethe* (OI, 531–53) and, in particular: 'Il porte toute sa volonté d'observation, toute la maîtrise de sa vaste faculté imaginative dans l'étude et la représentation du monde sensible. [. . .] il vit par les yeux, et ses grands yeux ne se lassent de s'imprégner de figures et de couleurs. Il s'enivre de tout objet qui lui répète la lumière; il vit de voir' (OI, 542).

19. 'Ce qui me caractérise — ma vertu particulière, mon don, c'est presque seulement la capacité de percevoir des phénomènes subjectifs *non significatifs*. Je me tiens toujours en relation avec l'informe, comme degré le plus pur du réel, du non interpreté. C'est comme le carrefour des métaphores. Certains ont eu ce don à un degré plus éminent, mais je ne l'utilise pas beaucoup comme moyen rhétorique, je le conserve comme état critique de la conscience' (III, 364). Gifford highlights the significance of form in Valéry's activity as poet in *Paul Valéry: Charmes* (Introductory Guides to French Literature, 30; University of Glasgow French and German Publications: Glasgow, 1995), p. 41; and suggests that 'the commitment to form [in Valéry] is ethical, even spiritual in nature, and not simply a matter of aesthetic preference' (p. 12). Jarrety's interpretation of Valéry's conception of literature as deliberately distancing itself from reality emphasizes, similarly, the importance of producing a form which would be adequate to the expressive needs of the authentic self.

20. Suzanne Nash touches on both these aspects in highlighting the significance of both form and voice in her study of the process of critical self-revision which Valéry undertook in reworking his early poems for publication. She reads the *Album de vers anciens* as enabling him to discover his authentic voice by deepening his understanding of the creative process and quotes from *Notes diverses sur 'La Jeune Parque'*: 'Et deux "temps" bien distincts (au moins par le travail). Un temps de la matière imaginaire. un temps des formes' (*Paul Valéry's 'Album de vers anciens': A Past Transfigured* (Princeton: Princeton University Press, 1983), 13).

21. For further discussion of parallels between Freud and Valéry with respect to the symbolism of dreams, see Malcolm Bowie, 'Dream and the Unconscious', in

Gifford and Stimpson (eds.), *Reading Paul Valéry*, 262–79. See also Jacques
Derrida, 'Les Sources de Valéry qual quelle', *Modern Language Notes*, 87 (1972),
562–99, for a discussion of the notion of the 'implexe' in relation to the Freudian
unconscious. For discussion of the 'implexe' in the context of the *Cahiers écriture*
as the site of tension see M. Tsukamoto, 'La Notion de l'"Implexe" dans le
Cahier no. 240' in Pickering (ed.), *Paul Valéry: Se faire ou se refaire*, 97–107.

22. 'L'Homme de l'esprit. Intelligence. L'intelligence dirige les divers inconscients
qui sont des bêtes sans elle; et elle rien, sans eux; identiquement rien. [. . .] Il est
souverainement sot d'opposer ces choses qui ne vivent que de l'union. Je vois un
art tout fondé sur l'intelligence — c'est-à-dire non pas excluant les inconscients
(ce qui n'a même point de sens) mais les appelant et les recouchant selon
l'occasion' (VI, 603).

23. 'L'imagination "créatrice" se passe dans le latéral — c'est-à-dire dans la région
non coordonnée au présent — repère' (VII, 337).

24. See e.g. 'Les belles Œuvres sont filles de leur forme *qui naît avant elles*' (XI, 898);
and 'C'est par la *forme* que la fabrication consciente se rattache au plus profond'
(XIII, 550).

25. The next chapters examine psychoanalytic views of aesthetic form as uniting the
creation of the art object with a process of self-creation.

26. 'Le monde de l'inspiration (qu'elle soit poétique ou scientifique) n'est autre
d'ailleurs que celui — (ou le système vivant) — dans lequel est possible
l'équivalence parfaite (à la limite) du désir et de ce qui le satisfait. Le système où
ceci est possible est le système spirituel. Et dans ce monde-là, on peut supposer
que le désir lui-même est créé par une première conscience de l'existence cachée
ou *diffuse* de l'objet désirable, que nous ne cherchons jamais, *non sans l'avoir
trouvé*, mais du moins sans le posséder en quelque manière. [. . .] Nous le
possédons comme de l'or est dissous dans la mer. Si le liquide se sature et qu'un
germe y soit jeté, tout s'oriente et s'*éclaire*. Désirer une chose c'est percevoir
qu'elle manque au fonctionnement d'une machine non construite encore. Tout
acte demande qu'une machine appropriée soit construite. imaginer, désirer,
vouloir — sont des nuances qui désignent les divers états de cette machine' (VI,
664–5).

27. 'Créer, veut dire que l'on réduit dans l'imagination d'une fabrication, l'acte de
l'agent au *minimum que nous connaissions*. Ce minimum d'action est de la nature
d'un désir auquel répond une image — ou, si l'on veut, de la nature (immédiate,
parfaite etc) d'une *image* portant *désir*. On substitue alors la chose réelle à son
image' (XVIII, 258).

28. The guiding influence of unconsciously dictated form has a will of its own as the
following remark suggests: 'Il faut avoir de bons et secrets modèles, qui soient
pour chaque ouvrage ce qui enseigne que l'on n'est pas arrivé encore au point'
(VIII, 168). And the role of memory assures the consistency or coherence of the
aesthetic form being produced: 'Etudier, élaborer — c'est peu à peu apprendre
par cœur des parties de la chose — Ces parties sues par cœur tendent à engendrer
d'autres parties qui composent avec elles un système complet. [. . .] Ces parties
attendent, et finissent par contraindre le tout à se former, et ce tout, enfant de la
mémoire, *conforme à elle*' (VII, 852).

29. Of interest in the present context for the parallels which it indicates with Valéry's
thought, is the position of the voice in the phenomenological philosophy of

Edmund Husserl. I quote at some length from Derrida's dialogue with Husserl in *La Voix et le phénomène: introduction au problème du signe dans la phénoménologie de Husserl* (Paris: Presses Universitaires de France, 1967) since the hypothetical position of the voice as origin is relevant to Valéry's own exploration of this area of thought. The voice for Husserl is identified as the ideal object precisely because, for the consciousness which speaks and hears itself, there would appear to be no temporal or spatial interval separating consciousness from its productions, sound from its ideality. Paraphrasing Husserl, Derrida comments: 'Quand je parle, il appartient à l'essence phénoménologique de cette opération que *je m'entende dans le temps* que je parle. Le signifiant animé par mon souffle et par l'intention de signification [. . .] est absolument proche de moi. L'acte vivant, l'acte qui donne vie, [. . .] l'âme du langage semble ne pas se séparer d'elle-même, de sa présence à soi. Elle ne risque pas la mort dans le corps d'un signifiant abandonné au monde et à la visibilité de l'espace. Elle peut *montrer* l'objet idéal ou la *Bedeutung* idéale qui s'y rapporte sans s'aventurer hors de l'idéalité, hors de l'intériorité de la vie présente à soi' (p. 87). In Husserl's account the apparently transcendental capacity of the voice rests with the fact that what is signified, the meaning expressed (which is always of an ideal essence) is immediately present to/in the act of expression: 'Cette présence immédiate tient à ce que le "corps" phénoménologique du signifiant semble s'effacer dans le moment même où il est produit. Il semble appartenir d'ores et déjà à l'élément d'idéalité. Il se réduit phénoménologiquement lui-même, transforme en pure diaphanéité l'opacité mondaine de son corps. Cet effacement du corps sensible et de son extériorité est *pour la conscience* la forme même de la présence immédiate du signifié' (p. 86). Derrida takes issue with this conception of auto-affection or self-presence as grounded in a phonocentric view of language; for him, self-consciousness is not possible without the use of signs—the self is only constituted through signification which, in turn, contains an irreducible reference to something non-present.

30. In his essay on Svedenborg (OI, 867–83), he explores the area surrounding the source of imaginative inventivity, suggesting that where the average individual identifies this 'origin' as existing within himself, 'le mystique ressent, au contraire, l'extériorité, ou plutôt, l'extranéité de la *source* des images [. . .] qui lui parviennent par voie intérieure' (OI, 876). Derrida offers a close and fertile reading of the source as literary theme and stimulus in Valéry's writing in 'Les Sources de Valéry qual quelle'. Essentially he confirms that difference inhabits Valéry's conceptualization of the self so that the source, in his work, can never be anything other than metaphor. His analysis of the voice in relation to Valéry's understanding of 'le moi' stimulated my own reflections on this topic in respect of the autobiographical relevance of the voice, developed in Ch. 4.

31. For an amplification of these paradoxes in the context of Derridean thought, see Jonathan Culler, 'Jacques Derrida', in John Sturrock (ed.), *Structuralism and Since* (Oxford: Oxford University Press, 1979), 154–81.

32. 'Sensibilité pure. Le seul "mystère" — ce qu'on ne peut savoir. qu'est-ce qu'un *son*? On le perçoit. On sait le produire' (XXVI, 88).

33. 'La musique est une "métaphysique" des sensations de l'ouïe — Relations des sons selon la sensibilité' (XXIV, 469); music, like poetry, develops an area of specialized auditory awareness.

34. The pre-eminence of the faculty of hearing over vision, in certain contexts, emerges from the following remark: 'Puissance des Arts — La Musique — a *puissance directe* [. . .] puisqu'on ne peut si aisément se boucher les oreilles que l'on ferme les yeux. Et voici une classification des Arts [. . .] fondée sur la *Force sensorielle brute*' (XXIV, 564).

35. 'Le monologue continuel, ou dialogue (plutôt) du langage avec les événements sensations et perceptions' (XVIII, 28).

36. 'Le silence est une sensation auditive imaginaire' (XXVIII, 742). Pickering, exploring the close interrelation of sound and silence in the context of a mystical dimension in Valéry's prose writing, emphasizes the value of silence as the very 'ressort de sa création' (*Paul Valéry, poète en prose; la prose lyrique abstraite des 'Cahiers'* (Archives Paul Valéry, 5; Paris: Minard, 1983), 72–3).

37. 'Le Silence — terme qui représente la continuité de la fonction auditive. L'audition = o, mais l'audibilité existe et est *perçue*. sous forme d'attente. Perception du *pur* pouvoir d'entendre manque de réponse. [. . .] L'oreille ne connaît pas le silence, ni l'œil l'obscurité. Il y a un organe qui connaît le silence et le bruit et qui est donc plus *profond* que l'oreille [. . .] Ne rien percevoir c'est percevoir l'état de cet organe et non de l'autre' (III, 842).

38. A similar mood of detachment and of 'disponibilité' where no sense of urgency obtains is evoked in *Neige*, a poem of such restraint that its tone may be described as gently breathed rather than spoken. Valéry creates an atmosphere of lightness, absence, purity, and silence: 'Quel silence, battu d'un simple bruit de bêche!. . . / [. . .] / Quel pur désert tombé des ténèbres sans bruit / Vint effacer les traits de la terre enchantée / Sous cette ample candeur sourdement augmentée / Et la fondre en un lieu sans visage et sans voix' (OI, 325–6). All distinctive presences are effaced beneath the blanket of snow which muffles sound totally; once again, silence suggests intensity—in this case, intensity of attention.

39. Both Bourjea and Jarrety propose conceptions of a similar level or register of language of undeniable significance operating in Valéry's writing practice. Bourjea evokes the function of Valéry's *écriture* in relation to three areas— 'l'expérience sensible, l'expérience langagière et l'expérience mondaine'—as follows: 'l'écriture vient [. . .] non pour tenter de les dominer ou de les réduire en les assimulant [. . .]. Non pas même pour s'essayer à les exprimer [. . .]. Mais bien [. . .] pour les maintenir à l'état d'incompréhensibilité (de non-préhension par le sujet) [. . .]. De là, ce qui me paraît définir absolument ce que je démarque comme "écriture": cet instant et ce lieu [. . .] où celui qui écrit quitte le plan du discours et de la langue instituée, proprement le nie ou le ruine' ('Soutenir', *BEV* 71 (1996), 10–11). Jarrety's discussion of the role of 'mots imaginaires' in Valéry's scriptural activity points towards a similarly elusive category which, I suggest, might usefully be aligned with the term 'voice': 'Si nous acceptons d'appeler réels les mots concrets auxquels correspond une image également réelle — nous voyons alors plus clairement se faire jour la nécessité d'envisager une catégorie intermédiaire — les mots imaginaires — auxquels ne correspond aucune image réelle, mais une image imaginaire tout entière constituée, et dans le même temps modifiée à partir d'une réalité' (p. 58); 'les mots imaginaires, si imparfaitement que ce soit, nous aident à mieux savoir ce que sans eux nous ne saurions pas' (p. 61).

40. The sonnet *L'Oiseau cruel* (OI, 158) presents a similar network of themes and

images in a more elaborate form in which the elements of sound and silence, an ecstatic intensity of emotional response, create a tight fabric of language and feeling which translates an intensely charged disposition of the sensibility. Sound, that is the voice of the bird, emerges starkly from the thickness of night, drawing the poet's auditory sensibility tautly towards it, demanding that the ear should strain towards the joy of experiencing sound: 'L'oiseau cruel toute la nuit me tint / Au point aigu du délice d'entendre / Sa voix qu'adresse une fureur si tendre / Au ciel brûlant d'astres jusqu'au matin'. The second quatrain describes the effects produced by the voice of the bird: 'Tu perces l'âme et fixes le destin / De tel regard qui ne peut se reprendre; / Tout ce qui fut tu le changes en cendre, / O voix trop haute, extase de l'instinct [. . .]'. It is worth noting that the notions of tenderness, of height, and of instinctive response, all associated with the voice and studied in more detail below, are already present in this early sonnet. Two points of interest not noted by Hytier in his edition of 1975 arise from manuscript variants. First, Valéry's pencilled corrections to an edition of *Pièces diverses*, published in 1942, indicate that 'le chant', originally intended, gives way to 'sa voix' (l. 3) in the final version and that 'voix' (l. 8) initially bore a capital letter, which would suggest that even greater emphasis was to be placed on this theme in the poem. The manuscript in question, entitled *Poésies: Nouvelle Édition revue, corrigée et augmentée*, is held by the Bibliothèque Littéraire Jacques Doucet, Paris, and is catalogued in the Fonds Valéry, MS 584. Second, a *Cahiers* entry of 1935–6, where part of the sonnet is jotted in a variant form, indicates that voice was the object of closer analysis. The fifth line reads as follows: 'La voix vivace et violente et tendre / qui perce l'âme' (XVIII, 177).

41. An interesting and amusing comparison is supplied by Gide, who gives an objective point of view concerning Valéry's speech habits: 'Sa conversation cependant demeurait éblouissante, au point que j'en venais parfois à craindre qu'il ne s'y satisfît. [. . .] il se souciait peu d'être entendu, et c'est bien plus pour lui-même et à lui-même qu'il parlait, que pour les autres. De là le peu de soins qu'il accordait à son élocution, laquelle jusqu'à la fin de sa vie, est restée défectueuse' (André Gide, *Paul Valéry* (Paris: Domat, 1947), p. xvi). And, in more admiring tones, he observes: 'Remarquable discours de Valéry. D'une gravité, d'une ampleur, d'une solennité admirables, sans emphase aucune, d'une langue des plus particulières, mais noble et belle au point d'en être comme dépersonnalisée' (p. lxxxiii).

42. Nash, who reads *Album de vers anciens* as a kind of 'poeticized autobiography', comments on the Valéry–Mallarmé relationship in the context of the issue of influence and originality (*Paul Valéry's 'Album de vers anciens'*, 45–51). She interprets the *Album* as a vital transitional project thanks to which Valéry was able to come into his own, liberate himself from the impotence which he had experienced earlier in the face of other writers' achievements. As part of this discovery of his own vision and voice, he distances himself from the Mallarméan ideal, particularly in his recognition of the interdependence of form and meaning, body and mind, world and self (pp. 73–83). A quotation from a letter from Gustave Fourment to Valéry (12 Sept. 1889) stresses, yet again, the value of voice in this context: 'Si jamais tu entends la "voix intérieure", alors tu auras moins de peine à nous révéler les choses nouvelles dont elle te remplira l'esprit — la correspondance sera établie entre ta main et ton cerveau' (pp. 67–8).

43. Again, it is Gide who recalls the importance of the same trait in Valéry himself:
'Mais, méthode ou système, si excellent qu'il soit, que vaudrait-il pour réussir
une œuvre d'art, sans les particulières qualités de celui qui l'applique? Ce qu'il
me plaît surtout de retrouver dans les vers de Valéry, bien qu'ils l'offusquent, c'est
sa tendresse. Je me souviens que, dans les premiers temps de notre amitié, il me
citait avec admiration un mot de Cervantes (je crois): "Comment cacher un
homme?", mot dont alors je ne saisissais pas bien le sens. J'attendais l'oeuvre de
Valéry pour le comprendre' (*Paul Valéry*, pp. lxix–lxx). Bourjea's comments on
the significance of tenderness in Valéry's work seem particularly apposite:
'Concept freudien mou, ontologiquement peu marqué et pourtant finalement
"riche de sens", le concept de tendresse dit quelque chose de ce qu'écrire, de ce
que l'écriture du sujet, est chez Valéry [. . .]. Chez Freud comme chez Valéry le
tendre a une double fonction: il qualifie et permet de nommer le rapport à la
mère, un certain rapport au matriciel plus qu'au maternel' ('Soutenir', 15–16).

44. De Lussy's exploration of the intertwined thematics of the manuscript texts of
Charmes points in a similar direction in noting the elusive feminine presence
which haunts both *La Distraite* and a possible prototype of *Les Pas*: the poet's
urgent need to communicate summons an answering presence and voice into the
reality of the text ('*Charmes*', i. 98–101).

45. See also 'écouter le chant de lumière du Soleil s'élevant' (OI, 352); and the
totally opposite emotion of disgust and horror provoked by the periodicity of life
which is sensed most acutely with the dawn, is similarly evoked in terms of
sound: 'Ce chant du coq dans la nuit noire, au fond de laquelle il y a la guerre
et les misérables humains, m'exaspère. Ce Chant bête comme la vie, et
mécanique, rompant le silence et plus morne que lui — ce chant de
recommencement aveugle. Je comprends qu'on se soit hâté de *renier* avant qu'il
ait chanté 3 fois — Peut-être pour l'empêcher de chanter — et faute de pouvoir
lui couper la gorge. Quoi de plus morne, ô Coq, de plus sottement vif? et que
ne dis-tu: Merde! au venir de l'aurore, A l'enfant qui va naître, aux fleurs *qui vont*
éclore' (XXII, 650).

46. 'Psaume ou chant du Daimon comme celui du rossignol (à l'Aube-aurore) triste
et vie — chant de l'esprit. Esprit si universel et si bien perdu dans l'univers. le
tout et le rien' (X, 684).

47. The speed of their movement excites him because it seems to be the image
which best evokes the 'propriétés fabuleuses de "l'esprit"' (V, 631); he notes, in
particular, 'quelle brillante approximation de la décision rapide avec l'acte de *tout*
le corps' and pushes this line of thought to its extreme, thus envisaging so
perfected a development of the nervous system that the body would usurp the
mind's control: 'Si le corps obéissait cent mille fois plus aux impulsions, s'il avait
des modèles de mouvements, et des mouvements pour autant de problèmes et
de contrastes et d'incitations de transformations que les sens lui en proposent, —
que serait l'esprit? Rien' (V, 631).

48. A similar thematic nexus occurs in *Air de Sémiramis* where a state of elevated
emotion is transcribed through images of birds, sound, and structure: 'Qu'ils
flattent mon désir de temples implacables, / Les sons aigus de scie et les cris des
ciseaux, / Et ces gémissements de marbres et de câbles / Qui peuplent l'air vivant
de structure et d'oiseaux!' (OI, 93).

49. Bird and dawn recur together as Valéry observes that 'cet oiseau pique la nuit

finissante de cris faibles et aigus' (OI, 355). This 'moment par excellence' for Valéry is described on numerous occasions. See e.g. *Méditation avant pensée* (OI, 351–2); *Matin* (OI, 355–6); *A Grasse III* (OI, 292–3), and *Réversibilité* (OII, 657).

50. 'Oiseaux-chanteurs [. . .] . Son chant est spontané, tandis que le cri des autres animaux est occasionnel. [. . .] cela ne dit rien à personne. Point de "but". L'état, le regret, le désir vague, et encore l'accompagnement de la simple vie' (IX, 426).

51. 'Ce sont des monologues sur toutes choses — et en quelque sorte, des *pensées toutes nues*, parfaitement naturelles — comme la source — [. . .] ou la vie (vive et bête) chantée par le rossignol. [. . .] Et *cela* (car cette parole est l'acte du cerveau libre-isolé-donc *neutre*) est *pensée intrinsèque, émission non dirigée, élimination et vie localisée'* (XIX, 128). This passage implies a conception of the human voice and of its function very similar to that of the song of the bird examined above.

52. 'Ces hirondelles se meuvent comme un son meurt. Si haut vole l'oiseau que le regard s'élève à la source des larmes' (OII, 658).

53. 'L'oiseau, son activité folle me grise. Hirondelles ultra-sensibles, ultra-rapides, ultra-vivantes' (V, 631).

54. The central position of this image has been studied by a number of critics; see, in particular, Crow, *Paul Valéry: Consciousness and Nature* (Cambridge: Cambridge University Press, 1972), 107–22; and Pierre Laurette, *Le Thème de l'arbre chez Paul Valéry* (Paris: Klincksieck, 1967). It represents the striving towards light which characterizes the poet's intellectual endeavour and, at the same time, asserts the interdependence of all aspects of organic existence; light and shade, height and depth, stillness and movement indicate the complementary dimensions which constitute the unity of the tree. It embodies a pattern of natural evolution and of formal self-regeneration similar to that which Valéry seeks to introduce into his poems as organic entities.

55. The tree as oracle lives again in these lines from *Palme*: 'L'or léger qu'elle murmure / Sonne au simple doigt de l'air, / Et d'une soyeuse armure / Charge l'âme du désert. / Une voix impérissable / Qu'elle rend au vent de sable / Qui l'arrose de ses grains, / A soi-même sert d'oracle, / Et se flatte du miracle / Que se chantent les chagrins' (OI, 154); and this is the role refused by 'le platane' in the poem of the same name (OI, 113–15).

56. The tree's downward penetration in search of nourishment is evoked in *Ebauche d'un serpent*: 'Arbre, grand Arbre, Ombre des Cieux, / Irrésistible Arbre des arbres, / Qui dans les faiblesses des marbres, / Poursuis des sucs délicieux, [. . .]' (OI, 145); and in *Palme*, where the opposition of height and depth is clearly marked: 'Ces jours qui te semblent vides / Et perdus pour l'univers / Ont des racines avides / Qui travaillent les déserts. / La substance chevelue / Par les ténèbres élue / Ne peut s'arrêter jamais, / Jusqu'aux entrailles du monde, / De poursuivre l'eau profonde / Que demande les sommets' (OI, 155). See too the passage of *La Jeune Parque* evoking 'la montée de la sève' (ll. 245–52).

57. De Lussy's exploration of the intertwined geneses of various poems from *Charmes* uncovers the degree to which Valéry's imagination was fertilized by his empathy with trees, particularly the beech and the plane tree. The affinity verges on identification as tree, voice, and poet merge ('*Charmes*', i. 93–8).

58. The use of the passive mood to describe this function: 'Mais il était arrivé qu'un *poème avait été fait*, et que le cycle, dans son accomplissement, laissait quelque

chose après soi' (OI, 1319), suggests that the poem is produced, in some measure, by forces which remain beyond the poet's immediate control.

59. '*Amour* — (Passion) [. . .] Les harmoniques — organiques entrent en jeu' (XX, 403).

60. 'Er[os]. L'amour emprunte une note aiguë' (XXVI, 352); and 'Er[os]. L'homme couvre la femme. Et le tout forme le circuit fermé d'une transe — C'est une chose assez étrange que ce moment de trans-conscience, arraché au possible de la sensibilité, *arraché* comme un cri qu'*arrache* une douleur subite, une brûlure — Et d'où vient ce cri? Ici, ce rugissement et râle, avec interjections d'appel, d'offrande, émis par un temps trop bref pour laisser s'organiser une pensée?' (XXVI, 351).

61. The association which explains how love and a mystical yearning interrelate in his imagination is their shared ability to awaken an appreciation of an extreme dimension of existence, of some form of infinite: '*Infinis* — *Implexes* — Extrêmes. Il y a un certain "Infini" dans l'ordre de la "sensibilité" Sons suraigus insupportables — Extrêmes. [. . .] Dans la mécanique érotique, l'action poursuit la production d'un extrême, et sans doute dans la recherche mystique' (XXIII, 253). See too in this context Gifford's 'Self and Other: Valéry's "Lost object of desire"', in Gifford and Stimpson (eds.), *Reading Paul Valéry*, 280–96. Mysticism is notoriously difficult to define although many have attempted to do so. It embraces an affirmation of the perfectibility of the human being, a belief in the non-separateness of all creation; it has the character of revelation and is almost always an experience which cannot be adequately captured in words; it envisages love as the governing force in the universe and proposes, as its supreme goal, a state of total union with the ground of being. For recent explorations of the mystical aspect of Valéry's work see Gifford, *Paul Valéry: le dialogue des choses divines* (Paris: José Corti, 1989); and, with regard to the *Cahiers*, in particular, Robert Pickering observes: 'De même que la quête mystique de Dieu peut prendre la voie apophatique de la négation progressive, comme aussi celle de l'annulation de contraires dans une synthèse totale, de même la "poésie abstraite" des *Cahiers* naît d'un effort suivi pour résoudre la contradiction entre lyrisme et activité intellectuelle, entre poésie et prose' (*Paul Valéry, poète en prose*, 63).

62. 'Mystiques, ô vous! — et moi de ma façon, quel labeur singulier avons-nous entrepris! Faire et ne pas faire, — ne vouloir arrêter une œuvre matériellement circonscrite — [. . .] mais enfreindre incessamment notre définitif, et toujours, intérieurement, en travail, vous pour Dieu, et moi pour moi, et pour rien' (III, 528). Or, again, 'Mystique — Retour de tout, affreusement revenu de soi, y a-t-il autre chose à faire — que se plonger dans ce qui n'est ni soumis aux autres volontés, ni à Χαριν, ni à Lionardo [. . .] mais sombrement, délibérément, entrer dans sa mystique personnelle, dans son union avec le Singulier — universel et — Mais y a-t-il quelque chose là? — Ce que tu voudras. D'abord à traduire les vrais mystiques en langage absolu/intrinsèque — Il y a toujours eu un "mystique" en Moi' (VIII, 344).

63. 'Amour et moi. J'aurais pu apporter à l'amour si le destin l'eût voulu, une contribution: une cruauté envers moi-même, et une conscience rigoureuse, qui jointes à [. . .] ce mysticisme sans objet, qui est en moi, eussent peut-être, si quelque femme s'était rencontrée ayant du corps et de l'esprit un sens analogue, une fureur intelligente et expérimentale, un pressentiment de la volonté comme

moyen — c'est là le neuf — eussent, dis-je, [. . .] peut-être pu faire de l'Amour quelque chose' (V, 806).

64. 'Je ne crois pas à ce que je vois. En ceci, pareil à un "mystique" comme on dit. — Je vois ce que je vois avec un regard qui perçoit "en même temps" que les choses offertes ou imposées, leur champ, leur tangence, leur groupe, leurs références et les libertés aussi de celles-ci' (XIII, 778).

65. Gifford, discussing Valéry's conviction that, since the temple of the mystics lies empty in the modern era it is thus available as a metaphorical resource to the poet, suggests that 'the poet of *Charmes* is centrally engaged in re-inventing a specifically modern subjectivity or "soul", in implicit dialogue with a range of traditional sources which includes both poets [. . .] and mystics' (*Paul Valéry: Charmes*, 6).

66. 'Principe à la Carnot. Nous ne pouvons parler des choses ou les penser que par ignorance — c'est-à-dire qu'en les rendant bien distinctes de nous, bien étrangères à nous. En prendre connaissance, c'est s'en séparer. Les voir nettement, les prévoir, c'est ne pas y être. De là cette grande opposition entre la connaissance et l'être, et si on y réfléchit on voit des effets extraordinaires. On voit par.ex. la connaissance tendre à produire de l'extérieur de nouveaux êtres — comme fait le chimiste. On voit l'être tenter de bâtir une connaissance en Soi-même — comme fait le musicien, le mystique' (VI, 898). Or, again, 'La vie mystique — Pas du tout l'activité intellectuelle [. . .] Le contraire même de "l'objectivité"' (V, 31).

CHAPTER 3

Integrating the Feminine

In a brief but revealing remark on the limitations of his memory or of the potential of the self to recapture experience Valéry exclaims: 'O paresse de Moi! — ne pouvoir irriter le petit membre du cerveau qui ferait vibrer tel timbre depuis l'enfance inentendu!' (OII, 769). The tone of exasperation suggests a degree of urgency in the pursuit of past sensations, a desire to reactivate certain moments or moods, for the value which they once held and possibly still possess for the poet's consciousness. The power of sound and its associative resonances forms the link or connecting vibration which unites present and past instances of the self in a form of acoustically perceptible continuity. In this chapter it is voice as expression of desire that comes to the fore; desire as the energy which transcends the purely functional requirements of the individual human being and speaks of the longing for a satisfaction which can never be adequately defined or answered. Such a force animates those projects which embody the essence of what it means to be human: the striving to bring into being an object of beauty through creative transformation of the materials which the world offers; the reaching out towards a form of perfection that is the love for another being or for God; the endless appetite for experience which takes us beyond the known.

Already in preceding chapters the desiring energy of voice has clearly contributed a powerful impetus to the discussion: as the semiotic impulse within the organism which stimulates consciousness to transform this primary level into poetry and as the provocation of images furnishing the poet with the potential for text. It seems appropriate to consider now something of the underpinnings of the voice of desire, to approach it in the context of its potentially psychoanalytic implications since, as intermediary between the body and the world of meaning, it is a critical accomplice in the structuring of subjectivity. The aim of this chapter is to highlight parallels between certain features of Valéry's understanding of voice and its significance in the work of several psychoanalytical theorists. This is a somewhat different project from one which attempts a rigorously exhaustive psychoanalytical account of the role of voice in the Valéryan psyche.[1] A dynamic aiming towards integration of the self is at work within Valéry's creative consciousness; and this is projected textually, as a governing thematic, into a wide range of his writings. Voice in its various meanings expresses both the awareness of a lost state of oneness and, equally, the longing to recapture that experience of an integrated existence. Between the 'origin' of the self as one feeling-world with/in the mother matrix and the utopian or fantasized position where multiple dimensions of the self may be resynthesized lies the path of life, the trace of a perpetually self-questioning *écriture*, the voice of *ego poeta* in a constant state of reformulation.

As suggested in Chapter 1, voice as semiotic utterance can be located at the pre-Oedipal stage in the development of the human subject, a stage which precedes the symbolic structuring processes which accompany entry into language. It marks the formless and the chaotic, typical of the dyadic unity in which mother and child dwell before the advent of the Father's word as Law. Now in so far as the creative consciousness draws on all its resources, conscious and unconscious, in the process of bringing the text into being, this fundamental realm of non-symbolized experience can be interpreted as the necessary complement to the conscious, rational level of the self's activity. It forms the repressed material against which consciousness defines itself, the unstructured domain in relation to which structure can be affirmed. It is from here that primal sound emerges and that form is born.

Although, as earlier chapters argue, Valéry expresses reservations concerning the concept of an unconscious mind, voice as encom-passing an unconscious dimension holds a powerful place in his imaginative world both as a determining presence within the evolving psyche from the earliest stages of life and as representative of an ideal position or state projected into the future which guides or moulds the way in which the self generates itself from present moment to present moment. A number of psychoanalytic approaches offer accounts of the vital role played in the development of subjectivity by both visual and acoustic phenomena. In exploring certain key Valéryan texts in relation to these readings—reference is primarily to Freudian and Lacanian approaches—no claim is made to provide an 'explanation' of how Valéry's particular creative consciousness was able to give birth to its own mysteries. Rather a range of settings is proffered in the context of which his musings and meditations on the potency of voice acquire a certain relief.

He himself authorizes, if he does not quite invite, such an approach by commenting on experiences which evade rational explanation. One of these accounts, *Rêve. Rapport de mer* (OII, 653), not only refers the reader to the various elements of 'l'imaginaire de la voix' which have been discussed in the previous chapter but suggests how they may be seen to have a coherent and shared significance based on unconscious determinations.[2] In this evocation of an experience which may be read as a description of a phase of intra-uterine existence Valéry appears to posit a moment of pre-Oedipal awareness encompassing those themes and images which have emerged as peculiarly resonant within his imaginative world: infancy; a sense of solitude or separateness and the concomitant desire for unity; a feminine presence; tears and the associated emotion of tenderness. An exploration of this intriguing account of a dream will lead on into a psychoanalytically slanted account of voice within the context of a desire for integration.

Valéry's interest in dreams for the light which they throw on the processes of consciousness is undeniable but the question of how to reproduce faithfully in words the reality of the dream experience remains unresolved. Like Freud, he identifies the problem of dream interpretation as essentially linguistic: 'Nous ne connaissons nos propres rêves que dans une traduction que nous en donne le réveil, — dans un état qui est incompatible avec eux' (OII, 654). In other words, to recall or recount the experiences which occur in a state of dream-consciousness entails an inevitable distortion of that original experience. He then parts company with Freud when he identifies the value of dreams as being a question of form above all else: 'Je crois que nous ne pouvons absolument pas nous représenter toute l'*insignifiance* essentielle des rêves, leur incohérence constitutive' (OII, 654). Yet this perhaps rather suspect, even defensively overemphatic downgrading of the meaning of dreams does not prevent him pursuing his inquiry into the form of language which would come closest to an accurate rendering of their psychic reality. This suggests that the exercise of exploring the world of dreams was not totally without value for him: 'Notre langage répugne à l'expression de ces possibilités psychiques si éloignées de nos habitudes de *pensée utile*. Mais peut-être trouverait-on [. . .] des termes et des formes plus variés, plus complexes, plus généraux, — et en somme *plus savants* que les nôtres, — pour traduire avec approximation plus satisfaisante les informes et inhumains phénomènes du rêve' (OII, 654).

The 'récit de rêve' in question opens, significantly, with the neutral pronominal form: 'On est en mer' (OII, 653), and Valéry himself comments on this use of a linguistic form which reveals that he was fully aware of the ambiguity surrounding the identity of the narrator: 'Le mot: *On*, que j'ai dû employer tient lieu d'un *sujet* indistinct, à la fois spectateur, auteur, auditeur, acteur, en qui le voir et le être vu, l'agir et le subir, sont réunis et même curieusement composés' (OII, 654). He thus alerts the reader to the coexistence of different levels of consciousness operative during the interval in which a dream occurs; and warns against an oversimplifying identification of the level of consciousness which actually experiences the events enacted in the dream with that other level which merely recounts these events. In this respect, the ideal state of consciousness would be one which combined these two levels: 'Si nous pouvions trouver de même un état capable de la veille et du véritable rêve', Valéry observes regretfully, 'de belles observations deviendraient possibles' (OII, 651).

From the start the perceiving consciousness of *Rêve. Rapport de mer* is aware of the indeterminate nature of the boundaries of the self or selves encapsulated in the dream-space: '*On* est en mer, couchés dans un cadre; deux corps en un seul; étroitement unis, et il y a doute si l'*on* est un ou deux, à cause de ce resserrement dans le lit exigu de la cabine' (OII, 653). The curious juxtaposition of singular and plural linguistic forms is proof of Valéry's attempt to stretch the resources of syntax as far as possible towards capturing the elusiveness and ambiguity of the experience: is it a question of a unique body or of a body contained within another? This state of doubt persists, and the reader is reminded of the peculiar status of the foetus simultaneously at one with, and yet distinct from, the protective container of the maternal body (and the homonymic repercussions of 'en mer/mère' cannot easily be ignored): 'L'être simple et double est en proie à une tristesse infinie. Il y a une douleur et une tendresse sans bornes *avec lui*' (OII, 653). The tenderness which has already been shown to play an important part in Valéry's emotional life is, here, strangely unable to be attributed to any specific, individualized identity: a sadness and a tenderness exist, are present with, this being and the limitlessness of their extent makes itself powerfully felt.

The account shifts into a moment of tension, potential menace and an awareness of struggle where the sense of sound seems to predominate: 'Un vent de tempête souffle dans la nuit extérieure. Le navire roule et geint affreusement. L'être à l'être se cramponne et *on* perçoit le battement d'angoisse d'un cœur unique, les coups sourds de la machine qui cogne et lutte contre la mer' (OII, 653). The rocking rhythm of the supporting liquid environment; the evocation of the darkness outside and the fearful associations which it arouses; and, most significantly, the acute awareness of a single heart beating—these various insights could be read as evocations of different aspects of intra-uterine existence as it is perceived by the foetus, with the overwhelming presence of either the mother's or the foetal heartbeat occupying the acoustic space of the evolving consciousness.

The emotions evoked here are typical of those accompanying the birth trauma as described by Freud.[3] The passage develops with an increasingly urgent rhythm towards a point of climactic tension when the inevitable rupture occurs: 'La terreur, le danger, la tendresse, l'angoisse, le roulis, la puissance des ondes croissent jusqu'à un certain *point* de *rupture*' (OII, 653). An aperture is formed and the protective barrier between inner and outer worlds destroyed: 'Enfin la catastrophe se déclare. Le hublot cède à la mer; la paroi même s'entr'ouvre et vomit l'eau formidable' (OII, 653). Again the description of the dynamics involved in this episode remains ambiguous since it seems that a two-way movement of water is evoked; the port-hole would appear to allow the inner space to be invaded, flooded by the force of the sea outside; yet the use of the verb 'vomir' suggests an expulsion or rejection of 'l'eau formidable' at the same time. It is hard to be certain, either, as to the precise nature and function of 'la paroi' which evokes, perhaps, the membrane which ruptures on the breaking of the waters of the womb. (A similar uncertainty concerning the body's boundaries, the parameters defining self in relation to other, characterizes the drama of 'la Pythie', as demonstrated in Chapter 1, and of Narcisse, as the present chapter will examine in more detail).

At this point the perceiving consciousness describes the awakening out of the dream state: 'Je m'éveille. *Mon visage est baigné de larmes.* Elles ont coulé sur mes joues, jusques à mes lèvres, et ma première impression est le goût de ce sel, qui sans doute a créé tout à l'heure cette combinaison désespérée de tendresse, de tristesse et de mer' (OII, 653). The narrator, on regaining a state of full lucidity, seeks to diminish the mystery of the mind's unconscious activity by reducing it to a reflex response to the stimulus of the salt tears which he tastes on his lips. Another angle on this text might, however, read it as an account of the originary moment of psychic separation or individuation whereby subjectivity structures itself as difference and the 'spaltung' or splitting which constitutes consciousness, at least according to a Lacanian model, is re-enacted in the imagery and dynamics of the dream-telling.[4]

At stake in this evocation of the coexistence of opposites, the constantly mobile potential of consciousness to be both subjectively engaged in its reflection on the world or objectively aware of its own functioning, is the question of difference. Within the singular, unique subject lies also, always, its own otherness: otherness as unconscious mental activity; otherness as that gendered aspect of the self which is denied or disowned; otherness as death which inhabits the human subject from the start. In this dialectical play of identity and difference, of unity and disunity, the conception of an integrated harmonization of the polarities involved dances throughout Valéry's writings as both tempting *imago* and contemptuous betrayal. Underlying the texts explored in this chapter (and the main focus will be on *Poésie* and *Fragments du Narcisse*) there exists a fundamental psychodynamic which exploits the imaginative potential of a state of integrity, totality, or completeness in the imagery of the poet's translation. It operates according to two principal axes: either a unity symbolic of the 'origin' evokes a pre-Oedipal fantasy of dyadic bliss between maternal and infant body which is then lost; or an idealized projection of a similarly fantasized state of unity is set up as a form of imaginary construction which then functions as the goal or *telos* of desire. In the pages which follow, voice remains the central thread in an exploration of the original significance of the 'feminine' as structuring component of the poetic consciousness in the earliest stages of existence, and one which remains associated with a fantasy of unity or wholeness. The final chapter pursues it further in the context of Valéry's autobiographical quest to acknowledge the complementarity of masculine and feminine poles within the psyche.

One of the poems which embodies most explicitly the interconnected themes and images whose relevance was developed in the earlier chapters is *Poésie*. Here Valéry employs the 'mère–nourrisson' relationship as, in part, an allegory of that aspect of the creative process which requires an ability to judge exactly the degree of control to be exerted by consciousness over the less conscious areas of the mind in order to encourage rather than hinder its productive capacity.[5] Too great an insistence by consciousness and the flow from the unconscious dimension ceases. So, to the plaintive voice which seeks to know

> [. . .] par quelle crainte vaine,
> Par quelle ombre de dépit,
> Cette merveilleuse veine
> A mes lèvres se rompit? (OI, 119)

there can only be one answer from the source:

> — Si fort vous m'avez mordue
> Que mon cœur s'est arrêté! (OI, 120)

However, in addition to its allegorical dimension, the poem awakens resonances which reveal the polyvalent power of the image of a state of dyadic unity already evoked in *Rêve. Rapport de mer*, and exploits, too, the acoustic space of consciousness in a manner which prepares imaginatively the encounter between the masculine and feminine dimensions of voice enacted in *Fragments du Narcisse*. The narrative dimension of the text speaks of a harmony of relationship with the mother experienced by the infant prior to weaning, a blissful moment of *jouissance* which precedes the necessary drama of severance without which the evolving consciousness cannot accede to autonomous subject status. The dyadic relationship of *Rêve. Rapport de mer* is developed further by introducing the dimension of dialogue: mother and child relate through the exchange circuit of speech established within the enclosed space of their intimacy.

A remark in the *Cahiers* reveals Valéry's awareness of the curious combination of dependency and power which characterizes the attitude of the child at the mother's breast:

Er[os]. Le premier objet dont tu acquis la science, ne fut-ce pas un sein? Ta bouche et tes mains rouges se sont appliquées à ce tendre et ferme sein, source et asile, où de quoi boire et dormir attend le jeune humain. C'est là sa première oasis, sa première fête, sa première volupté.

La tendresse, plus tard, n'est peut-être qu'un souvenir de l'état d'avoir été si faible et d'avoir été traité avec des égards extraordinaires à cause de cette faiblesse. Sa faiblesse fait la puissance exigeante du nouveau-né. (XXIII, 318)[6]

The tenderness revealed in Chapter 2 as closely associated in Valéry's consciousness with childhood, vulnerability, and a feminine presence is thus placed unequivocally in its original emotional context. This same passage provides, in addition, an objective analysis of the mutual play of power enacted through that symbol of nourishment, the maternal breast, which dominates *Poésie*.[7] The central stanzas of the poem evoke the absolute contentment and perfect accord obtaining between mother and child:

> A peine sur ta poitrine,
> Accablé de blancs liens,
> Me berçait l'onde marine
> De ton cœur chargé de biens;
>
> A peine, dans ton ciel sombre,
> Abattu sur ta beauté,
> Je sentais, à boire l'ombre,
> M'envahir une clarté!
>
> Dieu perdu dans son essence,
> Et délicieusement
> Docile à la connaissance
> Du suprême apaisement,
>
> Je touchais à la nuit pure,
> Je ne savais plus mourir [. . .] (OI, 119)

Images of purity, liquidity, light, and dark convey an impression of such bliss, such intense 'volupté' that words fail in the evocation of this god-like mode of being. The pre-Oedipal *jouissance* which prevails here is a state of supreme, almost mystical, oneness bordering on ecstasy and of dissolution of boundaries between self and other.[8] However, earlier manuscript versions of the text describe with greater realism not only the act of sucking and the milk which is absorbed but, in a tone verging on brutality, the breast's rejection of the drinking mouth:

étais-je
ton
A peine, dans ~~un~~ ciel sombre

    abattu   Où se fuit le temps lacté
Ecrasé sur ta beauté

    buveur de
Goulûment buvais-je l'ombre — Infiniment buveur d'ombre

Où se perd le temps lacté,

A peine, totale enfance,

Et délicieusement

        âme sans défense
Ta chose. . . ~~que je t'offense~~!

   Contre un tel
~~Verse moi l'~~apaisement!
   Contre l'ample

   Et
~~A peine~~ coupe trop pure

J'étais heureux d'en mourir

Qu'inexplicablement dure

Tu cessas de me nourrir.

                    (*Ch* MS I, 63)[9]

Several points are noteworthy here: the emphasis on the child's greedy hunger implies that, at this stage, it is a question of a genuinely physical desire and a physical substance accorded in response by a 'good' breast in contrast to the final version where the stress on 'buveur' and 'le temps lacté' is lost; the infant's utter dependence on the mother is even more clearly depicted than in the definitive text ('ta chose, âme sans défense'); and, perhaps most significant of all, the moment of severance is evoked in the form of a direct address from the child as 'Je' to the breast ('Tu cessas de me nourrir') rather than, as in the final formulation, by way of indirect questioning. The final stanzas speak of the disturbing transition which precipitates the emerging consciousness into full awareness of its autonomy: this poetic account of the *spaltung* is a tale of loss, of refusal, of withdrawal for which no explanation is offered other than the hint that the demands of the 'nourrisson' have exhausted the vitalizing potential of its source.

As indicated in Chapter 1, Valéry gave close attention to the phenomenon of a discourse within consciousness as a precondition of thought. The auditory sensibility of the poet requires, similarly, to be sustained by the resonances, both sonorous and associative, of language; and his inner ear draws on, is nourished by the resonant cavities of the mind where the precarious joy of creativity depends on tension, self-observation, and will. The origins of a markedly auditory sensibility can be attributed to that phase of the evolution of the human organism which is characterized by the predominance of sound as the primary mode of contact with the surrounding world. The human subject is alive for approximately two years before the symbolization of language distances it from the immediacy of sound as its living, breathing environment. Research into the intra-uterine phase reveals how the first perceptions registered by the developing organism are the sounds which penetrate the liquid environment of the womb; that the means of exploring the world most accessible to the infant after birth are the air and the sounds absorbed; that these sounds are often the voices closest to the child during the early stages of linguistic development; and that acoustic nourishment is as vital to the growth of the organism as is the satisfaction of its physical demands.[10]

Now in *Poésie* this same scenario is clearly present; mother and child can be viewed as participants in the inner circuit of linguistic exchange, participants whose positions are evoked in the following remark as a mouth and an ear: 'Interno. La voix intérieure est une oreille qui parle. Entendre parle. La conscience est une bouche qui écoute' (VIII, 378). The mouth feeds as the ear absorbs; the breast nourishes as the voice confides. Returning to a psychoanalytic understanding of the development of identity, the maternal voice is considered by a substantial body of theorists to play a fundamental role.[11] A fairly broad consensus of views interprets this voice as a sonorous envelope or mobile receptacle expressing a powerful cultural fantasy: since it constitutes the original containing environment for the child it can be experienced either as blissful plenitude or as an entrapping state of impotence.

These observations have clear relevance to *Rêve. Rapport de mer* with its veiled references to the acoustic sensitivity of the foetus. They also shed light on the dramatization of acoustic consciousness depicted in *Poésie* where, as a close reading of the text has suggested, the identity of mouth and of source are intricately embedded in the auditory metaphor describing the linguistic circuit of consciousness: 'La conscience est une bouche qui écoute' (VIII, 378); there would appear to be an overlapping here of functions, a confusion of nourisher and nourished, of oral and aural. Research in this field suggests that the double organization of vocal and auditory systems in the infant permits it to function at the same time as speaker and as listener. The simultaneity of these two actions, in other words, makes it difficult for a young consciousness to know whether it is 'outside' or 'inside' the sounds which it hears and creates. With regard to the aural dimension of the formation of identity, this uncertain spatial anchoring of aural events may have profoundly destabilizing consequences for subjectivity.[12] Since the child's economy is, at this stage, organized around incorporation—surely the central metaphor of *Poésie*—and since what is incorporated is the auditory field articulated by the mother's voice, the child could be said to hear itself initially in and through that voice. Another conceptualization of this process which brings us closer to the reflexive thematic explored in *Poésie* and the *Narcisse* cycle is to acknowledge that the child first recognizes itself in the vocal mirror supplied by the mother.

A number of manuscript jottings involving the same network of images as in the previous chapter, those specifically associated with the vulnerability of the self, confirms the significance of the mirror in relation to acoustic nourishment. The attentive mouth is highlighted in *Poésie* through the initial image of the outstretched lips turned towards the source of nourishment:

> PAR la surprise saisie,
> Une bouche qui buvait
> Au sein de la Poésie
> En sépare son duvet: (OI, 119)

An early version of *Les Pas* which bears the significant subtitle *Nocturne*, pointing yet again to the role of darkness in this thematic grouping, explores the circuit established between the 'bouche–oreille' of auditory consciousness in a parallel way. An 'ajout marginal', 'cf Nourrice', suggests a connection with *Poésie* which is borne out by pencilled corrections to the typescript. Hesitations here reveal that, at this stage, the auditory dimension was more predominant than in the final version of *Les Pas*. So the first stanza appears as follows:

épris les fils   enfants
Tes pas, ~~fille~~ de mon silence,

Sourdement
~~Saintement~~, lentement placés,

        mon   traçant le silence
Vers le lit de ma vigilance

            chargés de silence
Procèdent muets et glacés.[13]

More relevant, perhaps, is the recurrence of the image of 'la bouche attentive' which receives greater emphasis here than in the definitive version of the poem, thereby suggesting a close connection with *Poésie*, where the gesture of the lips is implicitly present throughout. There may also be an increased impact of this image on the reader's imagination since the gesture of the outstretched lips is, in the earlier version, reciprocal, as the last two verses reveal:

Secrètes
Si de tes lèvres avancées

        prépares
Tu ~~présentes~~ pour l'apaiser

A l'habitant de mes pensées

La nourriture d'un baiser [. . .]
                Fantôme imité de ses draps
                Ruisselant
Sur Des amples drames de ma couche
Spectre surgi jetant ses draps

                ôta
Aux ténèbres je tends ~~ma~~ bouche

        lui
Donne ~~moi~~ ce que tu voudras
[. . .]

        Moi
            Dépouillé   spectre qui [. . .] la bouche
Je sens mon spectre tendre sa bouche
[. . .]
O Ténèbres, voici ma bouche
Demandez ce que vous voudrez[14]

The clear delineation offered to us here of two mouths reaching towards each other on the point of imminent juncture provides an image embodying reflection which functions on the visual level. The mind's eye perceives the physical outlines of the gestalt of two sets of lips outstretched towards each other. The anchoring of the environment of auditory consciousness in an image appealing to the faculty of sight thus seems to be better defined than its location in terms of sound. Boundaries can be clearly sketched by sight but easily overstepped in the world of hearing.[15] This discrepancy has its origins in the ambiguous location of the voice for the infant consciousness; since it is capable of being internalized at the same time as it is externalized it can spill over from subject to object and from object to subject, violating the bodily limits upon which classic subjectivity depends. Such a profoundly unsettling identificatory experience has important consequences for the acquisition of gender identity since a male child will be absorbing and identifying with a female voice at an early and crucially determining phase of development.[16] It may help to account, in some measure, for the tension and rivalry between the male and female voices in texts such as *Poésie* and *Fragments du Narcisse* since the masculine consciousness, struggling to assert its identity as autonomous, must come to terms with the feminine vocal presence which haunts the space in which he lives as, too, the space of his own auditory consciousness. At work in both poems is the notion of an acoustic mirror, that function which the female voice is called upon to perform for the male subject. The maternal voice introduces the child to its mirror reflection so that, in later life, the male subject continues to hear the maternal voice through himself in a range of ways. It comes to resonate for him with all that he transcends through language after his entry into the structures of the symbolic order.[17] Yet it may also represent that aspect of his fantasy life which nourishes his creative attempt to recapture the bliss of being sustained by the other, the mother, the feminine vocal substance of his beginnings.

In contrast to the antagonistic implications of the withdrawal of the feminine in *Poésie*, a more positive connotation is communicated in a text where Valéry shares one of his most profound emotional responses, that is, his acute sensitivity to the human voice: 'Thermométrie. Hypothèses. A un certain âge tendre, j'ai peut-être entendu une voix, un contr'alto profondément émouvant' (IV, 587). Moreover it is a particular quality and tone of this voice which touched his innermost being and conditioned him to respond to it with such intensity throughout his life: 'Ce chant me dut mettre dans un état dont nul objet ne m'avait donné l'idée. Il a imprimé en moi la tension, l'attitude suprême qu'il demandait, sans donner un objet, une idée, une cause, (comme fait la musique)' (IV, 587). The reader detects a sustained effort towards some goal which is no less real in its urgency for remaining unidentifiable. The voice in question has created a sense of need in the poet's consciousness: 'Et je l'ai pris sans le savoir pour mesure des états et j'ai tendu, toute ma vie, à faire, chercher, penser ce qui eût pu directement restituer en moi, nécessiter de moi — l'état correspondant à ce *chant de hasard*' (IV, 587); a sense of need which comes to assume absolute status for the consciousness involved: 'la chose réelle, introduite, absolue dont le creux était, depuis l'enfance, préparé par ce chant — *oublié*' (IV, 587).

It would be hard to find a more explicit acknowledgement than this of the seminal role of voice in the founding moments of affective life. Although Valéry does not identify the voice described here as his mother's, the qualities which he associates with this primordial listening experience fit within the context of a maternal symbolism which psychoanalytic theory identifies as the prototype of all subsequent auditory pleasure. The location of the experience in childhood, the conviction of its absolute, incontrovertible reality, and the reference to the satisfaction of desire—all entitle one to speak of a displacement of the maternal trope/fantasy from the authentic mother figure to a voice representative of the maternal function.[18] However, the maternal voice is not without its ambiguities and paradoxes. It not only grants access to the fantasy of a state of blissful union between infant and mother but is also, as *Poésie* indicated, the force which first ruptures the initial sensation of plenitude or in-tactness, first introduces difference. In so far as it is the first sound to be isolated by the infant consciousness from other sounds, and to the extent to which it initiates the child's own mastery of articulation by supplying it with a sound to be imitated, it can be seen as the force or presence that first introduces the infant subject to the other and to the reality of the symbolic order.

Lacanian theory includes the maternal voice within the category of 'objet (a)'; that is, those objects which are the first to be distinguished from the subject's own self and whose 'otherness' is never very strongly marked. However, this lost object assumes the proportions of an amputation. Once gone it comes to represent what alone can make good the subject's lack; this explains why it becomes the focus of such a powerful fantasy of recovery. It may well be that Valéry is registering an awareness of this kind, the loss or withdrawal of a familiar, nourishing vocal presence, in the remark quoted immediately above; and that his sensitivity to sound and preoccupation with the physical qualities of the voice and with the substantiality of language reflect his attempt to satisfy a sensation of almost physiological need. Certainly the concluding sentences of the remark correspond closely to the urgency of the need activated by the lost object in the Lacanian model: 'J'ai l'idée d'un maximum d'origine cachée, qui attend toujours en moi. Une voix qui touche aux larmes, aux entrailles; qui tient lieu de catastrophes et de découvertes; [. . .] On l'oublie et il n'en reste que le sentiment d'un degré dont la vie ne peut jamais approcher' (IV, 587). Although the identity of the voice is forgotten, the reactions which it provoked remain firmly imprinted on the poet's sensibility. He is left with an ambivalent emotion: a sense of frustration that life can never grant him full satisfaction of his hunger; and, at the same time, a desire none the less to continue striving towards fulfilment.

In this context the hunger for the voice which Valéry's writing expresses conveys all the force of the desire which Lacan defines as the 'something other' which is relegated to the place of its original impossibility.[19] It is the 'remainder' of the subject, something which is always left over but which has no content as such. Lacan, like Freud, distinguishes between need which is a purely organic energy or instinct, and desire which functions as the active principle of the psychical processes. It is, in fact, the transition from need to desire which signals the human subject's entry into language: the original object of need, of the instinct is relinquished forever to the un-conscious as the symbolic signifiers come to replace it. The primal division or *spaltung* of the subject is therefore based on the loss of his unconscious truth in his acquisition of language which can only ever partially reflect that truth. Perhaps, therefore, Valéry's relationship to voice in its full range of meanings can be interpreted as expressing this transition from need to desire. The tendency of his sensibility, originating in the physiological impact of the voice absorbed in infancy which activated a sense of need, traces a curve culminating in the metaphorical import of the voice characteristic of the finest poetry.[20] Only a certain 'plénitude du langage' can overcome the feeling of emptiness or lack left in the psyche since childhood ('ce creux préparé depuis l'enfance'). Valéry's sustained engagement with language, with the conflicting demands of its semiotic and symbolic dimensions; his reformulation of self through the labour on the signifier, that *poiein* which epitomizes his creative endeavour; his striving towards 'le point délicat de la poésie' which is 'l'obtention de la Voix' (VI, 176)—all may be seen as aspects of his transposition on to the level of *écriture* and of poetic theory, of the desire or imperative to regain the originary impression of intactness and non-separation from the maternal body when a strange sense of unity, closely linked with a female voice, predominated.

Fragments du Narcisse represents one of the most elusive aspects of Valéry's writings, a problematic that was central to his life and work as the notes which he made for a talk to be given on the Narcisse cycle as a whole make clear: 'V[ou]s entretenir du Narcisse — c'est pour moi ressaisir un des thèmes conducteurs les plus suivis de mon existence de poète'.[21] Narcisse as emblematic of the tension obtaining between pure and contingent modes of consciousness, as dramatic poeticization of the mind in the mirror, precursor of 'l'Ange', forms one of the best-trodden interpretive paths in the corpus of Valéry studies. In more recent years a welcome development, the genetic approach to these texts, has shed further light on their autobiographical import and has opened the way to a fuller appreciation of the erotic relationship which is a key aspect of their meaning.[22]

Narcisse may be read as the embodiment or incarnation of the desiring voice, the voice made flesh in that mysterious conjuncture of spirit and substance that lies at the heart of all creative endeavour; in this sense, *Fragments du Narcisse* can be situated in the context of the autobiographical project that Valéry pursued throughout his life. In redefining the status of his creative identity, Valéry is obliged to confront, albeit implicitly, the question of the extent to which subjectivity is marked by questions of gender. The drama in which Narcisse is caught up permits him to explore both the visual and the acoustic anchoring of the human subject in space and time; and the classical myth of Narcissus and Echo is the ideal narrative vehicle for such an exploration since it exploits reflection on both the visual and acoustic planes and with reference to a male and a female protagonist. Beneath its explicitly narrative guise of myth the poem embodies an encounter between masculine and feminine modes of subjectivity. The concern of Narcissus with his own body in Ovid's text automatically grants the body, so vital to Valéry's inquiry, a key position in the narrative; similarly, the presence of the elusive nymph Echo enables him to emphasize the importance of the voice in the development of self-consciousness. Narcisse explores, as it were, possible relations with the feminine; while apparently rejecting it on the level of the visual gestalt by preferring his own virginal male form he is, at the same time, seeking to incorporate its specific power as acoustic nourishment or protective envelope into his own substance.

In the drama of Narcisse, as in *Poésie*, the thematic of unity and separation, of identity and difference is acted out through a dialogue in which a masculine voice appeals for a response, or for some form of satisfaction, while a feminine voice retorts, in rebuke or mockery, that separateness is inevitable and insurmountable.[23] In both poems the abstraction that is the circuit of auditory consciousness on which the psychodynamic of identity and difference depends for its existence is given textual form on two levels. On the visual level body boundaries are clearly delineated; as readers we receive the precise gestalt of the child's mouth at the breast or of Narcisse's bodily silhouette and lips profiled against the waters of the fountain. In contrast, the acoustic level depicts sound as a flow, a wave, a shapeless presence which nourishes the child in the warm flux of *Poésie* or develops into a storm of uncontrollable sounds in *Fragments du Narcisse*. The sound image, in other words, does not possess the morphological clarity and self-containedness of the visual image.

One way of conceiving this difference in perceptual modes would be to situate it in the context of contemporary theorizing of masculine and feminine imaginaries. In her analysis of the dominant masculine imaginary of Western culture, Luce Irigaray argues that its speculative processes require, as the ground which enables them to function, a repressed dimension which she depicts as analogous to the dark backing of a mirror's reflective surface. This marginalized dimension is the location of the feminine imaginary, the other of Western culture, which exists as potential only.[24] According to this approach the genealogy of the self which is contained in the manuscripts of the Narcisse cycle reveals the temptations of its own bisexuality being explored by a subjectivity which is reconstructing the foundations of its being in the material of the textual labour.[25] *Fragments du Narcisse* can thus be interpreted in the light of an oscillation within Valéry's creative consciousness between the masculine position, characterized by its reliance on a scopic economy, and the feminine position, which is manifested primarily in relation to the less easily definable realm of acoustic phenomena. Within the textual space of the poem, the reader experiences this dichotomy in two ways. On the one hand, we sense the tension at work in the poetic text as the demands of the symbolic order with its reassuring structures of syntactic logic and traditional poetic constraints come up against the equally powerful imperatives of the semiotic realm embodied in the disruptions, suspensions, and silences of the fragmented vocal substance. On the other hand, the clear, parallel development of the poem's theme according to visual and acoustic determinations makes the oscillation between masculine and feminine manifest in the narrative also through the figures of Narcisse and Echo.

In a manuscript jotting for an early poem Valéry confides the secret urge of his mythic *persona* evoking 'le rêve d'être un Autre et surtout une femme', that longing to embrace within himself the mystery of absolute otherness which inhabits each human being.[26] In the pages which follow I shall argue that while this dream remains unrealized on the level of a scopic economy it can be more promisingly accommodated in the substance of the voice and its acoustic resonances which spill over beyond the defining limitations of this economy. The desiring voice of Narcisse encapsulates, on a genetic level of reformulation of subjectivity as textual process, an encounter between polarities of the psyche which might otherwise have remained radically sundered.[27] In this way, the masculine subject attempts to overcome the painful feelings of abandonment, rejection, and anxiety referred to in texts such as *Poésie* and *Rêve. Rapport de mer* by seeking to take back into himself, within the parameters of his own acoustic control and efficacy, the psychic nourishment which is essential to him but which cannot be fitted neatly within the categories of rationally organized discourse.

Conflicting evidence exists as to whether visual or acoustic considerations were uppermost in Valéry's mind as he explored the significance of Narcisse. Several comments point to the predominance of auditory concerns as, for example, when he remarks: 'Narcisse — Miroir parlant. Ce que je vois me parle par quoi il est Moi' (NA MS II, 161). It would seem from this that the capacity for utterance is the basis for identity.[28] Or, again, in a passage bearing the humorously ironic title *Etudes pour l'éternel Narcisse*, Valéry stresses that the dramatic confrontation between consciousness as absolute and its necessary accompaniment, embodied and contingent consciousness, is discernible essentially as sound. The passage quoted below describes in terms of the inner monologue precisely the theme that is externalized in the narrative and imagery of *Fragments du Narcisse*:

C'est un monologue infini que celui qui peut s'entendre, (si l'on y prête l'oreille de l'esprit), entre deux... pôles/celui que l'on est par les circonstances, par la mémoire, par l'observation de chaque figure particulière de l'instant, l'examen de son corps, l'état de son humeur —, en somme, tout ce qui peut être nommé, décrit, fixé; et d'autre part, en contraste absolu avec celui-là, l'autre, qui ne peut ni ne veut être défini, qui se refuse à toute spécification, qui ne consent à aucune détermination, qui se dégage automatiquement de tout acte de conscience. Pour moi, mon 'Narcisse' n'est pas tant occupé de sa beauté. (NA MS II, 160)

Yet ample evidence reveals, too, that the myth attracted Valéry quite simply because it focused on self-reflection, on the manner in which an image of the self could be perceived, whether the medium was visual or acoustic. It is the function of the image in shaping consciousness which captures his curiosity, the way in which the development of subjectivity requires mirroring if a secure sense of autonomous selfhood is to evolve:

L'idée simple et en somme assez importante était celle-ci: N[ou]s connaissons celui que n[ou]s sommes en tant qu'objet par le retour vers nous de ce que n[ou]s émettons.

Nous voyons notre image, nous pouvons recevoir d'autrui les effets de l'effet que produisent sur autrui notre personne, notre voix, nos actes, nos émanations, connues ou non directement par n[ou]s. P. ex. notre timbre de voix n[ou]s est inconnaissable. (NA MS II, 125)

Both Freud and Lacan provide accounts of the role of the image in the complex process of ego formation, accounts which support a reading of *Fragments du Narcisse* as a poeticized enactment of subjectivity structuring itself on a number of axes. In Freud's understanding of events, the ego is formed not only under the influence of the external world but also by the contributions from the individual's body, particularly its surface. The ego is, in part, the mental projection of the surface of the body. The numerous appellations to the body as form or texture which the poem contains suggest a measure of parallelism between the Freudian and Valéryan conceptions of ego formation. Yet it is Lacan, in his elaboration of the concept of the mirror stage ('le stade du miroir'), who draws us deeper into the problematic of Narcisse.[29] A brief outline of his understanding of the primordially alienating role of the self-image casts light on the magnetically destructive relationship which obtains between Narcisse and his reflected gestalt. In Lacan's view the formation of the ego commences at the moment of fascination with and alienation from one's own image. The image is the first organized form in which the individual identifies himself; so the ego is formed by the organizing and constitutive qualities of this image which may be detected in the mother's gaze or in some other reflective surface. The ego, for Lacan, develops on the basis of an imaginary relationship of the subject with his own body: the infant, between six and eighteen months, becomes aware of his body as a complete gestalt. His mastery of the image fills him with joy since it anticipates a mastery of his actual body which he has not yet, in reality, achieved. The consequence, Lacan argues, is that he falls in love with his image and, in contrast to the auto-erotic stage, in which he has an erotic relationship to his fragmented body, he now takes the image of his whole body as his love-object. This identification with his own body as other than himself structures the subject as a rival within himself, in constant tension between the lived body, invested with all the distress and fragmentation from earlier months, and the striving which continues throughout life towards an imaginary wholeness or unity.

The relevance of this account of the illusory foundations of subjectivity to Valéry's understanding of the self as a linguistically based myth seems hard to contest. *Fragments du Narcisse* can be read as a poetic re-enactment of the infant passage through the mirror stage.[30] The waters of the fountain ('eaux planes et profondes') furnish the specular surface in which the image is perceived; the addresses to his body-image which Narcisse formulates capture closely the compelling nature of the illusory gestalt ('mon corps tyrannique; ce que j'ai de plus cher; la chair lumineuse; délicieux démon désirable'); more specifically Valéry, in both *Narcisse parle* and *Fragments du Narcisse*, refers to the 'obedience' of the bodily gestalt ('forme obéissante') which evokes something of the mastery enjoyed by the infant consciousness over his externalized image. The tragedy of Narcisse when viewed in the light of the Lacanian model is that integration with the otherness that inhabits identity remains forever out of reach. Lacan emphasizes the disappointment that is inherent in the project of human subjectivity since the illusory completeness which the infant perceives can only ever exist in an externalized form. Fusion with the image is an ideal ('O forme obéissante à mes yeux opposée; plus parfait que moi-même'); it cannot ever be touched ('inaccessible enfant') for, if contact is attempted, the shattering of the subject is inevitable ('l'insaisissable amour [. . .] brise Narcisse').

On the level of the scopic imaginary, that aspect of the Western cultural consciousness which gives priority to the visual faculty as primary structuring force of the reality we inhabit, it is evident that Narcisse's yearning to blend with the other is an impossibility. The anxious attention accorded by the text to the clear delineation of forms and the visually derived situating of the subject within his nocturnal environment establish firm boundaries between self and other that brook no infringement. Yet the dream of being the other, of realizing the feminine within himself which haunts Narcisse leads ultimately towards the more fertile configurations which resonate within the voice. The song of Narcisse is also the embodiment of that marginalized or repressed dimension which escapes the controlling grasp of rationality, order, definition, visualization. The voice in this scheme of things possesses the power to subvert the privileging of sight as the predominant sense in the structuring of the cultural imaginary; it does not obey the logic of the proper form, the distinct boundary, the rational order but instead speaks of chaos, formlessness, and potential disintegration. It is in the honesty and courage required to face that radical otherness deep within its own structure that the textual subjectivity of *Fragments du Narcisse* marks an advance beyond the failure registered on the level of a visual theorization of the problematic.

Where the feminine element in *Poésie* and *Rêve. Rapport de mer* could be identified with a maternal symbolism, the situation is more complex in the case of Narcisse. It is perhaps justifiable to speak here of an occluded feminine, an implicit complementarity required by the masculine dimension of Narcisse yet never welcomed fully into the body of the text nor into the body of its protagonist.[31] To become the other, specifically as woman, may translate a desire in the consciousness of Narcisse/Valéry not so much to share with, as to protect himself against, the feminine by introjecting into his own essence certain qualities associated with it. According to this reading, Narcisse's attempt to become voice, to create his own acoustic environment independent of the source, mother or Echo, would represent a desire to regain control over the fearful, threatening, and highly uncertain acoustic envelope which the maternal voice of early life represented. Rejected by the source, Narcisse will become his own source. The principal voice heard throughout *Fragments du Narcisse* is that of Narcisse whose soliloquy, echoing in the resonant space of the natural setting, as, too, in the cavities of his own acoustic consciousness, sends back to him a reassuringly self-generated sonorous envelope. In this way, the masculine subject regains control of his acoustic environment, enveloping himself in an acoustic image which is not derived from the mother, and so protects himself from an invasion by the truly, radically other which may be silence, or woman or death.[32]

The poetic voice of Narcisse/Valéry, that 'voix d'une femme idéale', which epitomizes a certain ideal of poetic discourse, can be imagined as a form of recreated or substitute maternal body of reassuring because controllable sound. The text of *Fragments du Narcisse* constitutes a reformed genealogy of the maternal container in the very substance of the sounds which contribute to its functioning; and the success of the poet, as of his mythical protagonist, is to be measured by his willingness to attempt this literal re-creation of the acoustic mirror, to seek to give birth to an alternative positioning of the masculine subject in space and in time, those vital coordinates of the voice. Yet the *Fragments* remain fragments, the song of Narcisse sings of compromise; in a sense, the import of the voice in this text is to remind us that the Real lies forever beyond recovery. To become the voice, to embrace the other within the self entails an acceptance of the limitations that constitute subjectivity. In both Ovid's account and Valéry's rendering of the myth it is significant that a certain diminished efficacy characterizes both Narcissus and Echo. They share the awareness that their power of speech is ultimately restricted; his, because the minute he utters a sound, he destroys his visual image in the pool; hers, because it is never original, only ever imitation. Clearly what the text enacts is the subject's encounter with his mirrored self in sound; Narcisse is Echo as Echo is Narcisse.[33] She serves a dual function in the context of the creative psyche both as a necessary and fertilizing reminder of complementarity and, equally, as a potent and potentially destructive degree of difference.

This twofold role of the echo is apparent when comparisons between the Ovidian and Valéryan accounts are explored. In Ovid's story the narrator never informs us of the time when Echo was a whole person; when we know her she has wasted away to voice and her voice is powerless. Valéry similarly hints, in a remark in the *Cahiers*, that her role has been unduly limited in *Fragments du Narcisse*.

Picking up the idea of irony which has been present since the start of his preoccupation with Narcisse, he notes: 'Le préfixe RE. La terrible moquerie de l'Echo. Re-dire — comme dépréciation; Simplement re-dire, tue. Retour, — qui pourrait supporter ce qu'*il* a dit? cet *Il* qui a été *Soi*? Dans Narcisse, j'aurais dû jouer de l'Echo en comb[inaison] avec le miroir. Donner au *reflet* puissance d'*écho* — Insupportables doubles' (XX, 597). Yet, paradoxically, though her presence might seem to have remained underdeveloped in this sense, Valéry's text reveals that the effect of her voice on the masculine consciousness is potent in the extreme. It threatens the very boundaries of his being: 'le roc brise mon cœur' evokes the impact of her derisive reiteration as it jars him to his foundations. The text of Valéry's poem exploits to the full this ambiguity of the feminine voice, both reduced and amplified, limited and expanded as it translates the oscillating emotions of the precarious masculine consciousness which searches for a new accommodation within its acoustic environment.

The dream of Narcisse, to become woman, to take otherness fully into his own being, means, in effect, to embrace a position of non-mastery, of incompleteness. Narcisse comes to recognize himself as Echo, as fragment, diminished power, disrupted utterance. The journey which the text embodies is the coming to awareness in the creative consciousness that to be voice, to usurp the place of the m/other, is to renounce the position of mastery of the image which a scopic economy posits as the goal of human consciousness, forever condemned to an illusory striving towards this impossible idea. The wisdom of *Fragments du Narcisse* is found in its registering that acceptance of the rejected dimension of the self as integral to its nature is the surest path to fulfilment; to remain perpetually a desiring voice is to remain open to the complexity and unresolved nature of experience, to the challenge of its formlessness, to the potential creativity of its chaos. Texts such as *Rêve. Rapport de mer*, *Poésie*, and *Fragments du Narcisse* function as a form of therapeutic encounter between the poetic consciousness and its reminiscences of acoustic mastery and vocal power. In the final section of this chapter, a close reading of a selection of manuscripts from the Narcisse cycle draws together the images and themes explored at the start and argues that auditory preoccupations were highly significant in the first stages of the text's composition. The principal dynamic of *Fragments du Narcisse* is a longing for a healed relationship with the (m)other in the self, with the feminine dimension essential to a fully integrated subjectivity.

The mirrored mouth, lips outstretched towards lips, which functioned as focus in *Poésie*, is the pivotal image and instant of *Fragments*. Here, the narrative development leads the listener-reader from the start towards the most intimate moment of the inner mono-dialogue where source and recipient, to speak and to hear, are mirror images hovering on the point of fusion: 'Mais que ta bouche est belle en ce muet blasphème!' (121). These two modes of conceptualization of this potential union, in terms of the scopic economy in relation to the physical gestalt of the body image, and in terms of a wider, non-morphological awareness, embracing acoustic phenomena, may be read as references to the masculine and feminine positions available to consciousness: 'Entendre parle [. . .]. Parler écoute. Et là aussi, voir, être vu; ce qui est vu, voit, ce qui voit est vu' (VIII, 378). If these lips could join, the circuit of 'auto-écoute' would close upon itself, and a state of perfect communication would be achieved with no dissipation of vocal or psychic energy to the external world. Narcisse, reunified with the (m)other contained in his image, would enter once again the integrity of pre-Oedipal *jouissance*. However, paradoxes and ambiguities characterize Narcisse's relationship to his other. His desire for, yet fear of, reabsorption into the form which he glimpses in the water, as, too, his appropriation of sound as a vital instrument in his relationship with reality yet his simultaneous fear of the threatening noises which surround him, translate the unstable and precarious response of the masculine subject to the initial, crucially determining perceptions of the feminine as it was embodied in the first voice of infancy. The poem enacts both dimensions of this conflicting tension within the creative subjectivity. The feminine presence, whether as bodily gestalt or as voice, is rejected or silenced, yet the longing to be reintegrated with it, or to absorb it fully into his own shape and voice, remains as strong as ever.[34]

In its fantasmatic guise as pure sonorousness the maternal voice oscillates between two poles: it is either cherished as 'object (a)', as what alone can make good all lack, or despised and rejected as what is most abject, most culturally intolerable, as representative of everything within masculine subjectivity which is incompatible with the phallic function and which threatens to expose discursive mastery as an impossible ideal. Echo's mocking presence embodies the flinging back into the face of the male subject of that disorganized state of linguistic development which reminds him of his origins in the unstructured sounds of infancy. Similarly, the depiction of the fountain itself conveys further aspects of the despised maternal voice viewed as an anterior position to the paternal world. Since the infant associates it with the darkness and formlessness of its earliest experiences, it displaces onto the fountain those qualities more characteristic of the newborn child itself, conceptualizing it as a uterine night of non-meaning similar to the scene depicted in *Rêve. Rapport de mer*, expressive of the infant's perceptual and semiotic underdevelopment. Narcisse, in restricting the (m)other's power to the static water of the pool or to the limited, mimetic interventions of Echo, has ensured a reversal of the claustrophobic situation of the infant by reducing the feminine voice to a state of relative impotence. This revenge on the maternal voice, the auditory afterbirth which is no longer required as the masculine consciousness develops through the mirror stage towards access into the symbolic order, results from the fact that it functions as the acoustic mirror in which the subject hears all the repudiated elements of his infantile babble. Yet Narcisse/Valéry attempts to heal this dichotomization affecting the status of the maternal voice, through the nature and effect of the poetic discourse. Poetry as a complete or integrated functioning of language in which mind and body, consciousness and unconsciousness co-exist, reformulates the original voice of the mother, substituting for it the ideal voice of the poet.

In the opening lines of the poem the natural décor is sketched in and a liquid element introduced immediately in relation to the body and, more specifically, the mouth of Narcisse. The waters of the fountain, as the nourishing breast in *Poésie*, exert a powerful attraction on the emergent desiring subjectivity which seeks satisfaction:

> Que tu brilles enfin, terme pur de ma course!
>
> Ce soir, comme d'un cerf, la fuite vers la source
> Ne cesse qu'il ne tombe au milieu des roseaux,
> Ma soif me vient abattre au bord même des eaux. (1–4)

In a variant of the sonnet *Narcisse parle* greater emphasis is placed on the idea of the longing for an encounter with selfhood as a thirst, later to become more explicitly a thirst related to sound. A tentative jotting placed above the sonnet notes: 'Lèvres de Narcissus, [. . .] / Mes lèvres sont en vain vers mes lèvres tendues' and, further down the same page but scored out, 'Cher Narcissus! tes lèvres ont soif de tes lèvres'

(NA MS I, 1).[35] The graphic depiction of two mouths outstretched towards each other, reminiscent of the gesture of the lips which lay at the heart of *Poésie*, describes here an attitude of auto-erotic attentiveness whose full significance in the context of the maternal symbolism is uncovered as the poem unfolds.

This first movement is predominantly a dialogue involving Narcisse and nature as the ambient world is sketched in as, essentially, a sonorous space. Although his is the only voice to be heard, Narcisse interprets the environment as response or, at least, reaction to his utterances; even his solitude is defined or highlighted against a background of sound:

> Je suis seul!... Si les Dieux, les échos et les ondes
> Et si tant de soupirs permettent qu'on le soit!
> Seul!   (30–2)

From lines 29 to 47 the voices of nature occupy the foreground while none the less being viewed mainly in relation to the physical form of the speaker. Pencil jottings on a manuscript variant of this section, specifically relating to line 44, reveal that natural sounds were envisaged as voices and were represented as responding to or accompanying Narcisse's appeal; they were strategically important elements during the process of composition:

> Grand soupir
> sur ma chair!
> Passe comme une voix   comme leur voix
>   Sa voix fraîche à tes vœux ~~tremble de consentir~~
>
>   Les bois, la nuit ~~qui vient~~ former le fond des bois
>
>   à peine   La voix basse   (NA MS I, 60ᵛ)

In this sensitivity to the vocal presences or forces active around him, Narcisse would appear to be recalling something close to the infant subjectivity's awareness of the environment as primarily sonorous; where sound possesses, indeed, a material density capable of touching and stirring the body surface.

Again, with reference to lines 39–43, the voice of night is depicted as more insistent than in the final version of the poem; it is an invasive though perhaps welcomed force, penetrating the boundaries of the self:

Jusque dans les secrets, jusque dans cet espoir...

Jusque dans le repli de l'amour de soi-même ...

Rien ne peut échapper au silence du soir;

La nuit qui vient me parle
~~Cette paix me pénètre~~; elle ⓓⓘⓣ qu'elle m'aime
          voix

and silence itself is powerful, authoritative over the sensitive consciousness.

For a time thereafter the natural world fades from the central focus,
leaving the way clear for the emergence of the body-image trapped,
immobile, in the reflective surface of the static waters of the pool:

O douceur de survivre à la force du jour,
Quand elle se retire enfin rose d'amour, [. . .]
Tout m'appelle et m'enchaîne à la chair lumineuse
Que m'oppose des eaux la paix vertigineuse! (48–9/70–1)

There is danger here for the observing subject since the calmness of
the site invites a certain loss of consciousness (l. 56); and the waters,
strangely, offer nothing of the resource of freshness or renewal more
usually associated with a liquid environment. They awaken connotations of death and the fatal brilliance of their surface seems rather
like a tomb. Narcisse's magnetic attraction to the gaping hole in the
ground may express his desire to return to the familiarity of the
maternal body, however suffocating such an experience may be,
however castrating to the developing autonomy of the masculine
subject.

A partial explanation of the irresistible attraction which he feels for
his image would thus be that it is contained still within the embrace
of the amniotic fluid, that supportive liquid environment which, in
the pre-Oedipal moment, protected and nourished the foetus.[36]
Narcisse, exposed to the nakedness of his independent existence, feels
the world a chill presence on his skin, a turbulence of sound and air
that leaves him longing to be gathered back into the fullness and
steadiness of the dyadic state. His searching voice, in a similar way,
gropes acoustically towards a re-situating of the self in relation to the
original maternal envelope. The anxiety which the fragile, autonomous subject registers permeates his awareness in terms of envy for
his double:

Cessez, sombres esprits, cet ouvrage anxieux
    Qui se fait dans l'âme qui veille;
Ne cherchez pas [. . .]
    Le malheur d'être une merveille:
Trouvez dans la fontaine un corps délicieux... (80–4)

In seeking and desiring himself Narcisse, in fact, desires to possess or to be the mother, that lost object of his desire. He discovers in the pool 'a home reminiscent of the mother's genital—that door at which, according to Freud, children first seek the truth of human origin, later cultivate the delusion of female castration and finally, as adults, confront the return of the repressed'.[37]

In fact, what is at issue here is not the mother's exclusion from the Symbolic but the subject's own irreducible castration, the cleavage of the speaking subject from the subject of speech already traced in the radical severance that the weaning of child from source in *Poésie* represented. Narcisse is powerless to step back through the gate of the womb as he is unable to embrace his pre-natal self. He may, however, be able to come closer to possessing his m/other in the song of his loss, in the vocalized substance of his poeticized reality, in a re-positioning of subjectivity both spatially and temporally. Narcisse is paralysed within the specular logic of identity in which the feminine has no part other than as margin or negativity in relation to which the masculine subject defines his identity.[38] And yet, there is evidence in Valéry's *Cahiers* that voice in its fullness, embracing the limitations and complexities which it embodies for Narcisse, serves as a vehicle for a spiritual awareness transcending the limits of an isolated individual subject. As suggested in Chapter 2, the mystical resonances of voice are powerful for the Valéryan sensibility; and in the *Fragments* a possible avenue enabling a new economy of desire to come into being is located in the spatio-temporal references of the reflective paradigm. As long as subjectivity is conceptualized purely as reflection, whether visual or auditory, it remains, in a sense, one-dimensional, incomplete, unconsummated. Solitude, for example, is characterized by just such an unsatisfactory sensation of insubstantiality as a *Cahiers* entry evoking the dilemma of Narcisse suggests: 'Solitude — fondamentale. Ton essence est solitude. Solitude, échange interne. O Vie. Seul. Tout pour soi. Il faut avouer que le Moi — n'est qu'un — Echo' (VIII, 385).

The creative sensibility yearns to accomplish within its substance a more fertile interaction of its component dimensions, an exchange of identity and difference, mind and body, that Valéry envisages, on occasion, as a form of divine presence. 'Le dieu peut-être', he observes, 'cherche et se cherche et par toutes voies — dont l'*une* serait *nature* et l'*autre conscience* et sensibilité. Et peut-être tente-t-il de les rejoindre?' (XVIII, 904). The approach to his own divine or spiritual potential entails an ever deeper integration of what he refers to as a kind of internal femininity. Despite the tone of regret implied by certain admissions, significantly placed beneath the rubric 'Faust III'—'Il est peut-être impossible de rencontrer la forme femelle de cette étrange nature' (XXIV, 375)—their intrinsic value is undeniable, as the conclusion of the same remark indicates: 'Cependant c'est une grande pensée que d'avoir voulu inventer un amour de degré supérieur' (XXIV, 375).

The significance of the symbolic marriage of the male and female within the poetic consciousness occupies a fundamental position in the evolution of the autobiographical quest of *ego poeta*, as will be suggested in Chapter 4. It is equally central in the context of the struggle of Narcisse to redefine his position in relation to his visual and acoustic image where it may be interpreted as an attempt to situate the masculine and feminine aspects of subjectivity in a more productive relationship with each other, in a more fruitful economy of desire. Valéry's poetic theory and practice, understood in the broadest sense of the term 'poetic', share a concern explored by Irigaray in her analyses of the underpinnings of the cultural imaginary. She develops her understanding of a more fertile era in human relations in terms of the *copula*, emblematic of an interaction of male and female which would grant full recognition to the distinctiveness, the value, and the creative potential of these complementary dimensions of a culture. The terms which she employs to evoke a lost dimension of sacred or spiritual awareness in the Western imaginary return us to the resonances of the Valéryan quest. Voice, in the philosophical and psychoanalytical framework of Irigarayan thought, refers to an integrated subjectivity in much the same way that this concern traverses Valéry's writing.[39] In her identification of the crisis produced by the 'death of God', she emphasizes the extent to which the radical split between mind and body which characterizes Western cultural productions has profound transcendental implications. Discourse and thought are marked as the preserve of the masculine subject, the body as that of the feminine. As long as such an imbalanced economy holds sway a genuine sexual encounter, in all the resonances of that meta-phor, remains impossible.[40]

In defining more closely the question of desire, her text lends itself creatively to an alignment with Valéry's poetic and spiritual concerns and, more precisely, to the problematic position of Narcisse:

Le changement du corps et la modification de l'intervalle [entre corps et enveloppe] représentent une question importante dans l'économie du désir [. . .]. Le problème du désir étant de supprimer l'intervalle en ne supprimant pas l'autre [. . .]. Pour que le désir subsiste, il faut un double lieu [. . .] Ou Dieu comme subsistance de l'intervalle, report de l'intervalle à et dans l'infini [. . .]. La sexualité rencontre peut-être cette aporie [. . .] en laquelle elle devient rivale avec la question de Dieu.[41]

At the heart of Narcisse's encounter with the mystery of subjectivity lies a very similar awareness of its transcendent dimension. The intricate interplay of voice and an intuition of the divine as that dwelling of otherness within the subject emerged at an earlier stage. In the context of voice as a retranscription of the desiring self *Fragments du Narcisse* embodies the feminine as an attempt to maintain the openness of the interval posited by Irigaray as essential in delaying the habitual foreclosure of desire according to the reductive categories of over-rigid identificatory paradigms. Valéry notes in his *Cahiers* that Narcisse has reached an impasse, risks foundering in the abyss of auto-erotic attentiveness unless the potentially infinite dimension in desire can be sustained: 'Narcisse. A n'a plus l'appétit de A. Il faut se désirer — se trouver *infini* pour *vouloir être*' (XVIII, 765). The key to sustaining the thirst for the other lies in the voice, in its function as the force which creates and animates the interval without which the breath of life, of consciousness and of spirit, dies: 'La voix sort de l'instant et vient de la totalité du temps; Elle paraît dans l'intervalle, dans la coupure de la conscience, dans ce qui sépare le sentiment de l'acte, et ce qui oblige à parler de ce qui s'attend à comprendre. Mais ce qui demande à comprendre oblige à parler' (VII, 643). It is indeed an awareness of the critical import of the interval that governs the discoveries of Narcisse. He comes to realize that union or reunion with Echo is as threatening as to merge with his other in the pool. Although Echo represents, perhaps, initially another love-object for Narcisse, her intrusion into the text is sensed as hostile and harmful (ll. 93–7) and Narcisse welcomes the re-establishing of silence. In the *Cahiers* remark where Valéry reflects on the impact of the acoustic

double on the recipient consciousness, indicating that he could have
expanded its role further in a theatrical context, he points to the
destabilizing consequences of a slippage of voice beyond the subject's
control: 'Dans une pièce plus ou moins "antique" cet effet: L'*écho*. On
apporte dans (temple, caverne sacrée etc) un suppôt qui répète les
paroles du personnage, et s'entendant répéter d'une forte voix, celui-
ci ne peut supporter sa pensée [. . .] Et il finit par se jeter dans le trou
(abîme ou folie)' (XX, 597).[42]

With the rendering of the echo effect nature emerges once more as
a dominant sonorous force and the self-referential human voice of the
preceding section finds itself rivalled by the sounds of the natural
world. In contrast to the containment of the visual image in the pool,
there is no limit to the expansive spillage of sound which floods
Narcisse on all sides:

> [. . .]   Vous le dites, roseaux,
> Qui reprîtes des vents ma plainte vagabonde!
> Antres, qui me rendez mon l'âme plus profonde,
> Vous renflez de votre ombre une voix qui se meurt...
> Vous me le murmurez, ramures!... [. . .] (98–102)

As the danger of dusk draws nearer, sound functions increasingly as
the link between self and world, with nature amplifying the menace
which threatens the solo human voice dwindling to nothingness.
The reflexive form of 'une voix qui se meurt' lends added force to the
idea of a decrescendo as the voice of the subject loses control of
the situation and ambient sound gains the upper hand. A drama of
uncontrolled sound develops; the boundaries between self and world
are destroyed and Narcisse is invaded by the voice of nature coursing
through him:

> Tout se mêle de moi, brutes divinités!
> Mes secrets dans les airs sonnent ébruités,
> Le roc rit; l'arbre pleure; [. . .] (105–7)

In an attempt to regain some degree of mastery over a threatening
situation and by a form of osmosis, he fuses with the forces of the
natural world, voicing his feelings through them, seeking to make this
acoustic envelope his own:

> [. . .]   et par sa voix charmante,
> Je ne puis jusqu'aux cieux que je ne me lamente
> D'appartenir sans force à d'éternels attraits! (107–9)

Again, it is in a series of fragments revealing the process of com-position that the role of the natural world as an amplifier of the panic perceptible in the voice of the protagonist is more heavily emphasized. The following manuscript fragment, referring to lines 100–14 of the final version, indicates that, in earlier stages of the poem's develop-ment, natural forces were depicted as more active:

> Brutes divinités, rocs, fontaines, roseaux,
>
> Grand | Noir peuple | (masse)
> Haut | Mouvements| des forêts, peuple |calme| des eaux
>
>   rendez mon âme plus
>   Antres qui me ~~parlez~~ de mon âme profonde
> Arbres
>
>   sous l'image du monde
>   Vous qui de toutes parts, ~~de Narcisse~~
>
>   que soi-même à Narcisse
>   traits Ne rendez à Narcisse étonné de sa voix
>   au solitaire amant
>   Que son ombre, sa voix ses   délicat enfant
>
>   Donc
>   Toutefois, je vous aime je [ne me]* défends   [unclear]*
>   [nous]
>   [vous]
>
>   Arbres, tumultueux |esclaves| de la terre,
>
>   Semblez du seul Narcisse | occupés
> | une foule occupée
>   misérable
>   (NA, MS I, 76)

This state of solitude bordering on the paranoiac is thrown into relief by the unison of natural forms and sounds which surround him, directing their attention towards him. By a process of imaginative empathy and perhaps in an attempt to mitigate the attack, Narcisse expresses his anguish through the image of the trees, fellow sufferers who join their voice with his. A manuscript variant of lines 105–6 emphasizes especially the articulate capacity of the world around him.

>   Tous   témoins
> Vous ~~O vous de toutes parts,~~ (orateurs) sans figure,
>
>   Arbres, rochers, roseaux, brutes divinités   (NA, MS I, 86)

One last manuscript jotting relating to this section captures the fear provoked in the perceiving consciousness:

> parcelle   ensorcelle
> étincelle
> Les ~~mains~~ sur l'être ont ~~pouvoir~~   force universelle
>   des
>
> L'ombre   bouche — scelle
> La nuit qui vient les   ensorcelle ruisselle
>
> Grands cieux qui me percez de hauts cris tournoyés
>   tournoyants
>   (NA MS I, 189)

It is not clear to which part of the *Fragments* this sketch refers but it is of interest for two reasons: for its portrayal of the intrusive role of the outer world which reaches into the innermost depths of the protagonist as highly pitched sound; and for the 'rapprochement' which it suggests with *La Pythie*, where a similar violation of the self is evoked.[43] A parallelism in tone and vocabulary can be detected in her panic-stricken plea to the superhuman force from whose hands some unknown charge is to be communicated:

> Sois clémente, sois sans oracles!
> Et de tes merveilleuses mains,
> Change en caresses les miracles, [. . .]
> N'allez donc, mains universelles,
> Tirez de mon front orageux
> Quelques suprêmes étincelles! (OI, 134)

Both texts describe the meeting of spirit and flesh, of desiring energy and its embodiment in voice, which remains amongst the most mysterious and yet the most empowering moments in the journey of what it means to be human. Yet they do so in different ways. Where *La Pythie* presents the reader with the emergence of language as ordered discourse, the product of a fertile compromise with the structuring forces of the symbolic order, *Fragments du Narcisse* invites us rather to remain on the brink; the subject of speech can only operate within language by constantly repeating the moment of fundamental and irreducible division when the first object is lost. Valéry's interrogations of this mystery cannot, in so far as mystery is its essence, lead the reader to an answer, a solution, a revelation of the secret. In Lacan's conception of the manner in which desire animates human projects, the goal or longing for identity or wholeness must, of necessity, remain forever at the level of fantasy. Its value to consciousness is, indeed, precisely the fact that it lies outside the register of need or the economy of pleasure, touching on that area of excess to which he refers as *jouissance*, an intensity of experience bordering on a dissolution of the boundaries of the self similar to death. The fragmentary nature of Narcisse's song captures the tragic fragility of this reiterated awareness of desire's potentiality.

So it is that, in Valéry's text, we are led to the critical point of an encounter with such a state of non-being. After the outburst of panic expressed by Narcisse the tone alters as he gazes at his image in the waters of the pool:

> [. . .]   Le bruit
> Du souffle que j'enseigne à tes lèvres, mon double,
> Sur la limpide lame a fait courir un trouble!...
> Tu trembles!... Mais ces mots que j'expire à genoux
> Ne sont pourtant qu'une âme hésitante entre nous,
> Entre ce front si pur et ma lourde mémoire...
> Je suis si près de toi que je pourrais te boire, [. . .]
> (128–34)

Juncture of self and other seems imminent as lips stretch towards reflected lips across the critical interval in which subjectivity has its being as utterance; as Narcisse invites the waters of the maternal body to absorb him.[44] Yet Narcisse is trapped within the paradox of all desire. By reducing and controlling the feminine as voice he has made it difficult to have or to be that voice without threatening its extinction. The exchange circuit must be maintained if consciousness is to survive: 'Narcisse — Monologue. Duo avec son image — avec lui-même? Voix autre. Voix de l'image [. . .]. Echange' (NA MS II, 2). The genetic labour of subjectivity creating the possibility of its own textual existence faces the ground of all being: the gaping darkness of the unknown, the interval separating birth from death, that 'béance' in which the Real may perhaps hover still, perpetually beyond our grasp.[45] Narcisse stands at the entrance to the mystery, has the courage to remain perpetually in no-man's-land, embodying incompleteness as the essence of his obsessional 'plainte'.

The closing lines of the final movement of the text confront the tragedy which is the hallmark of the drama of Narcisse as he drowns in his own image:

> Hélas! corps misérable, il est temps de s'unir...
> Penche-toi... Baise-toi. Tremble de tout ton être!
> L'insaisissable amour que tu me vins promettre
> Passe, et dans un frisson, brise Narcisse, et fuit...

Yet a variant of these lines points to a significant ambiguity surrounding the effect of his embrace:

> L'insaisissable amour que tu me vins promettre
>
> brise
> Passe, et dans un frisson, ~~se fait~~ Narcisse, et fuit... (NA MS I, 96)

The reflexive form of the verb 'se faire' which originally figured here suggests that, within the creative consciousness of the poet, a very real uncertainty, a hovering in the space that separates consciousness from non-being, vocalized desire from the silence of death, exercised him. It is the oscillation between the temptation of mastery promised by the image as visual gestalt where shattering of the illusion is inevitable ('brise'); and the attraction of a fuller, more integrated form of subjectivity which the voice promises ('se fait'). Narcisse as poetic protagonist dies; as vocalized desire, as poetic voice, he lives on as text.

Ultimately the poetic consciousness comes closest to being/having the mother in the reformulated voice of desire which constitutes the autobiographical discourse of *ego poeta*. Valéry's quest as a writer is governed by the urgent imperative to restore a sensation of plenitude to his creative consciousness, to recreate 'la chose réelle [. . .] dont le creux était, depuis l'enfance, préparé par ce chant — *oublié*' (IV, 587). In transforming the substance of his life into the greater perfection of poetry, he is perhaps able to draw closer to that lost voice which he qualifies as singularly accomplished in a remark evoking the purity of poetic discourse as 'le langage *complet* [. . .], le langage dont la *forme*, c'est-à-dire l'action et la sensation de la *Voix*, est de même puissance que le *fond*' (OI, 1336).[46] A degree of satisfaction is available through the displacement of need on to the symbols of language in a ceaseless process of transformation, of alchemical modulation of desire. The voice of poetry offers the possibility of an acoustic wholeness, an aesthetically or formally redeemed object which compensates for the originary loss of childhood; 'la voix d'une femme idéale, Mlle. Ame' sings of a surrogate *jouissance*.

Notes to Chapter 3

1. De Lussy treats the delicate issue of how to approach Valéry with regard to the unconscious with intelligence and sensitivity, quoting Valéry appositely in this respect. A letter from him to Ernst Robert Curtius, dated 24 June 1924, observes: 'Chacun de nous, même quand il se pique de "conscience", — et je dirais presque — *surtout* quand il si pique de conscience, — ne se perçoit que dans la direction de sa volonté. Ce que nous ignorons le plus est ce qui ne se rapporte pas à cette volonté, et qui ne l'excite pas, ou bien qui ne lui résiste pas [. . .] Mais le témoin qui nous observe est mieux placé que nous' (*'Charmes'*, i. 17). She acknowledges that Valéry's relationship with his own unconscious— 'Chacun de nous n'est-il pas le poème le plus obscur et d'abord pour soi-même?', he asks (Bibliothèque Nationale, MSS Cahiers, copies dact., Eros, V, fo. 211)—'constitue le fil directeur qui court d'un extrême à l'autre de cette étude de genèse et tente d'en assurer l'unité' (p. 17).

2. This text first appeared in *La Revue de France* in Dec. 1926 and was later published as part of *Autres rhumbs* in 1927. See Hytier, OII, 1425.

3. Freud's lecture on anxiety discusses the birth trauma in terms of a situation involving 'unpleasurable feelings, impulses of discharge and bodily sensations which [have] become the prototype of the effects of a mortal danger'; and he mentions, too, the significance of darkness and solitude in the same context (*Introductory Lectures on Psychoanalysis*, ed. J. Strachey and A. Richards (Pelican Freud Library, 1; Harmondsworth: Penguin, 1976), 440–60).

4. In my discussion of Lacan's thought I refer principally to Anika Lemaire, *Jacques Lacan*, trans. David Macey (London: Routledge & Kegan Paul, 1977); and to Bice Benvenuto and Roger Kennedy, *The Works of Jacques Lacan: An Introduction* (London: Free Association Books, 1986).

5. The poem's original title was *La Nourrice* and remained so until 1921 (de Lussy, *'Charmes'*, i. 117). Gifford argues against too literal an interpretation of the text, reading it rather as a 'parable about the human soul or psyche weaned from its dream of communion with the source and essence of things' (*Paul Valéry: Charmes*, 63). De Lussy herself favours a metaphorical reading of the text as exploring 'les affres de la création poétique' (p. 117).

6. This remark, placed unambiguously under the rubric *Eros*, suggests that Valéry perfectly appreciated the complexities of pre-Oedipal sexuality. In the analysis of *Fragments du Narcisse* which concludes the present chapter, this erotic dimension of maternal–infantile sexuality may account for the hesitation in a manuscript variant between 'enfant/amant' in a similar context of dialogue. See below, n. 15.

7. The breast, as 'part object' in Kleinian theory, is the first object of the instinct; it proposes itself as a substitute for the lost anatomical complement, as capable of filling the lack of the maternal body experienced by the infant and of re-establishing the lost connection. Klein uses the concept of 'part object' to describe the manner in which, during the process of ego integration, the infantile ego relates to the objects which form its environment. Strategies of introjection and projection enable the ego to defend itself against destructive feelings by splitting itself and the object (prototypically the mother and her breast) into good and bad parts. See *The Selected Melanie Klein*, ed. Juliet Mitchell

(Harmondsworth: Penguin, 1986), 115–45. See also Lemaire, *Jacques Lacan*, for a discussion of how part objects, of which the breast is one, propose themselves from the outside as external objects capable of closing the *béance* of being: 'the original loss will be represented in the psyche, in the imaginary [. . .] by an image of the anatomical cut or aperture, or by the imaginary presentation of the erotogenic zone' (p. 128).

8. In a *Cahiers* jotting exploring tenderness, an emotion which assumed increasing importance for Valéry, the terms which he employs suggest a parallel with the thematic network of *Poésie*: '"Tendresse". Sens de ce terme? Evasion dans la faiblesse, dans un évanouissement doux et insupportable presque — — Opposer à tout une / sa faiblesse. — Nudité du moi qui se dépouille de tout ce qui le revêtait et le rendait tout autre qu'un petit enfant. Perdre connaissance dans la douceur. Cette faiblesse échappe à toute force' (XXIV, 824).

9. De Lussy, *'Charmes'*, i. 118–19.

10. Is it an intuition of this fact that prompts Valéry to envisage a 'poème du souffle, cette précieuse marée d'air, âme toujours nouvelle' (VII, 528) where the breath is evoked as a liquid flow and as an animating force which is of particular value to the organism on a more than purely physiological level? For a more detailed treatment of the specifically physiological aspect of sound in relation to the thematic nexus of darkness, solitude, femininity, and fragile infant subjectivity see my article 'Valéry et Tomatis: étude sur la conscience auditive du poète', *BEV* 20 (1979), 27–44.

11. Psychoanalytic theory suggests that, for the developing ego, the voice has greater command over space than the look; and that voice, before language, is the instrument of demand (Mary Anne Doane, 'The Voice in the Cinema: The Articulation of Body and Space', *YFS* 60 (1980), 33–50). *Poésie* might express residual memories of the play of power between the voices of mother and child. Guy Rosolato discusses this aspect in the chapter entitled 'La voix: entre corps et langage', in *La Relation d'inconnu* (Paris: Gallimard, 1978); see also the study by Alfred Tomatis, *L'Oreille et le langage* (Paris: Seuil, 1978).

12. Christian Metz, 'Aural Objects', *YFS* 60 (1980), 24–32; and Kaja Silverman, *The Acoustic Mirror: The Female Voice in Psychoanalysis and Cinema* (Bloomington, IN: Indiana University Press, 1988), 79–80.

13. Paris, Bibliothèque Littéraire Jacques Doucet, Fonds Valéry, 195.

14. Paris, Bibliothèque Littéraire Jacques Doucet, Fonds Valéry, 195.

15. De Lussy's study of the genesis of *Les Pas* points to its erotic dimension, perhaps deriving from its origins in the tale of Amour and Psyché (*'Charmes'*, i. 309–17). She also notes the intrusive mood of terror which breaks the tone of harmony characteristic of the poem as a whole (p. 317). This may be attributed, I suggest, to the uncertainty concerning its boundaries which is registered by the fragile ego at this stage of its development. For evidence of how rich a reading the genetic approach to a text can offer see also de Lussy's 'Manuscript Steps: "Les Pas"', in Gifford and Stimpson (eds.), *Reading Paul Valéry*, 200–16.

16. This is not necessarily a comfortable experience for the masculine subject since it means that the boundaries of male subjectivity must be constantly redrawn through the displacement, externally, and on occasion onto the female subject, of what Kristeva terms the abject. What has to be jettisoned is the vocal and

auditory 'afterbirth' which threatens to contaminate the order and system of 'proper speech' (Silverman, *The Acoustic Mirror*, 81).

17. See Ch. 1 for a discussion of the tension between semiotic and symbolic demands within subjectivity; and Ch. 4 for a discussion of this projection/ reflection of the abject onto feminine *personae* in the context of Valéry's auto-biographical identity.

18. Gilberte Aigrisse proposes what is, perhaps, too facile an identification: 'Le charme magique de la voix de la mère, il espérait inconsciemment le retrouver dans les poèmes qu'il écrivait' (*Psychanalyse de Paul Valéry* (Paris: Editions universitaires, 1964), 125). A more subtle view emerged in the course of a conversation which I was privileged to enjoy with Mme Agathe Rouart-Valéry. She revealed that her mother's voice was not a contralto and that it was probably too familiar to Valéry to be remarked upon; she suggested that the voice so often referred to could, perhaps, have been that of a cousin, Gaëta Cabella.

19. For an account of need and desire in Lacan's thought, see Juliet Mitchell and Jacqueline Rose (eds.), *Jacques Lacan and the Ecole Freudienne: Feminine Sexuality* (London: Macmillan, 1983), Introductions I, II.

20. Might this not account for Valéry's observation that 'la plus belle poésie a la voix d'une femme idéale, Mlle. Ame' (VI, 170)?

21. NA MS II, 127–9. I refer to the manuscripts of the Narcisse cycle according to the classification method established by Mme de Lussy of the Département des Manuscrits, Bibliothèque Nationale de France, Paris:

Volume I, microfiche 4236: *Narcisse Parle* and *Fragments du Narcisse*; hereafter NA MS I with appropriate page reference.

Volume II, microfiche 4237: *La Cantate du Narcisse* and *Conférence sur les Narcisse*; hereafter NA MS II with appropriate page reference.

For reasons of typographical convenience, the presentation of manuscript material from the Narcisse 'dossiers' does not always reproduce exactly the layout of the original. However, care has been taken to ensure that the sense is not altered.

22. See, in particular, Jean Levaillant (ed.), *Ecriture et génétique textuelle: Valéry à l'œuvre* (Lille: Presses universitaires, 1982).

23. It is worth noting that the first stages of Valéry's expansion of the Narcisse theme from the early sonnet *Narcisse parle* towards its ampler development in *Fragments du Narcisse* were jotted on the same manuscript pages which carry the 'brouillons' of *Poésie* (NA MS II, 127 and 129 respectively).

24. She further suggests that the dominance of masculine speculation/ specularization, understood as prizing rationality, logic, clarity, and teleology in the production of thought, depends on privileging the visual faculty, both literally and metaphorically—hence the term 'scopic economy'. The feminine, or, as yet, non-existent imaginary, might prioritize other senses, and thus allow for the emergence of new ways of experiencing and categorizing reality (*Ce Sexe qui n'en est pas un* (Paris: Minuit, 1977)).

25. Levaillant, in referring to two states in which language would appear to be operative in the 'brouillons' of the Narcisse cycle—as the mobility characteristic of the imaginary and in a more organized manner typical of the symbolic—speaks of 'un fantasme originaire de bisexualité, d'androgynie' in this context

(*Ecriture*, 23); similarly, Céline Sabbagh, in the same collection, evokes 'la part féminine et secrète de Narcisse' (p. 153).

26. From the unpublished sonnet *Artifice*, composed in 1890 and quoted in Céline Sabbagh, 'Transformations textuelles: le sourire funèbre'; in Levaillant (ed.), *Ecriture et génétique textuelle*, 133–56 at 135.

27. The collection of essays grouped in Levaillant, *Ecriture*, offers an exceedingly rich range of approaches to precisely this dimension of the creative subjectivity. Different critics explore a range of texts from the point of view of 'une archéologie du sentiment', revealing the extent to which considerations of erotic love played a significant role in the genesis of the Narcisse cycle.

28. A remark from the *Cahiers* bears out my hypothesis on the priority of the auditory over the visual: 'dans le domaine de l'ouïe, nous avons la *voix* productrice de sons, par quoi *nous ne sommes pas absents de tout ce que nous entendons*. Je m'entends — Je ne me vois pas' (XXVII, 664). Jarrety's analysis of the Narcisse texts (*Valéry devant la littérature*, 132–7) underlines their value as 'un modèle d'allocution autant qu'un modèle de réflexion spéculaire' (p. 132), arguing, too, the importance of the voice as guarantee of presentness to self and of a sense of subjective identity (p. 136).

29. Parallels between the thinking of Valéry and Lacan in this respect have not gone unnoticed; see e.g. Nicole Celeyrette-Pietri, *Valéry et le moi: des Cahiers à l'œuvre* (Paris: Klincksieck, 1979), 130–2. The following account of the mirror stage draws on Benvenuto and Kennedy, *The Works of Jacques Lacan*, ch. 2.

30. All subsequent references to the poem relate to OI, 122–30; line numbering is placed in brackets after lengthier quotations.

31. Ned Bastet in 'Genèse et affects: le Fragment II du *Narcisse*', in Levaillant (ed.), *Ecriture*, ch. 3, and Judith Robinson in 'Le Finale du *Narcisse*: genèse du texte et archéologie du sentiment' in Levaillant (ed.), *Ecriture*, ch. 4, both explore the significance of the feminine in the Narcisse cycle, relating it to a variety of aspects: the encounter with a fantasized, erotic other; the textual memory embedded in the imagery and thematic of the poem; the metaphysical resonances of emotional complexes relating to childhood vulnerability. Robinson cites (p. 124) a remark from the *Cahiers* dating from the period when Valéry was working on the last stages of the finale of *Narcisse* which seems apposite:

> Par grand vent d'O[uest] avec rafales — l'être se sent — se ressent en triste et comme *intense* isolement.
> Sentiment d'appartenir à ce que ce vent pourrait emporter.
> On voudrait se serrer contre sa / une / mère intérieure.
> Celle-ci est ce féminin de l'être, ce tendre et ce tiède idéaux, cette paix dans les larmes, cet adieu, cette détente, cette nuit sacrée, ce don du refuge que nous prêtons à ce que n[ou]s aimons le plus profondément, à la femme d'entre les femmes,
> Celle aussi qui ne comprend pas.
> Les animaux se serrent dans l'abri en entendant la tempête. (VIII, 547)

32. In her study of gender considerations as they are textualized in recreations of the myth of Narcissus and Echo Naomi Segal explores the significance of language learning and linguistic mirroring for the masculine consciousness: 'The earliest relation of speech between mother and infant is, then, part of the sexuality

which is without violence. If the breast gives forth milk, the face gives forth speech. The oral sexual intercourse that psychoanalysts, philosophers and authors are afraid of is the mutuality they left behind for the women and their daughters, while they oedipally struggled away and defined desire in their own terms. In the unconscious of adult men, the speech that is a mutuality of mother and child haunts the assertion of the *logos*': *Narcissus and Echo: Women in the French Récit* (Manchester: Manchester University Press, 1988), 222. My exploration of the classical myth in relation to Valéry's interpretation is indebted to Segal's reading.

33. According to psychoanalytic definitions Echo, 'that "personification of the acoustic self-reflection" (Rank), brings in a first element of symbolisation or difference to the structure of narcissism which is "outside the situation of sexual difference and also outside language"' (Jean Laplanche, *Vie et mort en psychanalyse* (Paris, 1970), 108; quoted in Segal, *Narcissus and Echo*, 3).

34. In one of the manuscript jottings of the Narcisse cycle Valéry, discussing the formal beauty of the protagonist's reflection, seems to hint at its feminine/ maternal dimension in describing its capacity as containing vessel which 'holds' Narcisse:

> La beauté (μορφν) du corps est ici
>   image de son attraction
> L'image [. . .]
> Ce que je considère est *moi*
> Tu me contiens
>
>   (NA MS II, 155)

35. Hytier reproduces a number of poems which are closely related to the manuscript in question but not the relevant page in its entirety (OI, 1557–9).

36. The account given by Segal is illuminating in this respect: 'Where Narcissus finds love is that place where he sees himself reflected: the hole shadowed by long grass and hidden away, where he comes for refreshment and rest [. . .]. His mother conceived him while entrapped in a swirling male current—he finds the prenatal self preserved immobile in the stilled image of her captivity. Thus [. . .] the narcissist seeks his own image within the frame of the mother's body' (*Narcissus and Echo*, 8–9).

37. Segal, *Narcissus and Echo*, 12. She also quotes appositely from Freud's essay, 'The "Uncanny"', *Pelican Freud Library*, 14, ed. J. Strachey and A. Richards (Harmondsworth: Penguin, 1985), 368: 'This *unheimlich* place [. . .] is the entrance to the former *Heim* [home] of all human beings, to the place where each one of us lived once upon a time and in the beginning. There is a joking saying that "Love is homesickness"; and whenever a man dreams of a place or a country and says to himself, while he is still dreaming: "this place is familiar to me, I've been here before", we may interpret this place as being his mother's genitals or her body. In this case, too, then, the *unheimlich* is what was once *heimisch*, familiar: the prefix "un" is the token of repression' (p. 8).

38. Irigaray's extended use of the metaphor of the mirror suggestively exploits the extent to which a masculine consciousness traps itself in its own self-reflective operations while, simultaneously, fixing the feminine imaginary in the position of the black component which guarantees the very possibility of the mirror's functioning.

39. 'Le fait que l'homme et la femme ne se parlent pas — depuis le premier jardin?

— se [dit] aussi à travers l'extinction de voix du discours, l'oubli de la voix dans le langage. Le texte de loi, des lois, impose en silence. Sans trace charnelle qui l'édicte' (Irigaray, *Ethique de la différence sexuelle*, Paris: Minuit, 1984), 133.

40. 'La question de la différence sexuelle, question à penser notamment après et avec "la mort de Dieu" [. . .] demande de revoir la schize entre corps et pensée [. . .] Pensée et corps sont demeurés séparés. Ce qui entraîne, au niveau social et culturel, des effets empiriques et transcendentaux importants: le *discours* et la *pensée* comme étant les privilèges d'un producteur *masculin* [. . .] Les tâches du corps demeurant jusqu'à présent, l'obligation ou le devoir d'un sujet féminin [. . .] Tant que la pensée ne peut limiter le corps, et réciproquement, il n'y a pas d'acte sexuel possible' (Irigaray, *Ethique*, 88).

41. Irigaray, *Ethique*, 53–4.

42. Psychoanalytic theory indicates that the child, unable to situate and identify the flux which washes over his skin surface, nourishing body and acoustic consciousness, can develop a form of paranoia, experiencing environmental sound as a threat to his body boundaries: 'The attribution of material density to hallucinatory sounds in paranoia is only one possible permutation of the slippage caused by confusion of the position of the acoustic mirror' (Silverman, *The Acoustic Mirror*, 79–80).

43. Since Valéry was working on *La Pythie* in the midst of the same period in which he was reworking the original sonnet *Narcisse parle* and developing it towards the more extensive exploration of the same thematic in *Fragments du Narcisse*, it seems probable that the two poems are, to a certain extent, variant developments of a shared preoccupation.

44. 'The image which Narcisse perceives in the pool is not simply an adaptation of today's gazing self, it is a past self conceivable only through the mediation of the image of the mother's body. In seeking and desiring himself, he turns to the mother and desires to have/to be her. The narrator of the text confirms his past self as he confronts the remembered woman [. . .]. He needs to keep her image under control because it is the mirror in which he seeks his own reflection' (Segal, *Narcissus and Echo*, 13).

45. As Segal notes, 'the silencing of women's speech is both symptom and cause of an obsession [. . .] which surfaces in the echoes of the confessional *récit*' (*Narcissus and Echo*, 223). Valéry's obsessional, self-referential exploration through the predicament of Narcisse translates his painful awareness of the implications of such a silencing of 'women's speech' as a part of his own psyche. It is intriguing to bear in mind, in this context, that Valéry rarely uses his mother's tongue; and that the few occasions on which he expressed himself in Italian tend to give voice to powerful emotional experiences. See, for example, VIII, 373, quoted on p. 71.

46. Segal explores the oscillation between incompleteness and completeness in the narcissistic text in terms which seem relevant to this fulfilment offered by poetic discourse: 'the speech and actions of the reflected self have a similarly attenuated status to those of the woman [. . .]. In other words, there is a complex mirroring at the heart of [the text], in which the narcissist seems to be looking at himself but is actually haunted by the face of [. . .] the mother he requires to return him a whole reflection, the enclosed, bisexed complete self that is narcissism's crucial myth' (*Narcissus and Echo*, 13).

CHAPTER 4

The Serpent Self

Peut-on composer un UN de tous ces moments et
mouvements? (XXIX, 85)

The question of the self, its nature, its potential, its function, stands at
the heart of Valéry's research into the capacity of the human organism
as consciousness, as sensibility. This might seem a somewhat un-
necessary observation given that most critical studies on Valéry have
identified 'le moi' as one of the core problematics of his work. My
reasons for asserting its centrality yet again relate to the issue which
the present chapter will address, namely the sense in which Valéry's
inquiry into the self may be considered, in part at least, as a specifically
autobiographical project; and the role which voice plays in this
framework. Now it may seem strange, not to say perverse, to attempt
to situate his writing within an autobiographical context in the light
of his apparent lack of interest in or enthusiasm for the traditional
concerns of the genre; the most obvious obstacle in the path of such
an approach is his profound scepticism concerning the possibility of
self-knowledge. Yet no explanation of the notion of voice in Valéry's
work would be satisfactory or representative without some
consideration of what may, at least provisionally, be termed its
autobiographical status as a part of his desire to redesign the very
nature and structure of subjectivity. For Valéry situates a wide range
of observations relating to the self within the organizing category
of voice: the role of 'dédoublement' within consciousness, the continuity of the self in space and time, the possibility of generating a
sense of identity if only potentially. These are all concerns which, in
one guise or another, inform the activity of an autobiographer in his
search for a fuller grasp of an elusive and complex entity.[1]

As suggested in earlier chapters, Valéry confers on the voice a power of integration on both the physiological and metaphorical levels: as vocal substance and as metaphor within his poetic theory the voice attempts to harmonize the polarization characteristic of those governing dimensions of experience, 'être' and 'connaître', existence and awareness. In the present chapter this interpretation of the integrative potential of the voice is extended to encompass an aspect of Valéry's activity as writer which can be called existential or auto-biographical; in other words, voice plays a significant part in the creation of an ideal self, a poetic or mythical reconstruction of selfhood which is accomplished in and through the act of inscription of the self as text. The creative will operates essentially as self-creation since a common motive unites the creativity which is at the root of all artistic experience and the shaping urge which underlines the experience of life itself: 'Vivre pour *créer* — *créer* pour vivre' (XIII, 429). Valéry, contemplating his own 'psychobiographie', points in the direction of this shared motivation in identifying the mythic import of form in the genealogy of the creative self: 'Il reconstruit en quelque sorte un formateur de l'ensemble réalisé, qui est un mythe — De même un enfant finit par donner à son père l'idée et comme la forme de la paternité' (VI, 818).[2]

It is in this broad sense, then, of a deliberately revised version of the self as textualization that Valéry's inquiry into the problematic of the self can be considered autobiographical since such a reformulation or recasting of the self and its sense is traditionally viewed as one of the purposes of autobiography.[3] What is not traditional, however, is the form in which Valéry selects to designate his textual self. His interpretation of the autobiographical project reveals the extent to which he rewrites the rules of the genre along lines which structuralist and post-structuralist thinking has followed in the years since his death. By locating Valéry in this context my aim is to highlight the originality of his contribution to a genre characterized by its openness to experimentation, his perceptiveness in anticipating many of the insights and impasses which a literature of the self has been forced to confront rather than to allocate him a position within any kind of generic norm, a constraint which he would have abhorred.[4] The first part of the chapter provides an assessment of various aspects of contemporary autobiographical theory as context for Valéry's experimentation; the second part develops in more detail the precise form with associated function, that of the serpent as *mélos*, which he adopts as emblematic reincarnation of selfhood; and the closing pages explore the autobiographical voice as vehicle for the integration of the masculine and feminine dimensions of the desiring consciousness with all its mystical implications.

A curious autophagic intention animates the innermost layer of the Valéryan autobiographical palimpsest and, in this sense, his approach confirms the suicidal implications identified by certain critics as inherent in the genre.[5] The ultimate aim of the writing self as transcribed in Valéry's texts is to bridge the gap which holds the successive instances of the 'I' of enunciation apart from the apprehension of the self as 'énoncé' in the present moment. Valéry's ambition as autobiographer is, at some level, to defeat the time of writing itself, to transcend the scriptural instant/instance, yet without abolishing the scriptural trace.[6] In this impatient self-resuming or self-synthesizing gesture one detects the trace of a distinctively Valéryan 'caligulisme', a desire to abolish the self as existing in time which lies at the heart of Valéry's autobiographical vision.[7]

A note in the *Cahiers*, indicating the degree of imaginative 'parenté' which unites various manifestations of the self, reveals certain fundamental dynamics of the mythical autobiography in whose writing Valéry is engaged. Eros and Thanatos are shown to be tightly fused in the following lucid yet ambiguous formulation of the paradox shaping Valéry's life and writing career: 'Daimon. Narkissos. Testis. — Je cherchais à me posséder — Et voilà mon mythe — — à me posséder pour me détruire — je veux dire pour *être une fois pour toutes*' (XXIII, 289).[8] The longing for an absolute comprehension of the reality of one's existence can only be satisfied in death, and perhaps not even then. And this is certainly one of the major threads in Valéry's reading of the Narcissus myth. Yet the closing words of the remark lend themselves to at least two interpretations; 'être une fois pour toutes' may signify the shedding of the mortal coil, the concluding of the chapter of contingent existence in a realization of the suicidal impulse which traverses Valéry's thought.[9] Or these same words may be read as expressing a desire for a form of everlasting existence, a kind of eternity in which the reiterative function can be tolerated because it has transformed its sense, no longer implying monotonous sameness but promising instead a mode of non-contingent, purified continuity.

One reading does not preclude the other since both tendencies are at work in Valéry's sensibility. The critical concept is that of voice for it is in the formal properties and through the redemptive powers of the poetic voice that the secret of spiritual renewal is to be found.[10] It is in the detail of Valéry's analyses of the voice and in the song of his poetic self that the key to his unique interpretation of the autobiographical project can be read. Dispersed throughout a range of fields of inquiry relating to time, musical theory, memory, the body, poetry, form, aesthetics, an attentive eye discerns the virtual presence of an elusive continuity embedded in an apparently discontinuous sequence of isolated inscriptions of a theoretical nature. This fragmented, segmented self, strangely reminiscent of a serpent in its form and movement, unwittingly betrays its own presence in the substance of its song, that 'mélomanie du serpent' which is the voice of Valéry;[11] the mythical reality of the creative self, no matter how well disguised as theoretical formulation, cannot stifle its own statement. Nor can it completely eradicate the autobiographical import of that statement, however much the serpent seeks to devour its own substance.[12]

The autobiographical project has long been considered a means of transcending the banal, day-to-day function of memory in favour of that 'true' memory which offers a conquest or redemption of time. The way in which Valéry secures this immolation of the contingent self is the story of the present chapter, a narrative whose 'fil conduc-teur' is voice, a principle of structure within the organic sensibility and simultaneously a significant form on the level of aesthetic awareness.[13] It is the voice, conceptualized here in its aspect of *mélos*, which holds the secret to the problematic continuity of the mythic self; and which establishes the radically other nature of the Valéryan autobiographical project as above all a question of form.[14]

'Une application possible du mythe de Narcisse', Valéry notes in a central text from the *Cahiers*, would be to envisage 'la vraie "création" artistique [comme] l'œuvre de quelque fonction particulière qui *tend à se faire elle-même sa propre excitation et sa propre réponse*. Vient alors le travail de donner à ces formations du besoin ou de la surabondance [. . .] une présence, une extériorité, une durée ou une répétibilité' (XVIII, 598). Such a function is none other than the voice of desire, that deep-flowing current or 'mélisme' which animates and fertilizes Valéry's creativity as both poet and analyst.[15] Many of the most significant aspects of a theory of the creative self as progressive expansion or deepening of the founding myth of Narcisse are suggested here and its crucial dimension is identified as the formalization of a given function. Considered from a psychoanalytic viewpoint, Valéry's interaction with the substance and significance of the voice demonstrates the parallel progression of a creative process which struggles to give birth to the artistic personality in the same moment as it brings the work of art into existence. Valéry's effort is directed towards achieving a form of identity and developmental coherence through the medium of the voice, a structured object, whose elements possess iconographic significance for him. During the process of invention it is essential that some function establish itself as capable of conferring adequate shape on the arbitrary and formless products of the sensibility; such a function should enable these products to become recognizable and reproducible in time and space, to become, in other words, a significant form. As vocal form proved itself capable of self-generation and reiteration in Chapter 1, so now, here, the self as reconstructed formal entity endowed with the same properties, yet beyond the reach of contingent reality, emerges in the emblematic guise of the serpent self so characteristic of the Valéryan quest for knowledge.

No major biography of Valéry has yet been published and few studies of autobiography as a genre invoke him. A number of works have attempted to link the life and the work in a more or less successful fashion but none has sought to address the life of Valéry in a detailed and sustained manner.[16] At first sight this is somewhat surprising when one considers the proliferation of biographical approaches to contemporaries such as Proust or Gide. However, this paucity of biographical production becomes more comprehensible in the light of a range of factors each of which prepares the terrain for an evaluation of the specifically Valéryan interpretation of what autobiographical writing should ideally be.

First, and recurrently insistent throughout Valéry's writing, are his strictures concerning the undertaking of 'l'homme et l'œuvre' style studies which seem to him fated to omit the only vital dimension of a life precisely because they choose to focus on what is stated, visible, public.[17] He constantly asserts his belief that reducing a life to summary form is inevitably to lose the texture of that life.[18] With precise reference to his own fate at the hands of biographers, he registers the disappointment and fear aroused in him by the extent to which external perceptions and interpretations so often fall wide of the mark in assessing his output.[19] A second factor is the existence until relatively recently of taboos concerning the material that prospective biographers could be allowed access to when this related to Valéry's private life.

Most importantly, though, Valéry himself rendered the would-be biographer's task rather tricky by a variety of strategies which, whether conscious or unconscious, achieved the effect of pre-empting such an undertaking. It is his own highly lucid articulation of the difficulties posed by the biographical project which frustrates any attempt by others to give a successful account of his own life. And it is Faust, one of his self-substitutes, who speaks for him in observing of his own 'mémoires', significantly suspended, that the real and the imaginary become so intermingled in the living of a life that it would be difficult and perhaps not even desirable to attempt to separate them in any account of that life. He acknowledges how fine the dividing line is between material worthy of inclusion and that which is to be excluded when he affirms that what he has sought to achieve is no less revealing and vital a dimension of his being than what he has actually accomplished. Imagination is as real a force in the shaping of a life as the historical surface of daily events and should be given its place accordingly in any retelling of that life.[20]

Yet it is also Faust who provides an insight into the kind of account of a life that would be desirable: a book, that is, which would enable him to jettison the burden of selfhood once and for all, a text which would embrace the entire range of the mind's power to invent, to desire, a *summum* or 'traité' which, in its richness and exhaustiveness, would satisfy his 'volonté d'épuisement'.[21] Above all, these 'mémoires', despite their name, have nothing to do with memory as it is normally understood, a fact whose full significance will emerge later in the chapter.[22] It is clear that if Faustian ambitions are to be taken seriously a redefining of the parameters of confessional literature is required. Valéry's manipulation of a range of related terms—'journal', 'mémoires', 'autobiographie'—indicates that the question of his own practice as *Cahiers* annotator exercised him more than a little.[23] The metadiscourse on his activity as *Ego Scriptor*, embedded in the *Cahiers*, is proof of the extent to which the inscription of the self in the text is a fundamental concern. This theoretical discourse, as much by way of negation as affirmation, permits one to approach Valéry's own understanding of the aims and potential of autobiographical writing obliquely. So that, although he might not initially seem a likely candidate for discussion in this context, it becomes almost inevitable that his mode of writing (about) the self permits it to be considered retrospectively, in the light of the problematization of autobiography as a genre since his death, as belonging to this field.

Valéry affirms his opposition to the principal confessional modes available to him on countless occasions, thereby distinguishing his own practice as, in some sense, quite differently slanted. Although he shows no hesitation in employing the terms 'Mémoires de moi' or 'Journal de moi' to describe some of his entries, it is often in a slightly ironic or despairing fashion, with full awareness of their inadequacy as definitions of what he is attempting to achieve through the capture of the self in language.[24] His inquiry leads him to challenge at least three of the premisses on which traditional autobiographical discourse is based: the assumption that a relatively stable self exists to be known; the importance of the past in any account of that self; and the possibility of some degree of sincerity in the structuring and communication of that account. Yet to challenge conventions need not be interpreted as dismissal of them. It is in the rereading of each of these paradigmatic aspects of autobiography as genre which Valéry's theory and practice of the writing self offers, that its value as both subversion and renewal of that genre is to be found.[25] For this reason I shall explore in more detail the precise terms of his critique on each of these scores before discussing his alternative solution to the problematic of contemporary autobiography.

Valéry's governing dissatisfaction with the impoverished existence of a finite, contingent, all-too-human and imperfect self constantly limiting the potential of a pure self, or consciousness refined to a maximum of perfection in its functioning and untroubled by the contingencies of everyday existence, is well known. Throughout his writing life he reiterates that the definition of the self is impossible since, as soon as any of its contours or characteristics are defined, it ceases to be a self understood as ceaseless organic metamorphosis, becoming instead a static, fixed form.[26] Now if this problematic is transposed to the level of text and, specifically, to the question of how the self may be textualized, it is immediately apparent where Valéry's difficulties with traditional autobiographical pursuits lie. He has never had any clear sense of who he is;[27] he has always directed his energies towards transcending the very notion of personality seen as a fixation or obsessional idea rather than a reality;[28] and he early perceived that the concept of a self is but a convenient or inconvenient myth or fiction born of and sustained by language.[29] How then can any credence be given to a literary mode whose central preoccupations have been shown to be illusory?

Valéry postulates from the outset what mid- to late twentieth-century theory has since confirmed, that is, the instability and funda-mental insubstantiality of the concept of the self and of the notion of the subject.[30] Clearly anticipating Lacan's narrative of the alienated origins of selfhood in its own mirror image, Valéry, in the privacy of his *Cahiers* jottings, had encountered, and in strikingly similar terms, that same original fiction;[31] well in advance of structuralism's hypo-thesis concerning the death of the author subsumed in the tomb of the text, he had grasped the same basic truth, that language simul-taneously transcends and disappoints the subject in his desire for expression;[32] before Barthes gave parodic coverage to the arbitrary nature of the appropriate structures for autobiographical discourse, before Foucault advanced a view of the author as an artificially imposed limitation on the proliferation of meaning, Valéry had problematized in his practice and in the theoretical reflections on that practice, the elusive and fragile nature of the self as source of enun-ciation and the inaccuracy of narrative closure or totalization as a mode of textualizing that statement. Incompleteness, fragmentation, dispersion are characteristic of Valéry's *écriture* and bear witness to the essential paradox at the root of any attempt to transpose lived reality into textual trace: no form can represent accurately the dynamic process of consciousness without threatening to rigidify it.

With regard to time, that other constituent of autobiography, similarly categorical refutations characterize Valéry's views. He repeat-edly affirms his lack of interest in the past inasmuch as it is a sequence of events, of surface details of a life, like waves spread across the body of water that is the sea. This historical detail strikes him as so arbitrary as to be of no relevance to his inquiry into what a life may be said to be about; much more intriguing, he argues, is the nature of the sea.[33] He regards the past as, most often, utterly without importance if not indeed the locus of pain; and stresses how essential it is to be able to forget, to cancel out the 'poison' of the past (XXIX, 194). This 'prodigieuse *faculté d'oubli*' (XXVIII, 89) is valuable in so far as it represents the selective capacity of memory which functions to retain only what is of benefit to the growth of the self. He denies all interest in a Proustian-style recovery of lost time and points to a feature of his own personal memory which, once again, sets his quest apart from more conventional autobiographical journeys from past to present moments of the self: he has very few memories of his childhood and the past as a chronologically narratable dimension is, for him, non-existent.[34] The same disclosure, however, hints at how he will use memory in his own redrawing of the autobiographical project; he perceives its value to be virtual in so far as it creates a resource on which future developments of the self can draw. Memory is a bringing of the past into the present through its actualization as voice in the functioning of the body. The function of memory for Valéry should be to eliminate the past by bringing experience alive again in the actuality of the present moment. Yet not as sheer reiteration since this would amount to an intensification of the ontological claustrophobia provoked in Valéry by his acute sensitivity to 'l'éternel retour'. Memory as he conceives it is a faculty in the service of the imagination (III, 265); its value is creative as much as functional and this accounts for its crucial role in the restructuring of the self. It provides the idea of a self separate from time (XIII, 201), a self redeemed from the insidiously destructive implications of temporal flow as passage towards death. Yet his interpretation differs somewhat from that of Proust.[35] He is not seeking to reconnect the present moment of the self with past moments, which would enable consciousness to conceive of a transcendent, extratemporal dimension. He seems rather to be preoccupied with how the creative consciousness can have access to its own reality as continuous in the present instant, can project that perception towards future developments of the self without stultifying the self in monotonous and uncreative self-reiteration.[36]

A vital aspect of Valéry's theory of memory, particularly in its applicability to aesthetic form, is that it derives from the body, to be understood, however, as a particular manner in which consciousness inhabits the sensibility which is only available through the structures and effects of art. Valéry's ambition as creative artist is to devise a means of experiencing the richness afforded by the senses without allowing himself to be overwhelmed by the radically disruptive power of sensation. Through a harmonic awareness, a transformation of the brute substance of physiological reality into its symbolic equivalence in the aesthetic realm can be accomplished: 'La véritable voie qui mène aux cieux de l'être', he notes in a central remark,

passe par les sens particuliers, dont chacun est *superficiellement* significatif, et *profondément* formel; [. . .].[37] Rien de plus difficile que de ne pas fuir la sensation et de trouver sa suite dans le temps corporel sans le quitter pour les idées ou les actes — [. . .] Or les arts seuls ont conduit parfois à cette attention qui essaye de suivre le réel pur — qui divise l'indivisible ordinaire, et peut finir par trouver ou créer des correspondances dans la sensibilité — jusqu'à donner l'idée d'un monde fermé contenant un ou plusieurs infinis au retour — l'homme est changé. (XIII, 504)

I have quoted at some length here since this observation encapsulates the fundamental aspects of Valéry's vision of creation and self-recreation as the transformation of bodily awareness into the imagined forms of art. It is the figure of Faust, the ultimate modulation of the voice of mythic selfhood, who demonstrates most clearly this reincarnation in the purified structures of a harmonic universe, a reincarnation dependent on a new experience of temporality.[38]

The third and final question which is usually considered significant in matters autobiographical is that of sincerity, a yardstick established in order to assess the accuracy of an autobiographer's ambitions and achievements. Yet here again Valéry will not sit easily in the ranks of conventional historians of selfhood; his profound scepticism as to the possibility of achieving sincerity anticipates the insights of later theory concerning the validity of such a criterion in the context of the depiction of the evanescent and problematic self. Once more it is the figure of Faust who, referring to his own projected 'mémoires', neatly encapsulates the problem in observing: 'Je veux donner la plus forte, la plus poignante impression de sincérité que jamais livre ait pu donner' (OII, 286). It is not so much a problem of truth, highly questionable as a measure of worth in judging the authenticity of autobiographical statements, as of the multiplicity and relativity of various dimensions of the self and of the difficulty of avoiding a desire to impress: 'Ce n'est jamais soi-même que l'on veut exhiber tel quel,' Valéry observes in his discussion of Stendhal, that other inveterate note-taker; 'On écrit donc les aveux de quelque autre plus re-marquable [. . .] et même plus *soi* qu'il n'est permis, car le soi a des degrés' (OI, 571). These gradations or levels of self render the enterprise of accurate self-representation highly complex. The ideal would be, as Valéry suggests in evoking Faust's imaginary biography/autobiography, to develop a literary form capable of sustaining in their multiplicity the virtually infinite potential realizations of self that each individual contains.

It is in his discussion of Stendhal that Valéry addresses most explicitly the thorny issue of accuracy in the expression of the self.[39]

He attributes to the nineteenth-century writer the problems which he himself faces, suggesting that sincerity is less a question of the relationship between author and public, more to do with the intricate and irresolvable issue of the self's 'rapport' with its multiple potential for identity: 'Lui-même se feignait, se donnait sa sincérité,' he remarks of Stendhal. 'Qu'est-ce donc qu'être sincère? — Presque point de difficulté, s'il s'agit des rapports des individus avec les individus; mais de soi-même à soi-même? — Comme je l'ai dit ici et redit, à peine la "volonté" s'en mêle, ce *vouloir-être-sincère-avec-soi* est un principe inévitable de falsification' (OI, 572). This is precisely the core of Valéry's debate with Gide about whose own intentions as confessional writer Valéry expressed grave reservations.[40] Any self-avowed confession is by its very nature a translation and therefore liable to error in that it attempts to bind two irreconcilable orders, thought and language.[41] The 'décalage' between the self that speaks and the self that is spoken, the essential interval from which the activity of consciousness as discourse derives, precludes a coincidence of 'énonciation' and 'énoncé' which would, were it possible, indicate that sincerity of expression had been attained. It is precisely this 'split intentionality'[42] that provokes Valéry's comment on the impasse confronting Stendhal in his desire for literary sincerity: 'Qui se confesse ment, et fuit le véritable vrai, lequel est nul, ou informe, et, en général, indistinct' (OI, 571).

The reasons for Valéry's unwillingness, incapacity, or refusal to accept the existence of a contingent self are manifold.[43] They range from profound impatience at the limits imposed on consciousness by the reiterative monotony of the 'sensibilité générale', incapable of innovation;[44] to disgust with the undistinguished nature of the lower self's concerns which tend to reduce human potential to the lowest common denominator;[45] to a passionate conviction that only what is difficult to attain possesses any worth. It is his desire to transcend this disappointing dimension of the self which prompts the ambition to reconstruct it along more exemplary lines. Two possible approaches to this remodelling process are suggested by Valéry in one of his essays on Leonardo da Vinci in a discussion of the strategies available to the would-be biographer. He may choose to imagine, to create *ab nihilo*, certain *personae* or figures to embody his vision — in Valéry's application of the method to his own renovated self Monsieur Teste is a clear example of this imaginative approach. The alternative is to annex already existing cultural forms or figures, to inhabit them in surrogate fashion — Narcisse, Leonardo, Faust are colonized in this way as, also, are more strictly philosophical or literary models such as Descartes, Stendhal, Goethe. In this manner Valéry can explore his central concerns obliquely, as it were, while disowning any participation in the contamination of selfhood.[46] He evades having to acknowledge his own contingent self as source by projecting certain important themes, images, ideas onto figures, whether imaginary, historical, or mythical, who thus absolve him of responsibility in a traditionally autobiographical sense. This strategy is not so much evidence of 'mauvaise foi' as a response to the imperative of creative freedom similar to that which the actor exploits: to live as many lives as possible by refusing the permanence of any one mask or role.[47]

Now although these selected *personae* are distinct in many ways they share a common project in which the Valéryan preoccupation with transcendence of the self is inscribed. At the heart of their activity is a concern with realizing the potential of the self in a systematic manner, whether this is termed 'égotisme', 'méthode', or 'thème de soi'. It is with reference to what he names Stendhal's 'égotisme littéraire' that Valéry outlines a mode or model of self-creation in the materiality of the text which in fact expresses precisely his own understanding of how such a reformulation of self as and in the text is possible. 'Donnant à ses impulsions ou impressions un *suppôt* conscient qui, à force de différer'—and once more this key notion is seen to be determining—'de s'attendre à soi-même, et surtout de *prendre des notes* se dessine de plus en plus, et *se perfectionne* d'œuvre en œuvre *selon le progrès même de l'art de l'écrivain*, on se substitue un personnage d'invention que l'on arrive insensiblement à prendre pour modèle' (OI, 566).[48] In this analysis of a method attributed to an alter ego Valéry lays bare the central features of his theory of a creative self or *ego poeta*, a theory founded in the capacity of any given form or formal disposition within the subject to regenerate itself by means of a process of self-imitation. Stendhal's technique as Valéry interprets it, is but a positive application of the 'dédoublement' within consciousness which haunts Narcisse: it is the ability of the creative sensibility to be both self and other, to embrace difference within the terms of its own nature and structure that permits a degree of self-distancing and self-recognition to be accomplished. Without this, no willed projection of the self beyond the given is feasible.[49]

Undoubtedly one of the mythical figures whose identity has become almost synonymous with Valéryan selfhood to the extent of coming to function as emblem for that problematic notion, is the elusive and complex Narcisse. From the earliest stages of Valéry's literary career through to the late manuscripts where he features in the guise of 'l'Ange', Narcisse forms the most obsessive refrain in the history of the mythical self.[50] The critical distance or interval determining the reality of Narcisse is graphically represented within the text on two levels: that of visual perception—the 'moi-reflet' in love with its own image glimpsed in the waters of the pool; and that of auditory perception—the 'moi-écho' encountering the full burden of irony in its own sonorous self-duplication.[51] This same impasse or paradox functions not only on the level of the psycholinguistic phenomenon of voice as evidence of the structure of consciousness and its capacity to generate a sense of identity, but, extending the notion to embrace the idea of an autobiographical identity, indicates how voice serves as a measure, constitutes indeed the very possibility of establishing a narrative identity or ideal self. It is the *mélos* of the serpent as connecting function, guarantor of continuity, that Valéry highlights in a remark describing his systematic pursuit of the self as an exploration of the potential of consciousness, rather than a study of a historically situated personality: 'En somme — ceci (cahiers carnets) ce sont des tas d'études pour some "philosophy" (whose name I dislike) — or a *Miso-sophy*, better — un tas de croquis for [an] abstract scheme of the complexity of thoughts — in order to recall and possess in the shortest time a clearest sense of the manifold and possibilities involved in the appearance of *person, single-voiced*, Ego — I and Me, that consciousness, at each moment it exists, imposes' (XV, 72).[52]

The declared intention underlying the process of self-inscription is to achieve and maximize control over the resources of consciousness, developing its powers beyond the point with which human endeavour so often satisfies itself. Valéry creates a text in order to create a self according to a consciously constructed, willed model of self-functioning which is then adopted for imitation serving as an ideal towards which the contingent self strives. Set into this model as contributory aspects of its exemplary value are figures such as Leonardo, Descartes, Stendhal, imaginative reconstructions rather than historically accurate representations, through whom Valéry feels able to explore certain vital features of a reconstructed self. Each of these pseudo-selves modulates a variation on the theme of 'single-voiced Ego'; uniting them is their common point of origin in the problematic of Narcisse–Valéry. The 'méthode' identified by Valéry as the distinguishing feature of Leonardo's research as, too, of Descartes's enterprise, and the 'égotisme' characteristic of Stendhal, reveal themselves as belonging to the same critical area of inquiry, that is, the distancing potential inherent in consciousness and its attendant propensity for self-deferral and self-projection. The uniquely Valéryan redefinition of autobiography as it unfolds from the tragedy of Narcisse through to its ultimate, though incomplete, manifestation in the complex summation of self that is Faust, articulates itself as a question of form rather than content, of function before fact, of structure rather than substance. The governing principle throughout, that voice of the self or sustained resonance of being, can be seen to operate on two levels: as the theme which runs through a series of essays apparently dealing with other writers or artists but in fact permitting Valéry to explore displaced concerns of the self in oblique fashion; and as the generative principle motivating the progressive evolution of a mythic self, absolving it of all impurity and limitation in the redemptive ambit of the aesthetic realm.

A brief foray into the theatre of substitute selves makes clearer how the (re)construction of a transcendent formal self may be achieved. Stendhal's perception and exploitation of the self-differentiating potential of consciousness, Descartes's systematic doubt and Leonardo's preoccupation with form as primordial in the structuring response of the organism to reality modulate in slightly different ways Valéry's own concern to devise a method of tolerable self-reiteration.[53] Borrowing the term 'égotisme' from Stendhal, Valéry applies it to Descartes in a definition of the philosopher's approach which is, at heart, a stating of his own most cherished ambition: 'je dirai', he observes, 'que la vraie Méthode de Descartes devrait se nommer l'*égotisme*, le développement de la conscience pour les fins de la connaissance' (OI, 806). In the case of this particular imaginative identification the debate focuses on what is perhaps one of the most pressing aims of the personal mythology of the self in whose construction Valéry invests so much energy, namely, that of increasing his control over the functioning of the self and thereby enhancing its effectiveness. Closer scrutiny of the precise detail of his usurpation of the supposedly Cartesian problematic reveals that the real issue is the dilemma confronting Narcisse. In his interpretation of the seventeenth-century philosopher's technique of systematic doubt, Valéry attributes to Descartes the same intuition of the radical division structuring the interaction of existence and knowledge as informs the consciousness of Valéry–Narcisse: 'On pourrait écrire *moi* pour désigner sa personne... et *Moi* pour désigner l'origine [. . .]. Le fameux doute cartésien n'est sans doute qu'un jeu mental entre M et m' (XV, 170).[54]

In thus attributing to Descartes one of his most painful insights Valéry would appear to absolve himself of autobiographical responsibility. Yet this is only a gesture at absolution. Elsewhere he acknowledges as his own the distinguishing feature of 'method' and goes on to reveal that it is, in fact, essential to his personal project of self-recuperation. 'Ma méthode', he admits in a *Cahiers* entry of 1931, this time confessing the correct source of the notion, 'c'est moi. Mais moi récapitulé, reconnu' (XV, 164). The term 'method' then can be read as a convenient shorthand referring to an entire theory of creativity in which the vital factor attaches to the prefix *re*, simultaneously a function of reiteration and self-propagation. The concern with the recapitulation and recognition of the self voiced here and explored in the succession of mythic representations of self who bear the burden of Valéry's sustained speculation on the mysterious processes of invention which lie outwith the reach of consciousness, can be located in the troublesome realm of that supremely incomprehensible entity, the body. Leonardo, Descartes, Stendhal—each in his own manner gives voice to a 'magnifique et mémorable Moi' (OI, 842); each of these strategically selected authorial *personae* gives expression to that 'thème de l'égotisme égotiste' identified by Valéry as the principle of cohesion, the betrayer of a self-identical presence throughout a corpus of texts. It is to the poetico-autobiographical voice of Valéry himself, to that voice which thematizes his own egotism, that the path must now lead.[55] And into its very density as substance and structure, for it is only when the self has been rendered memorable quite literally, in other words according to certain precise criteria and obeying an alchemical methodology or formula, that it may be considered magnificent.

Biography as a genre has been challenged, the very bases of autobiography called into question, the notion of journal or diary refuted as an appropriate definition of his daily *Cahiers* notation; and yet I have persisted in applying the term autobiographical to Valéry's quest as annotator of the self. In part this is because no other term seems suitable or has yet been coined to describe certain texts which fit uneasily within the established schema of confessional literature; in part because I consider Valéry's fundamental preoccupations in his daily notation of self to be broadly akin to those explored in more conventional autobiographies.[56] However, I stressed earlier that Valéry's contribution is most significant in terms of his redefinition of the manner in which he inscribes the self in the text. And it is to the innovative aspect of his work that I shall now turn. The term 'autobiographical' functions, for the purposes of the present discussion, as an inadequate but provisionally acceptable way of referring to a body of texts that have come to be viewed in recent years as amongst the most experimental in the literary production of the twentieth century.[57] Valéry can be situated legitimately within this frame of introspective literature in so far as his own theory and practice contribute to the radical redrawing of parameters which at present distinguish the genre.

Very broadly speaking, autobiography can be defined as the writing of the 'life' of the 'self'; both these notions lie at the heart of Valéry's inquiry into the nature of human potential, as 'le moi', the central mystery calling for elucidation and as 'bios', the living reality of organic existence, similarly enigmatic in its functioning and equally needful of demystification. In this general sense the entirety of Valéry's literary production can be viewed as autobiographical.[58] Clearly, though, so wide a definition is of limited usefulness since, following its logic, virtually all writing may be interpreted in this light. The task of arriving at an averagely satisfying definition of autobiography has exercised many capable critical minds in recent decades. The standard definitions are often not particularly helpful with regard to Valéry for reasons which have already been discussed: the account of the self which he gives is not retrospective for the most part, it is not primarily a prose narrative, and it does not aim to create an effect of unity in its depiction of an individual life perceived in the main as the evolving history of a personality. If, instead, autobiography is viewed in the light of its postmodern characterization, it becomes easier and more fruitful to situate Valéry's discourse meaningfully. Rather than seeking unity or consistency as a defining feature of subjectivity, fragmentation, displacement, and dispersal of the self in time and space become valid modes of self-representation. The various techniques employed by the autobiographer in the structuring of her/his discourse can be seen as exploratory instruments of a subject in search of her/himself. In this light the autobiographical text 'has a performative quality, that of a working-model of the new paradigm of subjectivity which it investigates'.[59] It is with this emphasis on inquiry, a self-reflexive focus on the provisional nature of the self's reality, that we come closer to the Valéryan premiss and project: not the projection of a stable image of a completed self but rather an open-ended interrogation in language of the sense and status of the very concept of selfhood.

Throughout his life Valéry emphasized how process not product was, in his eyes, more interesting, more valuable. He finds little of worth in a perfected object, be it text or 'objet d'art', far more stimulus to reflection in the trials and errors of the creative journey which lead to the final state. And this vision can be applied to his appreciation of how a life unfolds. The self is not given in advance but is progressively constructed through time, language, experience. Equally, the written production of that self should not be regarded, as is sometimes naïvely the case, as merely an effect of the life lived but much more as a force influencing the direction and form of the life. Valéry's exploration in and through the *écriture* of his *Cahiers* is a journey towards enlightenment by means of which the self perceives something of its being as externalized in the graphic mirror of the textual trace; and then proceeds to integrate the awareness gained in this way in the future or continuing creation of its own being.[60] A journey assumes a destination whether known or unknown; and one of the fundamental assumptions of autobiography is that the subject, in transcribing her/his experience, does so in full awareness that s/he is writing in the context of an ideological constraint, a literary code which expects the autobiographical act to be intentional. Now once more we find that this normative requirement is not applicable to Valéry. He may on occasion refer to himself and his life as material from which a given text is derived (*Le Cimetière marin*; *La Pythie*); significant sites, recurrent themes, dominant rhythms are all identified as contributing to his literary output. But he nowhere proffers an authorizing statement inviting the reader to interpret his work, or any one text, as an autobiography.[61] He leaves no recognizable narrative of the self which would fit conventional formal definitions. The text about which he confesses most explicitly to have entertained auto-biographical preoccupations, *La Jeune Parque*, as a monologue in alexandrines, is disqualified from a genre most commonly associated with prose narrative. It further challenges conventions by overturning traditional gender assumptions about what constitutes the appropriate narrative voice for the autobiography of a male writer.

However, the secret of its subversiveness and the clue to Valéry's personal motives for his particular conception of autobiography lie in his definition of the meaning of this text: 'Qui saura me lire', he hints seductively, 'lira une autobiographie, dans la forme' (OI, 1631). In other words, the sense of this specific autobiographical statement and, I would argue, by extension, the entirety of his literary production, lies far below the surface level, that superficial inscription of despised personal historicity as 'événement'; it is to be located in his understanding and application of form as realized in the substance of his texts, and also in his theoretical formulations of the constituent elements which constitute the functioning of the organism and voice, deeply embedded in the materiality of the *Cahiers* as text. The Valéryan self is not to be read in the usual episodic narrative of a life, although a number of texts and comments of this sort are scattered throughout Valéry's writings.[62] It is to be found rather in the diffuse, fragmented, and oblique formulation which he selects as the most accurate and representative transcription of his understanding of that improbable being which we call the self. Valéry can only tolerate a textual self if that self has been quite literally transformed in the process of becoming text; by purifying the concept of selfhood, formalizing it in terms of those constituent components of the aesthetic sensibility termed *mélos*, voice, rhythm, restructured temporality, he is able to reveal the key to his own functioning. This disguised self-inscription forms the body of texts known to us as the *Cahiers*; and it is in the myriad observations concerning the voice, as, too, in the genesis of Valéry's poetic practice that a reading of this self, though not easy, is made possible.[63]

The quest of *ego scriptor* is motivated by the desire to reconcile fragment and totality, instant and eternity; and the power of the illusion which artistic form creates depends precisely on its capacity to exemplify permanence while at the same time symbolizing change, thus carrying with it the concept of growth ('La Poésie, Métaphysique de Mnémosyné'; IV, 214). The desired form of liaison operative between moments of selfhood hints at the structure and dynamic of that Valéryan form par excellence, *ouroboros*, the serpent self. In a brief definition of literary form, in which he acknowledges the extent to which creative responsibility lies less with himself as conscious agent and more with unconscious promptings of formal requirements, Valéry observes: 'J'ajoute, — ou plutôt: il *s'ajoute* — à une diversité ce qu'il faut de *moi* [. . .] pour engendrer une *Unité* — à répétition'

(XXVIII, 648). At work in this dialectic between part and whole, between discrete segments and ultimate continuity, the recurrent informing vector of the *Cahiers* inscriptions reveals itself. What is the status of the *Cahiers* inscription for Valéry if so many of the more usual concerns of confessional literature have been discounted? What were his motives in sustaining his morning meditation on paper over a period of approximately fifty years? An intuition emerges from his extensive self-commentary that some form of self, however difficult to define, exists in and through the trace which it leaves on the page. Any reader of the *Cahiers* can be in no doubt that s/he is listening to the voice of a recognizable entity which demonstrates certain recurrent characteristics, chief amongst which is the sustained output of *Cahiers* notations. It is legitimate to ask what induced Valéry to pursue his activity as writer, given his own reluctance to view the literary product as anything other than the debris of mental activity. One answer is the urgent need to earn a living, and this cannot be entirely discounted in any evaluation of Valéry's attitude to his creative activity.[64] Yet such a reason, though perhaps adequate in accounting for much of his published work, must fail with regard to the *Cahiers* since no external obligation operated here. And it is chiefly on the *Cahiers* as the most fertile laboratory of the self that the following discussion will be focused.

Valéry observes that the function of his daily jottings is not clear to him other than as providing proof of the self's production much in the same way as does a spider's web or the excreted shell of a mollusc; as inevitably yet also as inexplicably he continues to secrete a trace, 'ne voyant pas pourquoi ni comment il cesserait de la secréter, de pas en pas' (XXIII, 387).[65] He registers also a strange sense of separateness from his written production as though, having once externalized his thoughts, he is not sure whether he will recognize them as his own; he is not transcribing them so much as serving as a medium for ideas which can be acknowledged as originating in him but only if he chooses to legitimate them by granting them recognition (VI, 563). Clearly this process of regular self-inscription is not motivated by the common ambitions of the authors of confessional texts, although, since some sections of his *Cahiers* were published during his lifetime, a certain caution is advisable in interpreting Valéry's disclaimers at face value.[66] On the whole his attitude in this respect is well summarized in the contrast which he draws between Gide's desire to personalize the creative self and his own intention to depersonalize it, to reduce to a minimum the discernible connections between author and artefact, in favour of the intrinsic and, ideally, autonomous properties of literary language itself (XV, 511). Valéry shows nothing but scorn for those who see literature as a form of propaganda or excuse for proselytizing;[67] he disclaims any intention of manipulating his reader or of persuading her/him to adopt an attitude of complicity.[68] All in all there would appear to be no attempt at self-justification, no desire for self-glorification in his case: the value of writing for him is in its inner application, as a form of mental and spiritual exercise.[69]

What emerges from his comments on his *Cahiers* activity is its value to him in a variety of ways. He notes his impression that he only feels himself existing when he is engaged in some form of inventive process (XX, 518) as though the identity of the self, however elusive and problematic, were intimately related to the externalization of the word in written form.[70] Regular noting in the *Cahiers* is rather like practice exercises enabling him to 'keep his hand in' at certain recurrent preoccupations; it answers, too, a physical need which can only be satisfied by the daily production of ideas.[71] The material pleasure which he derives from secreting a visible trace seems to relate to a form of fetishism; the text, or simply the act of inscription, functions as a kind of 'transitional object' or surrogate activity capable of provisionally comforting the disquiet experienced by the ego in the face of its inability to achieve total satisfaction of its desire.[72] He is conscious as he writes that some kind of process is at work, that some form of continuity is implied by the sheer persistence of this particular habit.[73] He senses that his writing somehow precedes him, leading him towards an important yet unspecified goal: 'Je n'*arrive* pas à ce que j'écris, mais j'écris ce qui me conduit — où?' (V, 753). There would appear to be an implicit teleology in this process of self-notation albeit not of a narrative or linear nature.[74] The writing process itself possesses a momentum which permits it to assume responsibility in the defining of a direction. And he observes, too, how as he writes he is simultaneously engaged in the attempted 'lecture' of a text composed, as he puts it significantly, of 'des foules de fragments clairs. L'ensemble est noir' (II, 479). A projected totality is implied although quite on what level remains unclear; an imaginary textual body as totality pre-exists, summons, inspires. Almost, one might imagine an intuited serpentine form tempting him, elusively, towards the future of his own desire, beckoning him onwards with the insinuating stylistic virtuosity of his song. Yet Valéry is emphatic that the coherence of his auto-text is quite distinctive; he stresses that its fragmentary nature and lack of apparent order is of the essence and warns any prospective reader against the temptation to unify these isolated revelations of selfhood in any traditional manner.[75]

By enabling him to perceive himself as the being who has produced the *Cahiers* inscriptions, those same marks function as the mirror in which his identity as *scriptor* is confirmed if not actually created. Thus, although unlike most conventional autobiographers' treatment of the self, Valéry's approach, more similar to the diary method, implies that there is no clearly defined goal, none the less it does allow the potential future self a topology in which it may develop. The text as graphic trace functions as a mirror but of a special sort, reflecting not what already exists, the actual, so much as the potential.[76] In other words, one of the principal motivations for Valéry's pursuit of his *Cahiers* notation may be the urgent need to bring some form of self into being. Out of the void and formlessness that consciousness registers as the ground of its functioning, the desiring self seeks to give birth to itself as form, trace, proof of existence: 'Il n'est pas impossible', he observes revealingly, 'que ces écritures, ce mode de noter ce qui vient à l'esprit ne soient pour moi, une forme du désir d'être *avec moi* et comme d'être *moi*' (XXI, 349). And yet, for this dialectic to be sustained within the creative self, this endless shifting between present and future moments of consciousness, between reality and myth, words are required, those inadequate yet essential embodiments of dissatisfaction and desire. The torment of Valéry 'autobiographe', as of Stendhal hoist with the petard of his ambitions of transparency, is voiced in the tragic avowal of Narcisse: 'Je ne puis pas me reconnaître dans une figure finie. Et MOI s'enfuit toujours de ma personne, que cependant il dessine ou imprime en la fuyant' (OII, 572).

The Valéryan self, though denied, despised, disowned in all its contingent imperfection, continues to secrete its trace from page to page, moment to moment so that, ultimately, a sustained form exists, the recurrent voice has expressed its own, singular note so divulging the most intimate dimension of *ego scriptor*.[77] This textual trace comes to form another body, or 'espace textuel', which gains coherence in the material continuity of the graphic trace.[78] It is surely in the context of the mythic self envisaged as a kind of vector drawing the writing self onwards to its future potential as totality that one can situate a remark where Valéry evokes his 'Mémoires de moi' as 'une perspective de *souvenirs d'avenir*' (XXIX, 115); a remark made, interestingly, in the very final volume of those memoirs when the potential future of the writing self would soon come to constitute its past.[79] Valéry points to the fact that the meanderings of *ouroboros*, spawning their proteiform identity in the graphic texture of the *Cahiers* script, contribute to the emergence of a governing form outwith the control of the conscious self. A remark placed beneath the heading 'Sub-conscience' suggests that the formal continuity at work in the constitution of selfhood and re-enacted in the symbolic form of the work of art is situated very deep in the unconscious of the organism's function, having the force of an *imago* or archetypal image within the imaginative world of the psyche. In evoking a degree of permanence in the self he uses the category of 'le Même', a sameness or identity born of a process of reiteration, and sees it as the result of 'ce travail inconnu et inconnaissable qui s'opère sans doute dans un "temps" et à une échelle où la personnalité n'existe pas — c'est-à-dire où elle n'est qu'un élément' (XIII, 252). He then further characterizes the self-perpetuating mechanism at work on an unconscious level in terms which could also be a description of the form of motricity or self-projection typical of the serpent: 'Or le Même est lié au même, continué, alimenté, prolongé par une infinité de ces actions intimes, impersonnelles, Et qui *nourrissent* à la longue la personnalité mais qui n'en dépendent pas' (XIII, 254).[80]

An apparently paradoxical awareness of time in its implications for consciousness is a motivating dynamic in the restructuring of subjectivity which Valéry is exploring here. Just as the critical interval in the circuit of inner language marked a temporal difference essential to the production of voice so, now, in the extended context of the production of a mythical, narrative, or autobiographical *persona*, the crucial issue remains the same. In other words, what form or trace will be capable of registering simultaneously both its distinctiveness or punctuality and the continuity or connectedness on which the interval depends? Valéry's attempted solution to this impasse, a predicament acknowledged as inherent in the autobiographical project as problematic tension between structure and event, proposes that the inscription of self be envisaged not as a locus of self-annulment but as a space for change and growth. If the process of notation is conceived not as conferring closure but as enabling a perpetual deferral of self-definition, then it may acquire exemplary, even redemptive, value. It is surely in this sense that Valéry's assertion 'Je ne travaille qu'à différer

— devenir différent' (IV, 197) is to be interpreted. The presence of such claims makes it difficult to read the *Cahiers* as simply a form of diary since their function is clearly posited by Valéry as transcending the limited punctual attitude implied by such a form. In so far as one of the motives of autobiography is to produce difference through repetition, Valéry's yearning for the fabrication of the difference or otherness of the self—'*se faire* soi-même un autre' (XXVII, 274)— would seem to allow his approach to qualify for inclusion in this genre.[81] Valéry devises a formally constituted autobiographical self capable of integrating time as instant and time as succession; it is towards the paradigm of '*mélos*' that the pursuit of the authorial self now leads.[82]

A parallel can be drawn here between the substance of the autobiographical voice as realized in the topos of *l'écriture* and the process outlined above by which the personality develops itself. They both depend on the crucial role of imitative—and specifically self-imitative—action that was earlier shown to be essential to the creative consciousness.[83] Valéry stresses repeatedly that no development of idea, theme, or structure can be accomplished successfully without this capacity of the sensibility to echo itself productively. In the case of the aesthetic or autobiographical self precisely such a process is at work; *mélos*, the substance of the self as it is embedded in language, constitutes the basic reiterable form or fragment from which a summation of self can be generated (XIV, 206). It is this critical mechanism which is described in the following remark: 'Le fragment impose le tout. [. . .] Tantôt par une sorte de nécessité comme de volonté (!) esthétique que le morceau-moment d'une forme imprime [. . .] Forme. corrélation [. . .] entre successif et simultané — et réciproque — Sommation' (XXIX, 502). The creative will, striving towards a totality, exploits the materials offered by the aesthetic realm in a process of individuation which cannot be denied. The vital moment is that in which a synthesizing experience of the self is made possible and it is towards such a moment that the autobiographical project is directed.[84] In the mythic projection of self as Faust Valéry voices this summative perception of being: '*Sommations*. Cette notion est capitale — [. . .] Elimination ou annulation de "temps"; échange réciproque entre succession et simultanéité; [. . .]. L'unité qui est l'essence de ces entités et qui est suite, ou somme, ou figure est celle de l'acte générateur' (XXIII, 79). It is through Faust that he explores in greatest detail this intricate figure whose essence is founded in a different conception of temporality and whose integral nature as perfected form stems from the generative power of the voice.

Valéry claims that, in the creation of poetry, it is its nature as a formal art that interests him above all else; he is absorbed in the construction of 'la figure de la forme' (XXII, 783), in the abstracting of a self-sufficient conceptual embodiment expressive of the sensibility yet not identical to it.[85] Equally, in the context of his poetico-autobiographical construction of self as text, the aim is to transform the contingent self into a significant form or figure, an ideal version of the self which possesses the additional value of being available to a modelling process, capable of being reconstructed as an 'ideal self' or 'self object'.[86] The term used by Valéry to describe this artificial embodiment of self, what might be termed a rhetorically redeemed being, is *mélos*.[87] The borrowing from musical terminology is significant, for although Valéry accepted the limitations of language and, as poet, derived benefit from the constraints which it imposes, the ambition to achieve the power and richness of manipulative control which the musician can command never left him. In his imaginative recreation of self as perfected form it is on musical theory and practice that he draws. Faust is that *alter ego* 'qui sent une *perfection* vouloir se tirer de lui, un produit comme un "mélos", ou une forme — état dans lequel il y a une étrange combinaison du maximum d'égoisme avec le maximum de dépassement de soi' (XXVI, 153). This 'forme-état' enables a pattern of continuity to function in the sensibility while also allowing a reaching beyond the immediacy of lived experience towards the aesthetic realm. In his analysis of how *mélos* functions Valéry emphasizes the fact that time is of its essence: it works as a succession of notes or punctual instants which simultaneously contribute to a totality, to an overall effect of meaning, without however condemning the sensibility to the sterile, monotonous repetition characteristic of the physiological rhythms of the organism.[88] When this insight is transposed to the level of the mythic self it enables Valéry to elaborate a conception of a tolerable self-continuity or poetico-narrative identity, to conceive of a magnificent and memorable self, able to combine existence in successive moments of linear time with a mode of being in the instant, as a kind of summation of self.

Now the key concept is memory for it is this faculty which serves as connection between physiological reality and aesthetic re-creation of that reality. To create form is to create what can be reiterated (XXIX, 886); and he speaks of an 'intelligible form' as one which generates also the means to be imitated and so indefinitely reproduced (XXIX, 505). Without memory no degree of continuity in formal development could be achieved, no punctual perception could be expanded and sustained in the production of an integral form. In the same way, without memory there can be no self, no identity; and without the recurrent inscription of self in language, no mythical or ideal self as goal or *telos* of desire.[89] Within the space-time of the act and mark of writing Valéry exploits a topography in which the precise nature of the self as a mnemonic function can be observed; it is in this locus of language that memory and form interact in the substance of the sensibility in such a way that its provisional or instantaneous productions acquire a degree of continuity: 'L'expression (langage etc) [est] [. . .] une notation/excitation qui permette de reconstituer, retrouver [. . .] certaines valeurs de ma mémoire ou même de construire — Ce qui implique les postulats de l'existence d'une sorte d'espace où l'on peut se reconnaître' (IX, 582).[90] The secret of this self-propagating activity is the relationship between the perceiving of a given form within the substance of the sensibility and an accompanying application of will-power, what Valéry refers to as '*relations — forme — volonté*' (XXVIII, 648) between the instantaneous manifestation of the self and its successive prolongation.[91]

The alternative manner of living time made available to the poetic consciousness in the formal properties of the voice is a space or site where the transformative potential of the organism is re-enacted on the level of significant form: 'La voix. Poésie du changement pur dans un domaine de la structure [. . .] duquel nous avons le sentiment'.[92] Within the vocal substance, whether literally or metaphorically understood, a mechanism enables the construction of a functional present or continuity out of isolated, past instants, precisely the self-imitative mechanism which has been shown to lie at the heart of Valéry's conception of the creative consciousness. By transmitting its own structure it translates a basic stimulus into a lasting form: '*La voix communique une imitation de sa condition d'émission* [. . .] *et d'abord elle donne* [. . .] *le modelé — la dimension — 3 du discours* [. . .] *c'est à dire ce qui permet* [. . .] *de former un simultané, — condition de la compréhension*' (XXIX, 76). In terms of the autobiographical project the voice of the self is, in this sense, a precondition of any perception of the continuity of that self.

Faust's redemption from contingent selfhood relies on his encounter with time in a different mode, time, that is, as the intensely present exploitation of bodily sensation. Once more it is an analysis of the voice which sheds light on how his escape from linear time into an expanded or intensified consciousness of its substance and duration is accomplished: 'La notion de *présent*', Valéry argues, 'est liée profondément à [l']excursion de la [voix] et à sa limite. Ce présent est bien différent d'un élément de "temps". Il a une *durée* qui n'est pas du *temps* (du coulant): mais une résistance, et cette durée est mesurée par l'échange intérieur au système — réciprocité' (XVI, 245). Aware of the tragic impossibility of escaping bodily existence which anchors the self in the flow of time, Faust adopts a strategy of aesthetic redemption.[93] Rather than seek to escape time, he will maximize his experience of it by becoming time itself; in other words, that time of musical awareness which is composed of sensation, rhythm, change, and continuity.[94] It is in this sense that Valéry's desire to rival music can be seen to reach its most evolved expression in the Faustian *mélos*, a 'forme chantable, figure du temps' (IX, 314). The critical move returns us to the concept of self-identity mentioned earlier. Some mode of breaking free of reiteration is vital, for, 'si tout redevient, et repasse au même, rien ne le distinguant de l'état reproduit, ce retour n'a pas [. . .] de sens. Si quelqu'un s'en avise, il est donc hors du retour et il n'y a pas retour. Il ne pourrait s'en aviser que par quelque chose qui n'est pas le même' (XII, 394). For Faust, the means of transcending recurrence is, specifically, to become *mélos*, 'cet écart modulé, modelé entre deux *mêmes*' (XIV, 282). He opens up the precious space existing between the punctual moments of linear time, expanding the interval to its maximum capacity for sensitive awareness.[95] The mythic self thus accedes to a form of transcendence that is a restructured present deriving from the body, its rhythms and sensations, an awareness expressed in the substance and structure of the voice.

It becomes increasingly difficult to distinguish between his conception of the present and the notion of the voice in Valéry's exploration of the creative self since both designate an intensified consciousness of organic functioning transposed into the structure of language and, specifically, into the theoretical formulation of the self that makes up his autobiographical statement.[96] Faust, as the most highly refined of the selves to emerge from the alchemical transubstantiation of the Valéryan *Grand œuvre*, becomes voice in the same way that he expresses himself as pure presence in an encounter enacted as a dialogue between two dimensions of the same being: 'Mais... voyez que tout mon être n'est qu'une voix' is the appeal of Faust-Lust in the unpublished fourth act of *Mon Faust*.[97] And in his song of joy marking the rare point of equilibrium that a life sometimes achieves it is as 'le présent même' that he names his experience of heightened self-perception (OII, 321).

It is to the serpent that the quest for a fuller understanding of Valéry's autobiographical self returns in so far as it may be interpreted not only in its associations with form but equally as emblematic of the tendency towards integration within the creative consciousness. Rather than restrict the significance of *ouroboros* to more traditional readings which interpret it as symbolic of the limited nature of analytic self-consciousness, it lends itself to an approach which values its function as an archetypal form or image translating certain very deeply located dimensions of the personality.[98] In this third section of the chapter the focus returns to the gendered nature of subjectivity, already revealed as significant at earlier stages of the argument but explored here in the context of an interpretation of Valéry's authorial subjectivity as the ground in which conflicting energies, associated with masculine or feminine imagery, are at work. 'La mélomanie du serpent' sings of the dialogue, conflict, and potential integration of these distinct yet dependent aspects of the creative sensibility yearning for, though aware of the elusiveness of, a combining of their energies in fertile communion.

The question of the gendered nature of subjectivity can be approached from a variety of angles. In Chapter 1 it was situated in the context of the dynamics of pre-Oedipal sexuality and of the tension between semiotic and symbolic determinations within the developing psyche. There, the dichotomy discernible in the Valéryan *écriture* between the controlled register representative of ego mastery, and other forms of textual statement attributable to more vulnerably accessible states of the sensibility was located in the wider context of the mind/body divide characteristic of Western culture. Chapter 3 examined the masculine imaginary's emphasis on the visual faculty as providing access to scopic mastery in contrast to the repression of the feminine imaginary as associated with formlessness, sound, and the sense of hearing. In the present chapter, the idea of an inherent psychic bisexuality can be developed further by relating it to the question of a formal self, realized on the aesthetic level in the substance and structure of the voice.[99] Faust, to cite but one example, encounters Lust as the other within the self, as an integral part of his own melodic nature; so the voice of Valéry's autobiographical or serpent self owes its value to its status as symbolic acknowledgement of the feminine within the creative sensibility.

Valéry himself comments on the psychology of his own creative process in terms which appear to suggest such an awareness of psychical gendering.[100] In a *Cahiers* entry envisaging the value of complementary aspects of the mind's creative process, he proposes the model of a form of psychic androgyny as suggestive:

Mâle et femelle forment un système complet [. . .] — L'idée de Platon était bonne. On pourrait traiter un amour en partant d'un système complet d'où l'on dégagerait les 2 membres. L'idée de ce système serait l'idée constante et directrice de celui qui ferait l'ouvrage. Il ne la donnerait jamais explicitement. Dépendance préétablie d'où se tirerait ensuite l'indépendance des êtres. [. . .] C'est au fond l'idée d'Eureka — la désunion antérieure/l'attraction actuelle 'expliquée' par l'unité primitive. (XIII, 315)[101]

The unitive tendency or dynamic which animates Valéry's *œuvre* has been widely recognized.[102] His ambition as a writer to facilitate a more harmonious cooperation of 'être' and 'connaître', to establish a more tolerable level of coexistence between mind and heart, may also be conceptualized as a desire to embrace the difference within identity as, quite specifically, a gendered difference: 'Tout homme', as he states, 'contient une femme' (OI, 387). In the context of what may be termed a phenomenology of creative intelligence, desire finds its embodiment in both masculine and feminine guise. Valéry's particular conception of this division or distribution of roles within the authorial subjectivity—'Ma pensée est, je crois, toute... mâle, ma sensibilité — des féminines' (XXI, 884)—justifies a reading which classifies the concern with control, separateness, and purity, characteristic of the angelic intelligence, as 'masculine'; while the 'feminine' would describe all that escapes the position of mastery, yearning rather for openness, a relaxation of anxiety over ego boundaries, and an acceptance of fusion and flux as necessary and inevitable.[103] A revealing comment from the *Cahiers* hints that, despite his detailed and thorough engagement with his mythic *persona* Narcisse, the problematic nature of the self's otherness had not been adequately confronted; the intimacy of identity and difference enacted within consciousness merits a more fertile conjugation of mind and heart:

Amour — L'intelligence mêlée à l'amour, ou se substituant à lui insensiblement, peut faire quelque chose de ce trouble étranger. Etre vivant contre être vivant. Origine contre origine. Deux sphères d'action interférant. Et il ne s'agit plus de sexes mais de la différence pure des moi. La proximité est chose extraordinaire. Je n'ai pas su le dire dans le *Narcisse*, dont c'était le vrai sujet. (VII, 627)

This conception of a sexual complementarity within the creative consciousness, based on a psychoanalytical model, resonates with the dimension of the sacred in Western thought. Several strands in contemporary thinking posit, as a lost yet essential dimension of Western cultural symbolism, the living reality and implications of the couple, the androgyny, the masculine and feminine components of the cultural imaginary. For Lacan, the androgynous ideal is simply one of the myths promoted by the symbolic order with the aim of perpetuating the illusion of an imaginary unity. Yet interestingly, the dimension of otherness, that heterogeneity inherent in subjectivity, is connoted feminine in his writing; and the attempt to experience the supreme bliss of integrated subjectivity which he terms 'jouissance' functions as an approach to the divine within the human.[104] In Irigaray's vision of an ethical imperative informing the sexual relationship, an ethics embracing an awareness of its transcendent dimension, it is the concept of the *copula* which represents the renewed interaction of masculine and feminine which she envisages as a prerequisite of any spiritual renewal. In Jung's understanding of the journey of the human psyche, according to which 'male' and 'female' function as metaphors for the psychic conditions of conscious and unconscious, the recent history of Western society reveals the dangers incurred through the neglect of the dual nature of the subject. By overvaluing the rational capacity of the mind at the expense of a sound knowledge of its unconscious dimension, a culture risks a form of spiritual death.[105]

If, as argued in the opening section of the present chapter, the autobiographical writing project in its Valéryan sense offers a space for the creation of a different self; and if, too, as psychoanalytic theories of aesthetic form suggest, the formal pursuit of the organic integration of elements of content in the creation of a work of art is analogous to the ego's attempt to integrate aspects of conscious and unconscious functioning into a workable synthesis; then voice in Valéry's *écriture* may be read as the *locus* in which the feminine can be encountered, in which the *copula* may be enacted, the *mysterium coniunctionis* or marriage of male and female, as Jungian terminology evokes it, consummated. The substance of the voice permits a stepping beyond the conceptual parameters of a purely self-reflexive dynamic and the conjoining of the desiring polarities within the psyche. It is the symbolic power of the serpent which functions as self-motivating, self-perpetuating impulse possessed, too, of the capacity to guarantee the union of male and female, of mind and body. In a note from a *Cahier* of 1913, Valéry envisages the tension between instinct and consciousness in terms of the serpent which haunts the poetic intelligence:

[J]ouer au plus fin avec ce système étrange. Passer entre l'excitation et la réponse, ou entre deux réflexes. Tromper ce trompeur dont le cerveau, son fils, a fini par se dégoûter [. . .]. Quelle situation! Mythe et drame possible! Le cerveau loyal, nu, pas *profond*, toujours trompé par la clarté, cocufié, mais honnête — enchaîné à ce serpent ou femme nerveuse — qui en sait plus que lui, moins que lui, chacun d'eux y voyant dans un monde inconnu de l'autre, réagissant à sa mode se jouant les plus mauvais tours nécessairement et pourtant se continuant l'un l'autre, s'alimentant s'aidant et s'entretuant. (V, 11)[106]

The rational mind may achieve a kind of totality through its self-reflexive capacity yet such a simulated state of oneness lacks the vibrant depth that an integration of its unknown aspects brings to the one–dimensionality of consciousness. There must, in other words, exist the posssibility for the creative consciousness to fecundate itself if it is to remain fully alive. The serpent signifies body, flesh, voice in so far as these are interpreted as metaphors expressing the psyche's power to heal itself through an acknowledgement of its own unconscious; they are images which function as guides enabling the alienated mind to leave a state of disunion for a more integrated mode of experience.[107]

The figure and form of the serpent has been widely acknowledged as one of the most elusively obsessive self-refrains to haunt Valéry's work. Both an absent presence, and the presence of an absence, it can be identified with that 'mélisme' or voice of creative desire from which the complex interconnected genesis of the poems of *Charmes* derives;[108] and with the 'hydre inhérente au héros',[109] a feminine creativity and flow whose meanderings and sinuous interpenetration with the masculine make possible the process of fecundation on which all psychological, affective, and spiritual nourishment depends.[110]

The serpent, then, is not to be conceived as uniquely masculine, locked in onanistic pursuit and repetition of his own substance, or cast in the stereotypical role of seducer; it is also feminine, and Valéry's unconscious or imaginary envisages this feminine in multiple guises;[111] and, equally, it embodies the coming together of masculine and feminine, however provisionally, in an integration of energies. The voice of the authorial self, itself a multi-tongued serpent, unlike that of Narcisse, can adopt now the tone and perspective of the masculine (*Ebauche d'un serpent*), now those of the feminine (*La Jeune Parque, La Pythie*); or the masculine and feminine in conflict, as in the Pythia's struggle with the emerging 'Saint Langage' or Eve's tribulations at the hands of her seducer; or, finally, the masculine battling with the masculine as the voice of the serpent challenges the powerful voice of God.

What all these texts reveal is the interplay of forces or struggle for authority within the acoustic space of consciousness; they are texts about power, the power of the voice, of desire, of the struggle of self with self, of serpent as container with serpent as contained. This splitting of his own status as subject into distinct selves, songs, voicings ('le chant de la Parque', *Chanson du serpent, Eve au serpent, Air de Sémiramis*) enables Valéry to give widely ranging expressions to the contradictions, disparities, and conflicts which he recognized as integral to his own personality.[112] He is, as is the Pythia, that 'être divinement contradictoire' (*Cah. Ch.* IV, 5 in de Lussy, p. 214), powerful and powerless, voice and voiced, fragment and whole, condemned to the song of his search.

Two texts which may be read as seminally autobiographical in the sense that both, though differently, articulate such a serpentine complexity of desire are *La Pythie* and *Ebauche d'un serpent*. Study of their genesis through various manuscript stages provides an insight into the microscopic level at which the formulation of the poetic subjectivity occurs: composed concurrently, each borrowing from the other in terms of strophic structure, rhythm, idea, image, they reveal the rich and mutually fertilizing process of germination and interconnected structuring which demonstrates the development of that deepest level of autobiographical inscription of the self. These, significantly, are the poetic texts which took the longest time to achieve their 'definitive' state, perhaps those which posed the greatest challenge to Valéry and which bear witness to his aim to make 'l'air du serpent [. . .] l'une des pièces maîtresses du recueil'.[113] Both poems offer a vocal enactment of the 'Chanson du Serpent', one of the titles originally envisaged for *Ebauche*, whose theoretical origins in the voice as existential *mélos* were traced in the opening section of the chapter. As readers we are witnesses to the literal metamorphoses of desire into form which constitute the foundations of creativity. In their origin, genesis, structure, and thematic both texts exploit the dialectic which simultaneously unites and divides part and whole, fragment and continuity, that underpins Valéry's autobiographical dilemma.[114]

The question, however, remains: why did he choose to separate them, what led to this bifurcation of an initially shared inspiration? One answer, though not exclusive of others, might be his desire to differentiate more clearly the gendered poles of the imagination through the serpent in/as textual (re)formulation of the creative subject. In one of his marginal notes on *La Jeune Parque*, for instance, he asks himself: 'Pourquoi femme' (XVIII, 265). And in writing about Valéry's autobiography, or inscription of self as *écriture*, the degree to which it is permeated by the sinuous forms of the feminine as serpent cannot be ignored. Much of the transcription of the self as *écriture*, whether in the *Cahiers* notations or in the manuscripts which ultimately give birth to the collection now recognized as *Charmes*, reveals that the serpent is also woman; and woman as voice. 'Karin, étroit serpent' (de Lussy, p. 175); the Parque, originally christened Pandore, providing access to the monsters of the deep;[115] the Pythia, whose name, truncated body, and disrupted speech, mime, incarnate the motricity of the serpent, fragmented yet entire; and Eve, seductive in her turn, born from the same soil as the Pythoness.[116]

Indeed one might argue that a great deal of Valéry's poetic autobiography, that level of imaginative activity out of which the definitive texts emerge,[117] is as heavily dominated by the presence of female figures, as male. Many manuscript versions, as, too, published poems, evoke the significant presence or participation of a woman: Pandore, to become *La Jeune Parque*; *La Distraite*; *La Nourrice*, later rechristened *Poésie*; *Eve au serpent*; *La Pythie*; *Sémiramis* in her various textual forms—to name but some of the most important. Much of the nourishment from which these poems derive is thus explicitly associated with femininity as inspiration, theme or connotation.[118] This may be simply evidence that Valéry continued to draw on the traditional trope of the muse as source of poetic genius. Yet it might also be read as proof that he fully understood how necessary for the fertilization of the poetic consciousness was the participation of the female. For the poet's voice, that 'chanson ou mélisme du serpent', to resonate fully, fecundation must occur within its embrace.[119]

Viewing it as a theme 'qu'il juge d'une "poésie suprême"' (de Lussy, p. 270), Valéry returns on several occasions to his sense of wonder before 'le mystère de la femme fécondée' (pp. 269–70). Not only is it implicit in the varying degrees of violation of their bodies and being undergone by the Pythia and Eve; it provides the central theme of a text such as L'Abeille and, at least as regards manuscript development, is implicit in the inspiration of Air de Sémiramis.[120] Returning to La Pythie and Ebauche viewed as sites of tension or conflict between masculine and feminine aspects of the creative psyche, it is clear that the presence and even participation of the feminine is essential. In La Pythie, the serpent is woman: her fragmented body is the object of rape, her disrupted voice nostalgically evokes a lost virginity, her final achievement is to give birth. Yet the Pythia is not entirely victim since, without her physical and psychological form as container of the onslaught, akin to an alchemical retort in its transformative potential, the new voice could not have come into being. Equally, in Ebauche, there would be no triumph for the seductive serpent, this time in masculine mode, unless he were able to wield his verbal power in the manipulation of naïve Eve. Nor is she entirely reduced to the status of gullible pawn since her own seductive power threatens to catch her seducer out at his own game.

There is, then, no definitive victory in either text viewed as the field of a conflict enacted in sound between competing voices. In La Pythie and Ebauche, as elsewhere, it is the rebellion of self against self that finds voice in the space-time or acoustic theatre of the auto-biographical mélos. For victory, understood not as the triumph of one vocal force over the other but as integration of one with the other, masculine with feminine, one must await the emergence of the triumphant figure of Sémiramis out of the tormented genetic labourings of the Pythia.[121] As 'Parole et reine', she takes her stand, proud, free, and 'Divinement contradictoire Sous les ailes d'une victoire'.[122]

It is the curiously hybrid nature of this striking figure in the gallery of 'autoportraits' or substitute selves which explains her powerful resonance within the Valéryan imaginary. She is, as he notes in his *Final de Sémiramis*, both 'enchanteresse et roi'; in other words, an image, emblem, or form which blends attributes more commonly associated with a masculine role—power, authority, constructive competence[123] —with qualities evoking feminine creativity and seductiveness.[124] She is able to accomplish this merging of contrasting dimensions in so far as she represents for Valéry a literal embodiment of the energy of the voice.[125] Her autobiographical significance for Valéry can be read as somewhat similar to that of Faust, though inverted. She is woman yet encapsulates a masculine dimension understood as a preoccupation with dominance, order, the emergence of form; while he, as man, yet contains qualities of the feminine such as tenderness and vulnerability, thus encapsulating Lust within himself. In both figures, this synergy or psychosexual complementarity of energies is accomplished in the medium of the voice.[126]

In many cultures the serpent symbolizes chthonic forces, darkness, and the unknown dimensions of life; yet it possesses value also as a symbol of transcendence.[127] The recurrence of the serpent image in Valéry's imaginative world may be read as a fundamental aspect of the psyche's capacity to heal its inner conflicts. By engaging with the imaginal other, or serpent self in Valéry's private mythology, psychic images which often reside *in potentia*, outside consciousness, can be concretized in the vividness of symbolic form. According to a Jungian reading, this collaboration between soul and image is part of the soul's instinctive process of caring for itself.[128] Jung's thinking, rooted deeply in the value of the imagination, offers a number of avenues which enrich a reading of the voice as an expression of the serpent self, the feminine self, in the context of Valéry's restructuring of his authorial subjectivity through artistic creation. At the heart of Jungian thought lies the concept of individuation, an imperceptible process of psychic growth which cannot be brought about by a conscious effort of will but must be allowed to follow its own hidden regulating or directing tendency over a long period. The organizing centre from which this natural effect stems is the self, a creatively active aspect of the psychic nucleus, an inner guiding factor quite distinct from the conscious personality which can only come into play when the ego rids itself of its purposive aims, allowing the unconscious to follow its course, expressed in symbolic images deriving from personal and collective structures.

There is much here that suggests parallels with Valéry's own understanding of identity in relation to the creation of art and to the creation of a transformed self: his view of the pure and contingent self as connected yet distinct; his intuition of the vital importance of a mythic transformation of the substance of the self in and through the products of the imagination; his according of value to central images donated by the psyche.[129] Pursuing these parallels further, voice can be interpreted as expressing the imperatives of the specifically Valéryan path of individuation; it speaks to the poet of his shadow self, guiding him through the unconscious realm towards the acknowledgement of his psychic femininity and thus to the more complete state of self-realization which Jung envisages symbolically in terms of the divine marriage or *coniunctio oppositorum*.[130] Voice weds in its compass the conscious and the unconscious, blends the Gladiatorial register and all that escapes that register in an autobiographical *mélos* integrating self and personality.[131] More specifically, it embodies characteristics of the shadow, that aspect of the individual which contains values that are needed by consciousness but exist in a form that makes it difficult to integrate them into the individual's conscious life.[132]

It is here that the relevance of the feminine, already signalled within the context of otherness as representative of a repressed dimension of the cultural imaginary, gains increased impact when Jungian interpretations are brought to bear on Valéry's project of a reintegrated subjectivity. The notion of *anima* consciousness is central to Jung's view of the creative complementarity of male and female within the psyche.[133] *Anima* as expression of life, becoming, feeling, exists over and against *animus* as *logos*, idea, intellect, *ratio*, *nous*. Since Western cultural symbolism functions by repressing its unconscious aspect, *anima*, linked in with a fantasy of opposites, becomes associated with the shadow. It is thus relegated to the position of the feminine, the shadow realm of the masculine position.[134] When Valéry evokes the woman within himself; when he yearns for the plenitude of the truly mystical encounter with the complementary other; when woman is characterized as cosmos (VII, 738), as devourer (XIV, 324), as soul (VIII, 777), his imagination recognizes the power of the *anima* archetype. These remarks suggest that he intuited the shadow dimension borne by the *anima* archetype—the fear entertained by the masculine consciousness of a cosmic energy; of the immense, impersonal, and indifferent cycle of life itself; of a sexuality radically other than its own—in accordance with a projective tendency in the male psyche which casts out onto woman the threatening and intolerable components of itself, yet still requires these same elements to be available in order to feel complete. In the sequence of mythical *personae* which inhabit Valéry's writing, those projective identifications which span the progress of his autobiographical project, the recurrence of the couple as symbol or emblem belongs, also, to Jung's conception of a coming together within the creative sensibility of the divine pair.[135]

Teste and Emilie, Gladiator and Sémiramis, Leonardo and the Parque, Faust and Lust, Assem and Rachel, partners in the creative quest of selfhood, can be situated within the framework of this *hierosgamos* or sacred marriage, considered the goal of the alchemists' research, emblematic of a point of synthesis or creative supremacy. The Valéryan transubstantiation of self is equally a search for that integrated existence, conceived of as godlike in its power to harmonize aspects of the poetic sensibility: 'Le dieu peut-être, cherche et se cherche et par toutes voies — dont l'une serait nature et l'autre conscience et sensibilité. — Et peut-être tente-t-il de les rejoindre?' (XVIII, 904). The complex couplet of *La Pythie* and *Ebauche* come to mind here, born from the same soil and somehow, each in its own way, seeking reunion with the lost half or Other. An acknowledgement of the sacred significance of this moment emerges from the supreme import of the conjunction of male and female in the aesthetico-mystical *copula* realized through Faust and Lust; and it is towards this synergy within the creative sensibility as, above all, voice that the concluding pages return. In the Faustian figure or function, the final avatar of the desiring voice of Valéry, an attempt is made to integrate the 'forme femelle' of his 'étrange nature'; the fragments of the *Quatrième acte* lend close attention to the sacred significance of the embrace of male and female, to that *jouissance* which marks the radical extraneity of human desire identified by the mystical tradition as beyond language. In Valéry's universe the feminine dimension grants access to this transcendent moment, as Faust seeks to absorb it into his very being: 'Car Lust et Faust sont *moi* — et rien que moi [. . .]. L'expérience m'a montré que ce que j'ai le plus désiré ne se trouve pas dans l'autrui [. . .]. Je m'aperçois ici que je poursuis [. . .] mon idée de la "mystique sans dieu" [. . .]. Dans ce — système — la jouissance elle-même est un symbole, un sacrement' (XXIX, 804–5).

Faust contains Lust, lends his voice symbolically as container for the transformed relationship of self with other in a process of self-embrace which encompasses the unconscious realms of his personality hitherto distanced as the feminine, the abject, the intolerable.[136] As voice deploys the topography in which the individuated self comes into being as textual practice and transformative *écriture*, so, too, it is *in* voice and *as* voice that the embrace with the feminine is enacted in *Mon Faust*: 'Mais [. . .] voyez-vous que tout mon être n'est qu'une voix' (60) is Faust's joyous realization as the point of fullest encounter approaches. Voice is an integral part of the realization of the *copula* on which the possibility of a renewed cultural creativity depends; and in the manuscripts of the *Quatrième acte*, the alchemical retort in which the traces of the complementarity and interaction of opposing elements in the creative subjectivity can be read, we are privy to the process of purification, that ordeal by fire, which contributes to the refining of the autobiographical voice of *ego poeta*. In the mono-dialogue of Faust and Lust, a vocal osmosis manifesting on the level of syntax, a conjuncture if not identity of masculine and feminine, desire borders on a *jouissance* which tests the limits of expression.[137] As Faust gives voice to his longing to 'porter l'amour où il ne fut jamais' (120), he admits that the distinction between separate aspects of his being has been transcended as voice blends with voice in a harmony: 'Mais voici que tout ce qui se dit entre nous, nous ne savons plus qui le dit, de vous ou de moi' (120).

One reading of the Faustian endeavour in the context of Valéry's creative life interprets the attempt to redeem the self through the aesthetic embodiment of *mélos* as a sublimation rather than a solution of the problem of contingent existence. In the yearning to attain a higher form of communication with, or love for, another human being, Faust's ambition appears to meet with failure: the object of desire, forever displaced, remains inaccessible, as Valéry's inability to give final form to the *Quatrième acte* seems to confirm. Faust ultimately confronts an irrefutable force, the order of a resistant awareness: 'Voilà, leur dit le Réel, voilà ce qui ne peut pas être. Brisez-vous la tête contre ma substance de granit' (140). Yet, in the pursuit of a more adequate statement of the nature of subjectivity, in redeploying the coordinates of his authorial persona, Valéry's writing does not register failure. Rather it affirms the strength and sustained relevance of the voice of creative intelligence as fragment, as question, as experiment. The real achievement lies not in the attaining of perfection—as self, as syntax—but in the willingness to allow the incomplete, the hesitant, and the searching self to have its say; to remain open to the wound within the self, to the dark or secret sister.

One final group of texts remains to be considered in the context of

Valéry's autobiographical or alchemical quest for integrated selfhood. In *Histoires brisées*, those strange and unfathomable stories, the voice bears witness to its power as presence, sufficient in itself as articulation of the mysteries of creative intelligence, expression of the ceaseless modulation of desiring consciousness. Such dense and revealing texts lend themselves to many forms of exploration and interpretation; my own approach focuses briefly on the interplay established between male and female elements in the narrative, and on the mystical or visionary dimension which is implied.[138]

The narrative voice in several of the pieces communicates the phenomenological awareness of remaining close to the source, to that pure time-consciousness constitutive of identity. It speaks from the gap or interval, 'écart modulé, modelé entre deux mêmes' (XIV, 282), expressing desire as presentness to self; as upsurge of images; as creative flux emerging from latency.[139] It is, perhaps, the voice of the secret sister in a sequence of feminine embodiments—as Calypso, Héra, Emma, Rachel, Sophie, Agar—exploring the space of consciousness as acoustic theatre and screen.[140] And it is not afraid to acknowledge the fragmented, formless, and incomplete nature of its utterances.[141] Valéry relinquishes narrative responsibility from the outset, releasing the shadow, allowing the wider creative self to speak of matters which may not conform to the parameters of syntactic control: 'il m'arrive [. . .] de me faires des contes. Ou plutôt, il se fait des contes en moi' (OII, 407). The imaginative landscape opened up before the mind's eye and ear possesses all the mysterious precision and radical otherness of the world of dreams as the reader is drawn into a complex interplay of forces. Male and female protagonists align in a struggle for control; the faculties of vision and speech vie with each for dominance; clarity, precision, and detail are simultaneously undermined by the strangely obscure and enigmatic character of this other space, other time, brought into being through the experimental searching of a textuality which rejects all ambition of meaningfulness, structured coherence, or narrative closure. This is a scenario of orchestrated fluidity, potential chaos, ceaseless transformation of energies and impulses which relates, in part, to the semiotic dimension of the products of consciousness discussed in the opening chapter. It belongs, also, within the context of a psychoanalytic understanding of the role of sound, of the acoustic gestalt, in the creative sensibility explored in Chapters 2 and 3. In the present context, it offers evidence of the voice as revelation of a mystical insight reaching beyond the limitations of the real into the accomplishment of selfhood in the form of the quaternity identified by ancient symbolism as a yet more complex archetypal manifestation of the psyche's nature.[142]

It is in *Acem* that the radical otherness of the *Histoires brisées* is encountered in its fullest impact. The uncertain gender of its protagonist develops further the hermaphroditic potential of Gozon in *L'Ile Xiphos*; and it is his voice, initially limited to semiotic utterances, which animates the drama. It registers, as did that of Faust, the ineffability of the Real, and yet, when it comes into its own, orchestrates a thematic complex of extraordinary significance. It speaks, in the tones of a child, of love and tenderness and summons into the time of the text an embodiment of the androgyny as a young man and woman seat themselves on either side of Acem.[143] As the observing level of consciousness relaxes its hold, relinquishing scopic mastery, the voice can give full measure in bringing into being the mystical vision of the quaternity:

Je compris ou j'imaginai que les trois personnes qui composaient cette masse devaient avoir les yeux fermés. [. . .] Moi-même, je me sentais comme insidieusement contraint de fermer mes yeux. L'évanouissement de la lumière me faisait sentir je ne sais quel besoin de suivre ou de simuler sans le vouloir une diminution de ma faculté de regarder [. . .]. Bientôt nous étions QUATRE, sans doute, dans les pleines ténèbres. (OII, 456–7)

In the exchange of voices between male and female, brother and sister, contemplator and vision, desire interrogates the foundations of its being. The young man asks: 'Qu'as-tu fait des semences précieuses de ton vouloir créateur? Et pourquoi n'as-tu pas jeté dans la balance féminine de notre sort tout le poids des énergies de la perfection?' (OII, 455). This, the voice of self-reproach in Valéry, awakens its own response as the young girl answers: 'Nous sommes frère et sœur, et tout ce que nous sommes voudrait que nous partagions la même couche, et qu'il n'y ait entre nous que ce qu'il faut de différence pour aliment des divins efforts de l'union' (OII, 456).

In a life which has shaped itself, consciously and unconsciously, according to a search for that form best able to embody a mastery of death, the utterance confided during the visionary moment is valuable. Valéry's autobiographical journey leads, finally, towards an acceptance of the other within the self as an essentially different, creatively necessary participant: 'C'est pourquoi le vrai créateur doit avoir les *deux sexes*' (XIX, 135).

Notes to Chapter 4

1. Autobiography as a field of creative and critical production is a fertile ground in contemporary writing. A valuable collection of essays on contemporary approaches to the problems which it poses is James Olney (ed.), *Autobiography: Essays Theoretical and Critical* (Princeton: Princeton University Press, 1980); the present discussion has also been significantly informed by Michael Sheringham, *French Autobiography: Devices and Desires; Rousseau to Perec* (Oxford: Clarendon Press, 1993).

2. De Lussy proposes that Valéry's recourse to myth in this context serves as a defence against anxiety and the recurrent mental patterns which it provokes (*'Charmes'*, i. 221).

3. Michael Sheringham refers to the autobiographical subject as 'a hybrid, a fusion of past and present, document and desire, referential and textual, *énoncé* and *énonciation*—not a product but a process' (*French Autobiography*, 21).

4. The suggestion that autobiography may be considered as a form of resistance to ideology whereby 'the writer seeks to redraw the wider configuration within which his or her new approach to the self is to be viewed' (Sheringham, *French Autobiography*, 169) is apposite here.

5. Louis Renza develops this idea further in the context of the autobiographical act yielding 'a potential self-abnegation, a divorce between writing self and textual rendition' in 'The Veto of the Imagination: A Theory of Autobiography', in Olney, *Autobiography*, 278.

6. Monsieur Teste's remark seems relevant here: 'Et Moi! que je déchire, et que je nourris de sa propre substance toujours remâchée, seul aliment pour qu'il s'accroisse!' (OII, 42).

7. 'Mon Caligulisme. [. . .] Je fus ou suis l'idée de ce moment qui foudroie t[ou]s les autres possibles ou connus [. . .]. Pas de redites: construire pour se détruire' (XXVIII, 822).

8. The same insight is communicated in the following remark: 'Pour moi, on ne tue que pour et par création. Et d'ailleurs, l'instinct destructif n'est légitime que comme indication de quelque naissance ou construction qui veut sa place et son heure' (XXII, 207–8).

9. 'Tout ce qui intéresse l'homme, en sus des strictes nécessités de sa vie, tend à sa destruction — ou plutôt à sa négation. Il semble que le suicide *de sa* nature, (non de sa personne) soit l'objet, l'*apex* caché de tout son mouvement. Chacun se meut vers le non-humain. L'un tend vers le dieu, l'autre vers la machine, l'un et l'autre prenant modèle et idéal dans leurs moments les plus rares et se niant eux-mêmes tels qu'ils sont' (V, 914).

10. 'Orphée. Voix. L'opération qui consiste à tirer de ma douleur un chant magnifique — Cette douleur stupide a conduit mon sens à des extrêmes de détresse, [. . .] mais puisque je n'y suis pas demeuré, puisque je suis remonté des enfers pour pouvoir y redescendre, j'ai appris du moins, la continuité de cette chaîne de tourments, [. . .] toute la modulation de l'être, [. . .] voix rattachée aux entrailles, [. . . .] état élevé, tonique, tendu, fait uniquement d'énergie pure, libre, à haute puissance, ductile, [. . .] voilà, voilà le divin mystère' (VIII, 41).

11. De Lussy, in discussing the genesis of *La Pythie*, for example, notes that 'il convient de lire ici la présence obsédante pour la mémoire de la fameuse

dédicace à Arsène Houssaye par Baudelaire de ses *Petits poèmes en prose*. C'est aussi une manière d'hommage à un grand aîné que Valéry considérait comme le père de la poésie moderne: "Nous pouvons couper où nous voulons, moi ma rêverie, vous le manuscrit, le lecteur sa lecture; [. . .] Enlevez une vertèbre, et les deux morceaux de cette tortueuse fantaisie se rejoindront sans peine [. . .]. Dans l'espérance que quelques-uns de ces tronçons seront assez vivants pour vous plaire et vous amuser, j'ose vous dédier le serpent tout entier"' (*Charmes*, i. 169).

12. 'S'accoutumer à penser en Serpent qui s'avale par la queue. Car c'est toute la question. Je "contiens" ce qui me "contient"' (XXVIII, 417).

13. A passage from *Extraits du Log-Book de Monsieur Teste* develops such a gesture of self-immolation in more detail: 'Soumets-toi tout entier à ton meilleur moment [. . .]. L'état où doit te reconduire toute discipline. [. . .] Tout par rapport à Lui, qui installe dans ton développement une mesure, des degrés [. . .] Je m'immole intérieurement à ce que je voudrais être!' (OII, 40).

14. As is the case with his mythical projection Leonardo, identified with a central attitude governing the operations of knowledge and incarnating a symbolic mind, repository of a vast collection of forms, Valéry sets the question of form at the heart of his inquiry: 'Système — Chercher une forme pour l'ensemble de la connaissance' (VII, 890); or 'La maîtrise de la pensée est la présence presque immédiate de sa nature "formelle"' (VII, 63). Everything, he claims, is a formal problem to the extent that other categories lose their validity and the traditional opposition of form and content can be dismissed as a misconception of reality (IX, 135; VII, 596; VII, 652). Similarly, mental activity is reducible to the constant play of forms in a process of transformation (VII, 596). On a more personal level he frequently observes how much pleasure he derives from the formal properties of an object where others might respond more readily to its material dimension, its substance. In a late *Cahiers* entry he identifies the intense investment of imaginative energy in the pursuit of formal perfection as one of his governing characteristics. 'Quant à moi, *jusqu'au bout* fut mon désir 1. en fait d'*intellect* — arriver par manoeuvres et exercices d'imagination et self-conscience à former l'idée de nos possibilités [. . .] — par *voie de possession des formes* ou transformations' (XXIX, 765).

15. 'Ainsi voit-on apparaître dans un dossier, [. . .] l'existence de "mélismes", qui s'imposent avec force, demandant à prendre corps et à se fixer dans une structure... ces alliances de mots dont la présence a quelque chose d'obsédant' (de Lussy, '*Charmes*', i. 241).

16. Aigrisse, *Psychanalyse de Paul Valéry*, and Benoît Peeters, *Paul Valéry: une vie d'écrivain?* (Paris: Les Impressions nouvelles, 1989) study the notion of his 'life' in very different ways but neither can be seen as a sustained biographical account. A seminal article in this context is Peter Boa, 'Valéry's "Ego Poeta": Towards a Biography of the Authorial Self', *Neophilologus* 62 (1978), 51–62. I shall refer to this in greater detail later in the present chapter. Jarrety devotes a chapter to the question of the status of the author figure in Valéry's writing, distinguishing between Valéry's 'refus d'un sujet de l'écriture' and his postulation that 'un sujet de l'énonciation' exists (*Valéry devant la littérature*, 169). His emphasis on the imprint of individuality as form (p. 158) and on the role of the voice as offering a certain continuity to the fragmented subject (pp. 172–3) confirms some of my own interpretations of the autobiographical voice. Ned Bastet's chapter 'Towards

a Biography of the Mind', in Gifford and Stimpson (eds.), *Reading Paul Valéry*, 17–35, offers the most recent analysis of this issue.

17. 'L'idée que des parties entières de notre *vraie vie* puissent entrer dans une œuvre littéraire m'est [. . .] étrangère' (XV, 511); he notes that others work on the least important aspects of him because he has reserved the essential for himself: 'La volonté de cacher / garder ce qui me semblait le plus important de mes idées — observations — a fait que mes exégètes ou critiques travaillant sur ce qu'ils avaient [. . .] ne pouvaient que façonner un personnage non existant' (XVI, 493).

18. 'Réduire une vie à un "résumé"! / et vous perdrez de vue la texture de [la] vie' (OII, 1508).

19. In a letter to Gide he remarks: 'Qui dosera ce mélange extraordinaire de la crainte de n'être pas compris avec la terreur d'être compris?' (OII, 1489); and, elsewhere, he comments: 'Encore une étude [. . .] sur moi! On ne me connaît pas. Je mesure chaque fois la distance de l'œuvre à l'auteur' (XVI, 533).

20. 'Il résulte de tout ceci que ma vie, telle qu'il m'en souvient, se mêle de toutes ces vies non moins imaginaires, mais non moins authentiques, que l'on m'a attribuées' (OII, 284); or, 'je ne me suis jamais abstenu de façonner ainsi ce qui devait être mon histoire; [. . .] Ce que j'ai fait, ce que j'ai voulu faire, ce que j'aurais pu faire sont à l'état d'idées également vivantes devant moi' (OII, 284).

21. 'J'ai donc ce grand ouvrage en tête, qui doit finalement me débarrasser tout à fait de moi-même, duquel je suis déjà si détaché... Je veux finir léger, délié à jamais de tout ce qui ressemble à quelque chose' (OII, 298).

22. 'Je vous ai dit et redit', notes Faust, 'que ces Mémoires ne sont pas des souvenirs' (OII, 330–1).

23. See e.g. comments such as: 'Je n'écris, n'ai jamais écrit de journal de mes jours. Je prends note de mes idées' (OII, 1506); or, 'Ce n'est ici ni un journal, ni une autobiographie' (XXVII, 35).

24. See XXV, 617 and 879; OII, 1525–6.

25. In this context of autobiography as subversive of current generic norms, the proposal that 'the true self is disclosed, through friction with the categories which seek to circumscribe it' (Sheringham, *French Autobiography*, 171) is suggestive. He argues that a tendency exists in certain contemporary autobiographies for the subject to reappropriate his/her identity from the grip of ideology by the manner in which he/she takes up a position in discourse: 'the autobiographical work comes to reside in a process of "isolation" by which the current self is placed "outside the reach of existing ideological systems"' (pp. 171–2). Valéry's interpretation of vocal form demonstrates one such strategy for undermining the autobiographical *doxa*.

26. 'Touches de mon portrait. Si je cherchais ma définition je trouverais que je ne suis Rien. [. . .] une fois cette figure et ce système arrêtés, je ne puis jamais les tenir pour moi. Quoi que ce soit n'est pas moi' (V, 791).

27. 'Quant à moi, je n'ai jamais su qui j'étais' (OII, 1490); or, 'Je me perds dans tous ces "Moi" que l'on m'a faits' (OII, 1491).

28. 'La question est de surmonter la Personne, qui est une *Idole*. Et j'ai déclaré la guerre aux Idoles, il y a 50 ans passés!' (XXVII, 375).

29. 'Notre histoire, notre moment, notre corps, nos espoirs, [. . .] tout nous est *étranger*. Tout est extérieur [. . .] à un je ne sais quoi, qui est *moi*, — et qui est un mythe' (IX, 275).

30. 'To talk of the autobiographical subject is already to think of the individual as being constituted by, subject to, different orders of meaning defined by different discourses. We are dealing, in fact, with a plural subject—or a plurality of subjects: a subject of memory, of ideology, of desire; a subject oriented towards communication, towards death, towards the body. The process of autobiography does not resolve this diversity into unity so much as provide a context for the interaction of strands and forces' (Sheringham, *French Autobiography*, 21). See also Valéry's remark on one of the manuscripts of *Charmes*: 'Narcissus — c'est un dialogue entre lui et son image, roulant sur la passion de soi-même, qui est la seule — Il n'y aura jamais satisfaction de cette passion-là, qui met aux prises le stable et l'instable' (Cah. *Ch*. II, in de Lussy, 'Charmes', i. 284).

31. Something similar to Lacan's positing of the mirror as origin of subjectivity is caught in the following remark: 'Définir un son jusqu'au fond de soi-même. Mais il n'y a point de fond. Il y a un miroir dernier. L'être finit par un miroir, par un retour, par un foyer d'où il reçoit ce qu'il donne' (IX, 376).

32. 'Vais-je me vider dans la parole? Elle est infidèle; elle devient étrangère [. . .] Le plus délicat et le plus profond, le plus unique, — ne dit-on pas *inexprimable*?' (IV, 452).

33. This remark and those which follow are taken from a key text, *Propos me concernant* (OII, 1505–38), where Valéry does in fact supply the reader with details about his own personal interests, habits, likes, and dislikes.

34. 'Peu de souvenirs d'enfance, — et douteux... Le passé est donc pour moi plus aboli dans son développement *chronologique* et *narrable* qu'il ne l'est, me semble-t-il, pour la plupart' (OII, 1507).

35. 'Je n'aime pas du tout me retrouver en esprit sur les voies anciennes de ma vie. Ce n'est pas moi qui rechercherais le Temps perdu!' (OII, 1506).

36. Bergson's 'durée' is obviously very similar to this notion in so far as it is an expanded, intensified consciousness of temporality as distinct from the flux of linear time. However, Valéry refutes any influence of Bergson on his work (OII, 1494). See, for further exploration of parallels between Valéry and Bergson, A. E. Pilkington, *Bergson and his Influence: A Reassessment* (Cambridge: Cambridge University Press, 1976), ch. 3.

37. It is in this sense of form that one should, I believe, interpret Valéry's oft-quoted remark concerning *La Jeune Parque*: 'Que la FORME de ce chant est une autobiographie' (VI, 508). It is worth noting, in the context of the autobiographical form of *La Jeune Parque*, that Valéry observes: 'Je sens bien que je n'ai allongé et disproportionné l'apostrophe au serpent que par le besoin de parler moi-même... L'histoire technique de ce fragment est d'ailleurs des plus curieuses. Elle est aussi un raccourci de l'histoire de tout le poème, qui se résume par cette étrange loi: une fabrication artificielle qui a pris une sorte de développement naturelle' (OI, 1633).

38. A discussion of this harmonic dimension occurs in a passage where Valéry defines the nature of 'les Fées' and 'le Solitaire' in *Mon Faust*: 'Quant aux "harmoniques" [. . .] ce sont ces valeurs supérieures de la sensibilité, *qui s'ordonnent en groupes* [. . .] et qui sont *la structure abstraite* de nos modifications les plus *concrètes* — *les sensations en soi, au-dessus de toute signification* [. . .]. C'est l'art qui a pour fonction de révéler ces groupes' (XXVI, 442).

39. '"Amiel" et M. Teste. Mais l'immense différence entre les Stendhal, les Amiel et

moi, ou M. Teste — c'est qu'ils s'intéressent à leurs états et à eux-mêmes en fonction du contenu de ces états, tandis que je ne m'intéresse au contraire qu'à ce qui dans ces états n'est pas *encore* personnel, que les contenus, la *personne* me semblent subordonnés à des conditions 1. de conscience impersonnelle 2. de mécanique et de statistique' (XIV, 351).

40. 'Gide a la curiosité des *individus*, le désir de les confesser et de se confesser à eux, il les tient pour beaucoup, et moi pour rien. Nous sommes tout opposés quant aux valeurs que nous donnons à l'être. J'ai l'instinct de ne pas me livrer et de ne pas aimer qu'on se livre, et lui le contraire' (XII, 847).

41. 'L'objet de l'écriture d'une pensée est tout différent de l'objet de cette pensée. La production de l'*œuvre* de l'*esprit* se distingue de la production de l'esprit' (XX, 555).

42. Renza in Olney, *Autobiography*, 279.

43. 'L'ange [. . .] s'aperçoit [. . .] que la loi de ses goûts est de s'éloigner de ce qui est "Humain"' (XV, 716).

44. 'Ego ou Faust III. [. . .]. Cette rage éphémère d'impuissance m'irrite elle-même contre ce moi qui produit ce qu'il ne sert de rien de produire' (XXV, 182).

45. 'Faust III et Ego. Quel destin, quelle amertume parfois de percevoir si clairement la mécanique de l'esprit et de la sensibilité, de souffrir ou jouir avec mépris de ces modes tout-puissants, [. . .] de ressentir à la fois leur empire et leur niaiserie! — Tu es tout et je sais que tu n'es rien' (XXIV, 398).

46. Now although it has been argued that such a use of a pseudo-self is not permissible autobiographical strategy—Renza claims, for instance, that 'the nature of the autobiographical text precludes the possibility that the writer can deliberately adopt a persona behind which he conceals references to his own life' (Olney, *Autobiography*, 292)—Valéry does not try to deny this as his technique: 'Enfin, je le confesse, je ne trouvai pas mieux que d'attribuer à l'infortuné Léonard mes propres agitations, transportant le désordre de mon esprit dans la complexité du sien. [. . .] Je changeai mes embarras en sa puissance supposée. J'osai me considérer sous son nom, et utiliser ma personne' (OI, 1232). Such a strategy, in Michael Sheringham's opinion, is one example of the devices necessitated by the pressures of autobiography as a genre: 'a "device" can mean both a stratagem, a plan devised to fulfil a certain aim, and an emblematic figure [. . . .]. Such features [. . .] give [. . .] autobiographies their particular flavour, reflect the vicissitudes of autobiographical desire' (*French Autobiography*, p. ix). Pickering offers a recent reading of Valéry's self-modelling strategies in 'Paradigms of the Self: Valéry's Mythical Models', in Gifford and Stimpson (eds.), *Reading Paul Valéry*, 53–69.

47. 'Narcisse. L'esprit ne se reconnaît pas dans l'homme — et moi dans mon miroir. Car le possible ne peut avoir *un seul* objet pour image — C'est trop peu d'un seul personnage pour tant d'existences... virtuelles!' (XVIII, 45).

48. Valéry's 'suppôt' or henchman, offering him a means of controlling and directing material relevant to the self but at a safer remove, corresponds to a category identified by Sheringham in the context of autobiographical fetishism. 'Autobiographers often convey the impression that their textual effigies have the attraction of miniature or scale models, an appeal which may be associated with the mind's disposition to classify and order. The autobiographical manikin or homunculus [. . .] is [. . .] amenable [. . .] to scrutiny, a "transitional object" to

be cherished in the context of an otherwise unpromising environment' (*French Autobiography*, 6–7).

49. 'Toute connaissance n'est possible que grâce à l'incomplet (puisqu'elle ne consiste qu'à compléter, *fermer*). [. . .] C'est par quoi *connaissance* et *création* ou *invention*, sont voisines' (XIV, 472).

50. 'Ce thème de *Narcisse* que j'ai choisi, est une sorte d'auto-biographie poétique', Lecture on the Narcisse cycle, 1941, quoted in Nash, *Paul Valéry's 'Album'*, 182.

51. De Lussy, discussing the draft versions of brief 'autoportraits' in poetic form, quotes the following text entitled 'Désaveu':

> Je ne me trouve d'image
> Car l'hôte de mon miroir
> N'est qu'un certain personnage
> Que je m'étonne d'y voir;
>
> Si j'écoute dans la conque
> L'écho de mon cœur chanteur
> Cette musique quelconque
> M'en fait mépriser l'auteur

(BN MSS Petits vers, fo. 92^v, quoted p. 186).

52. Numerous remarks emphasize that aspect of his autobiographical ambition which envisages a study of the inner life, of the drama of the intellect: XXII, 280–1, XXIII, 8; OII, 1525.

53. 'It is his repetition that is his most interesting feature. [. . .] In the nature of his own repetition lies the form of Valéry's system of thinking; and that is as it should be, since he had a passion for form' (Elizabeth Sewell, *Paul Valéry: The Mind in the Mirror* (Cambridge: Bowes & Bowes, 1952), 12).

54. In the first of his studies of the genesis and history of autobiography as genre in Western literature Philippe Lejeune points to Valéry's pioneering interpretation of Descartes's *Discours de la méthode* as an autobiographical text (*L'Autobiographie en France* (Paris: Armand Colin, 1971), 59).

55. 'Thème. [. . .] C'est ici le Mélos dans le langage, un élément *naturel* de *mémoire*, une forme avec fond [. . .] qui s'impose à la voix' (VIII, 435).

56. Michel Beaujour in *Miroirs d'encre: rhétorique de l'autoportrait* (Paris: Seuil, 1980) contrasts the 'autoportrait' with the autobiographical text; in the former an absence of narrative structures, an emphasis on language as the rhetorical locus in which the self evolves, and a poetico-metaphorical mode of development inform a view of the text as a form of 'bricolage', fragmented, lacking in imposed coherence. Although he makes no sustained reference to Valéry, much of what he proposes could be suggestively related to Valéry's view of the self as textual entity. For an interesting refutation of the autoportrait/autobiography distinction established by Beaujour, see Sheringham, *French Autobiography*, 308–9.

57. Sheringham rightly identifies the vitality of the French autobiographical tradition as grounded in the 'problems and contradictions which beset [the autobiographer's] undertaking' (p. ix). His thesis is that the various devices developed by individual autobiographers spring precisely from their critical lucidity concerning the complexities inherent in the autobiographical project.

58. See, in this context, his remark: 'il n'est pas de théorie qui ne soit un fragment, soigneusement préparé, de quelque autobiographie' (OI, 1320).

59. Sheringham, *French Autobiography*, 200.

60. Sewell, developing the crucial significance of formal preoccupations in Valéry's work, highlights the self-reflexive dimension of the written trace: 'Clearly, a mind may construct its thoughts, may make them into something, a book perhaps or a poem. But at the same time that mind is undergoing its work as well as creating it, being constructed as well as constructing' (*Paul Valéry*, 13).

61. Lejeune's definition of the autobiographical pact as guaranteeing that cover name, author, and narrator refer to one and the same being provides an example of such a legitimizing statement (*Le Pacte autobiographique* (Paris: Seuil, 1975), 14).

62. *Propos me concernant* is a key text here; and a wide range of comments, particularly those bearing the rubric *Ego*, discuss features of a recognizably human personality. One finds also confidences and revelations of a more private nature, moments typical of the self-disclosure practised by conventional autobiographers. Indeed, one of the later *Cahiers* entries conveys Valéry's surprise on realizing that he does, in fact, possess a personality in the normal sense of the term: 'Le nouveau, c'est que je me trouve par-ci par-là en présence du seigneur *Yo-Mismo* — non de ce "moi pur", mon éternel agent — Mais d'un personnage *moi* — Auteur de telles œuvres, — situé, défini — donc le plus Antégo possible' (XXVIII, 89).

63. Highly relevant here is Beaujour's thesis that the technique of the 'autoportraitiste' is a variant of the procedures of ancient rhetoric (*Miroirs d'encre*, 11). The self-portraitist makes use of structures and devices inscribed in the linguistic code and grammatical forms operative in language but is often not conscious of what he is doing. It thus becomes possible to use the autoportrait-text as a means of disguising a personal identity in the wider community implied by the unconscious functioning of language as social code. Rhetoric as concealment has considerable relevance to Valéry's autobiographical strategy.

64. See OII, 1491; in response to a questionnaire circulated amongst writers of the period addressing the issue of 'Pourquoi écrivez-vous?' Valéry responded, 'Par faiblesse' (OII, 1485). We must make of this what we will.

65. A similar point is made in the following remark: 'Tout mon *travail naturel*, celui de ma nature — et que j'ai accompli toute ma vie [. . .] ne consiste que dans une sorte de *préparation perpétuelle, sans objet*, sans finalité — peut-être aussi instinctive que le labeur d'une fourmi, quoique de tendance additive, perfective; [. . .] quoiqu'enfin ayant pour orientation la *direction* d'une *conscience croissante* étrangement cherchée avec une obstination et une constance d'instinct! Tout le reste [. . .] est de mon travail *artificiel*' (XXII, 462).

66. 'Si je prends des fragments dans ces cahiers et que [. . .] je les publie, l'ensemble fera quelque chose. Le lecteur — et même moi-meme — en formera une *unité*' (OII, 1519). Jarrety explores the motives which led Valéry to publish some of his hitherto private, fragmentary notes, suggesting that he may have felt a certain frustration at the fact that his ideas were not effective in the external world (*Valéry devant la littérature*, 196). Jarrety's own view is clear: 'les propos écrits à l'adresse d'autrui éludent le plus vif et le plus aigu. [. . .] Lui-même demeure en ses silences' (p. 195).

67. 'Il est d'une grande importance dans toute étude sur "Moi" de relever ceci et ses

conséquences que je n'ai *jamais visé à convaincre qui que ce soit* de *quoi que ce soit*';
he concludes with self-directed irony, '*Toujours un aveu*' (XXVII, 820).

68. He interprets Gide's *Journal* as evidence of an attempt to achieve 'la puissance
    d'émouvoir les autres' whereas his own seeks to 'rejoindre ce qu'on voudrait être
    devant soi' (XXVI, 366).

69. 'Ma fin n'est pas littéraire. Elle n'est pas d'agir sur les autres tant que sur moi —
    Moi — en tant qu'il peut se traiter comme une œuvre... de l'esprit' (XVIII,
    703).

70. Although he is aware, too, of the limits of what writing can achieve or, at least,
    of the uses to which he puts it: 'Quand j'écris sur ces cahiers, *je m'écris*. Mais je
    ne m'écris pas tout' (XXVIII, 236).

71. 'La production d'idées est chez moi une fonction naturelle, quasi physiologique
    [. . .]. Je suis positivement malade tout le jour si je n'ai pu, à peine réveillé,
    pendant deux heures environ, me laisser faire par ma tête' (OII, 1526).
    Celeyrette-Pietri points to the sensation of 'volupté' experienced by Valéry in
    the creation of text: 'l'écriture est sans doute le type le plus raffiné d'action
    complète' (*Valéry et le moi*, 343). Relevant in this context is an observation by
    Valéry: 'Il écrivait de tout son corps' (XXVII, 161).

72. For a discussion of the fetishistic dimension of autobiography see Sheringham,
    French Autobiography, 6–8. Clearly, there are connections to be made with the
    view of the voice as transitional object outlined in Ch. 1.

73. Celeyrette-Pietri proposes that 'l'écriture valéryenne' may be 'avant tout celle
    d'un travail de deuil' but also sees the existence of the *Cahiers* as evidence of
    'l'espoir mis dans le langage par lequel l'homme échappe à la seule individualité
    biologique et se découvre autre qu'un corps souffrant' (*Valéry et le moi*, 298).

74. In this light Valéry's suggestion that biography would do better to follow a
    radiating pattern rather than a linear or chronological one seems apposite. Of
    similar interest for the light which it sheds on so seminal a text as the prose poem
    L'Ange is a remark pointing to the role of *écriture* as guide in the creative process:
    'en vérité, je ne savais où j'allais; point d'idée à suivre, fixant le *sujet narrable,
    résumable* de cet ouvrage —; mais, au contraire, l'idée du seul cheminement, une
    manière de s'avancer étant le *but* vrai; [. . .] Conduire — Reconduire? Qui? —
    qui ou quoi et où est conduit par le développement d'une symphonie? — *Mais
    faut-il toujours un sujet à un verbe?*' (XXII, 716).

75. What he refers to as 'prémunir le lecteur contre l'effet de "bloc" que peut
    produire un texte dont il est naturel de penser qu'il est le fruit d'un travail
    unitaire et constitue une ŒUVRE. Ceci n'en est pas une' (OII, 1506). The
    status of the unity or cohesiveness of the autobiographical text is one of the
    points of disagreement dividing Beaujour and Sheringham. Beaujour argues for
    the distinctiveness of the autoportrait on the grounds that it abandons the myth
    of subjectivity as unified, preferring the acceptance of the self as fragmentation.
    Sheringham takes the view that many so-called autobiographies share an
    identical conception of the self as plural, heterogeneous, and inconsistent. Both
    Bourjea and Jarrety speak of the danger of imposing a false unity on Valéry's
    essentially fragmentary approach to writing.

76. This prospective dimension of the reflective surface is voiced by Narcisse, who
    claims: 'ce miroir ne me sert qu'à considérer ce qui, pour moi, n'est pas moi.
    [. . .] J'ai toujours fini d'être celui que son image retrouve et contemple' (XVIII,

707). Once again it is Beaujour who explores the idea of the mirror as integral to the construction of a rhetorically grounded self-portrait in terms which are strikingly similar to those employed by Valéry: 'On peut démontrer que l'autoportrait littéraire est une variante transformationnelle d'une structure dont relève également le *speculum* encyclopédique du Moyen Age. Cette structure — qu'on peut appeler *miroir* — a pour trait distinctif d'être à dominante *topique*. [. . .] On peut donc parler d'une *topo-logie*, ou logique spatiale, par opposition à la *chronologie* des textes à dominante narrative' (*Miroirs d'encre*, 34).

77. 'Pour comprendre cette entreprise', Valéry notes with regard to the *Cahiers*, 'écartez toute habitude littéraire. [. . .] chaque page y commence quelque chose qui n'est liée à la précédente que par le but final — Et c'est cependant une seule phrase continuée' (I, 765).

78. Beaujour discusses how the practice of the autoportrait postulates a 'corps autre'; '"le vrai corps", celui de la chair, de la topographie et de l'espace vécu, s'est mué en topique et typographie' (*Miroirs d'encre*, 309). Of interest, also, in this respect are Sheringham's comments on the role of the body in the context of Roland Barthes's autobiography: 'the body's difference is rooted in desire, in the realm of affect, and in its barometric sensitivity to the unconscious and to the troubled life of the psyche. The body is *par excellence* spatial, but its topology favours dispersal—much of what pertains to the somatic area is unlocatable and involves displacement [. . .]. In the process of writing, the body is freed of its own *imaginaire* and becomes an agency which attenuates and relativizes the place of the imaginary in the production of discourse, creating clearings or vacancies where something other than the imaginary is *incorporated*. It leads to words as transitional objects' (*French Autobiography*, 198–9).

79. Renza evokes a 'vector' or 'orientation' communicated by the self-defining mode of self-referential language typical of autobiography (in Olney, *Autobiography*, 295). Of interest in the same context is the following comment by Valéry: 'Le mythe MOI. Le langage est d'emprunt. Il se fait notre intime — et il crée même cette intimité — Ne fut-ce que par le mot MOI. Ainsi, *nous apprenons à être Nous* — à grouper des moments et souvenirs — et à les ordonner *implexement*, hiérarchiquement par rapport au "Moi" ou plutôt tellement que la *direction* moi en résulte [. . .] et le *Mythe moi* se développe' (XXIV, 215).

80. Significant in the context of a discussion of the Faustian *mélos* as just such a continuous or integral form is the following remark: 'Troisième Faust. La vie (j'entends ici la succession d'événements, états et impressions directes) successivement éclaire [. . .] et montre au spectateur extérieur comme au spectateur intime — un Même — — quantité d'aspects qui semblent composer un UN. Mais, d'abord, cet UN fait supposer ce qui unirait ces aspects accidentels' (XXIII, 723–4). Rachel Killick's analysis of the strophic structure of *Ebauche d'un serpent* explores a similar tension, imitative of the movement of a snake, between part and whole, discontinuity and implied continuity ('La Ligne et le cercle: structures d'un serpent', *BEV* 50–1 (1981), 67–76).

81. Paul Ricoeur's theory of narrative identity proposes to mediate the tension experienced by the human subject torn between change and continuity, punctual instant and continuous existence. 'Narrative identity is not the product of organic unfolding based on passive, intuitive understanding, but a dynamic modelling process driven by active, constructive processes at work in our

engagement with [. . .] the enigmas of temporal experience' (Sheringham, *French Autobiography*, 26). This view of identity as a dynamic temporal structure akin to the composition of a narrative text sheds light on Valéry's prospective approach to autobiographical subjectivity, emphasizing, as it does, that 'identity is to be conceived of not in terms of the same (*idem*) but in terms of "un soi-même" (*ipse*)' (p. 25).

82. His avowed intention of perpetuating the inherent difference at the heart of subjectivity—'Je ne travaille qu'à [. . .] devenir différent'—shares a conceptual space with the Derridean exploration of 'différence'. Derrida, bringing his thinking to bear on the possibility of signification, considers the paradox of structure and event. Rather than seek, as Western thought normally does, to resolve the paradox in favour of one entity over the other, Derrida proposes instead a position or approach of 'différence'. This designates both a passive difference already in existence as the condition of existence and an act of differing or deferring which produces differences. See *L'Ecriture et la différence* (Paris: Minuit, 1979). For both thinkers the question of priority is paramount: if differences are themselves created by punctual instants then what is present at any given moment is itself complex and differential, marked by a series of differences, irreducible to identity.

83. See Ch. 1 for a discussion of this same idea with reference to the constitution of voice as metaphor in Valéry's poetic theory.

84. 'L'objet de l'homme est la synthèse de l'homme — la retrouvaille de soi comme extrême de sa recherche' (XI, 437)

85. For an instance of this see his remark on the composition of *Mon Faust*: 'Je m'aperçois par le Faust [. . .] de ma constante propension à définir organiquement. [. . .] je *commence à ressentir* [une] *forme* indépendamment de toute application, et le besoin s'impose à moi d'isoler nettement, de concevoir formellement sa fonction' (XXIV, 624).

86. Psychoanalytic theory views the notion of an 'ideal self' from a number of angles. Freud situates it in the context of narcissism in his work on the integration of the ego ideal; the British object relations approach explores its significance in the context of creativity as reparation for fantasized damage inflicted on the maternal object (L. Layton and B. A. Schapiro (eds.), *Narcissism and the Text: Studies in Literature and the Psychology of Self* (New York: New York University Press, 1986)).

87. *Mélos* for Valéry is that particular type of formal functioning which brings the body into the world of art; it is, in a sense, the mediating concept which permits one to appreciate an entire area of theoretical reflection where he is at pains to define form as rooted in the functioning of the body. Form in art exists, he claims, to remind the consumer that s/he occupies a body (VII, 552); or, again, the very structure or form of a work of art is what interests or concerns our body (IX, 660); quite simply, 'Forme, c'est le corps' (XXIV, 635).

88. 'La mélodie, — *continu* engendré par des impulsions distinctes, par *discontinu*' (XIV, 206).

89. Discussing further the distinction drawn by Beaujour between two forms of memory at work in the field of self-writing, Sheringham observes: 'Autobiography, he claims, rests on belief in a coherent self, constituted through time, which can be accessed through the contents of personal memory: in this

genre, selfhood, memory and narrative are mutually supportive, natural phenomena. By contrast, practitioners of the "autoportrait" [. . .] lack confidence in a unified self, and therefore construct textual self-representations—non-narrative "miroirs d'encre"—out of avowedly heterogeneous materials [. . .]. Rather than trying to rejoin his past—or historical—self, he seeks, through the act of writing, to apprehend himself in the present: "l'autoportrait n'est pas une mémoire mais une machine à perpétuer le présent de l'écriture"' (*French Autobiography*, 307). In Valéry's exploitation of a degree of presentness encapsulated within the form of the voice a similar awareness appears to be at work.

90. Again this comes close to Beaujour's thesis that the autoportraitist bases his portrait of the self on rhetorical premisses deriving from 'memoria' and 'inventio' (*Miroirs d'encre*, 81–131). See also a further remark by Valéry asserting the tight interdependence of memory, form, and creativity in the understanding and reconstruction of the self: 'La mélodie est une idée inséparable d'une forme [. . .] La forme, ce qui ressemble à quelque chose — et *singulièrement à soi-même*. [. . .] Mémoire, forme, idées, invention, compréhension (complète) sont choses étroitement liées' (VI, 712).

91. 'La *forme* (au sens esthétique) implique une continuation sensible et une sommation-acquisition' (XXVIII, 70).

92. The remark continues: 'la présence [. . .] ressentie du "domaine" engendre un système d'éléments-événements [. . .] Le fait qu'un élément devienne un élément (de contruction) est capital. Il est typique d'abord dans la fonction Mémoire. Ce qui fut passager devient régulier, permanent-en-puissance [. . .] ce qui fut isolé reviendra en série. L'accidentel est promu fonctionnel' (XIX, 885).

93. 'Que de fois ai-je fait ceci ou cela!', he notes. 'Mais on peut moyennant un autre *grossissement*, dire, au contraire, que *rien ne se répète*. On a le choix' (XXVIII, 921).

94. It has been argued that what music does is to create an order of 'virtual time', a symbolic image of time measured by the motion of forms which seem to give it substance, yet a substance that consists entirely of sound (Suzanne Langer, *Feeling and Form: A Theory of Art* (London: Routledge & Kegan Paul, 1979), 104–19). Within this idealized conception of time rhythm, the pattern of tensions within the functioning of the body, forms the most vital component since it ensures that musical time has more than one dimension. This is, I think, what Valéry attempts to achieve in the figure of Faust, who features as a kind of distillate of organic functioning very close to that communicated by music.

95. A wide range of comments reveals the extent of Valéry's interest in the nature of this expanded moment or instant: 'Faust III. Vue ou poème de l'*Instant même* [. . .] L'*énergie du moment* [. . .] Densité certaine. [. . .] Le rien de temps chargé de plus de *valeur* qu'il n'en peut porter' (XXV, 760); 'L'instant [. . .] n'est pas un petit temps. C'est un temps quelconque mais compté *dans* un simultané' (XIV, 629); 'L'univers de l'instant est le quoi que ce soit compris entre deux mêmes' (XVI, 518); 'L'instant n'est pas un fragment de Temps — mais un entier / un tout — dont le Temps est un des caractères' (XVI, 4). And finally a revealing remark about himself in this context: 'L'*instant* me domine au dépens de l'avenir — c'est pourquoi tant de fragments ou instants' (XXVI, 865).

96. 'J'ai songé à une forme qui représenterait ce que nous nommons Présent. Cette *forme* définie et adoptée, plus de Temps — Rien hors d'elle — mais elle

contiendrait ce que nous percevons comme temps — et qui est sensations. [. . .] La sensation essentielle peut se nommer *dilatation* ou *écart*. Cet écart est *intérieur au présent*' (XVII, 458).

97. Ned Bastet, 'Ulysse et la sirène: le quatrième acte de "Lust"', in *Cahiers Paul Valéry*, 2 (Paris: Gallimard, 1977), 60. The unity of Faust and Lust is evoked on several occasions as, for example, 'Ego. Lust. [. . .] Je suis mon seul modèle. Car Lust et Faust sont *moi* — et rien que *moi*' (XXIX, 804); or again, with regard to *Mon Faust*, 'je me suis surpris me parlant à deux voix' (OII, 276–7).

98. See *BEV* 50–1 (1989) for a rich range of contemporary readings of the serpent symbol in Valéry's writings. My own emphasis, though clearly preoccupied with related concerns, lies more with the gendering of the serpent in its function as the voice of desire.

99. Aesthetic and psychoanalytic theories recognize that the artistic consciousness embraces a bisexual capacity; in other words, the process of giving birth to any form of art seems to require a creative thrust emerging from the unconscious and an application of creative mastery on the part of the ego, or conscious mind. To label these dimensions as 'masculine' and 'feminine' is potentially problematic although contemporary psychoanalytic and gender studies legitimate a sensitive use of these terms on the understanding that they are of provisional value, a kind of shorthand permitting discussion of highly complex areas of human functioning. Some of the material in the following section has already been published in 'Valéry and the Feminine', in Gifford and Stimpson (eds.), *Reading Paul Valéry*, 251–61.

100. 'Ce qui ne me coûte rien ne me donne pas la sensation d'avoir vécu — pas plus que d'engendrer ne donne de mal et fait moins auteur qu'enfanter. En quoi, je suis femelle. Elle est plus "profonde" que le mâle' (XV, 140).

101. The ideal of the androgyny has a long history in human thought and has come to be understood in contemporary psychological usage as an integrative model whereby male and female dimensions form a synthesis on a symbolic level. This model functions as an ideal whose symbolism remains, however, profoundly ambivalent, since it may either be linked with the polarization of difference as culturally constructed according to sexual stereotyping, or as a symbol of transcendence representing the denial of all differences.

102. Boa, 'Valéry's "Ego Poeta"', 52 and Sewell, *Paul Valéry: The Mind in the Mirror*, 18–19 are but two of a number of critics who comment on the significance of this aspect, although current trends in Valéry criticism tend to refute the value of attempts to impose a unity which they regard as unjustifiable.

103. In the context of contemporary psychoanalytical and philosophical inquiry into the status of subjectivity and its modes of representation, the classical vision of the unified subject collapses under the pressure of modernity. The 'otherness' or 'difference' marking this modern subject gives rise to a proliferation of conceptualizations. In one of its modes, the question of difference is sexualized: 'masculine' and 'feminine' are read as privileged metaphors expressing the crisis of established rational values and the possibility of alternative values. Suggestive discussion of this question is offered in Teresa Brennan (ed.), *Between Feminism and Psychoanalysis* (London: Routledge, 1989).

104. In 'Dieu et la jouissance de *LA* femme' Lacan observes: 'Cette jouissance qu'on éprouve et dont on ne sait rien, n'est-ce pas ce qui nous met sur la voie de l'ex-

sistence? Et pourquoi ne pas interpréter une face de l'Autre, la face Dieu, comme supportée par la jouissance féminine?' (*Le Séminaire, Livre XX, Encore* (Paris: Seuil, 1975), 71).

105. C. G. Jung, *Psychology and Religion* (New Haven: Yale University Press, 1938, repr. 1976), 18–19.

106. I am indebted to Boa for drawing my attention to this remark. He traces the psychological pattern of separation and division in a number of texts by Valéry and argues that, in metaphoric form, this pattern reveals the points at which lived experience and its poeticized expression meet. He isolates for special consideration the theme of the separation of the couple and its catastrophic consequences as manifested in an early sonnet and, later, in *La Jeune Parque*. Most intriguing of all, in the context of my argument, is his mention of the 'emergence of the serpent symbol [as] a vital turning point in the evolution of authorial intention [. . .]. It is a complex symbol, [. . .] paradoxically, both instigator of the heroine's inner division, and as *ouroboros*, unconscious prefiguration of that totality and unity to which the heroine consciously aspires' ('Valéry's "Ego Poeta"', 57–8).

107. Highly intriguing in this respect is the similarity between Jung's definition of archetypal images whose specific energy exerts a peculiar fascination and Valéry's reference to the potent effect of certain key images, identified as critical by A. R. Chisholm in '"La Pythie" and its Place in Valéry's Work', *MLR* 58 (1963), 21–8. I quote at length here since the closeness in the terminology used by the two authors is striking. Jung's definition of the archetype reads as follows: 'Logical analysis is the prerogative of consciousness; we select with reason and knowledge. The unconscious, however, seems to be guided chiefly by instinctive trends, represented by corresponding thought forms—that is, by the archetypes' (*Man and his Symbols* (London: Aldus Books, 1979), 78). Valéry's *Cahiers* jotting, noted by Chisholm, evokes the power of the image thus: 'Les animaux qui font le plus horreur à l'homme, qui l'inquiètent dans ses pensées, le chat, la pieuvre, le reptile / l'araignée... sont ceux dont la figure, l'œil, les allures ont quelque chose de *psychologique*. Ils ressemblent à des pensées ou à des arrière-pensées et donnent, par conséquence, l'idée qu'ils en ont. Fantaisie: Peut-être, sont-ils ceux qui ont failli passer à l'intelligence et être à la place de l'homme. Peut-être de terribles expériences ont eu lieu contre des bêtes qui avaient quelque similitude avec celles-ci, et que des "associations" invincibles se sont formées? Ces antipathies toutes puissantes font voir qu'il y a en nous une mythologie, une fable latente — un folklore nerveux, difficile à isoler car il se confond sur ses bords, peut-être, avec des effets de la sensibilité qui, eux, sont purement moléculaires, extra psychiques' (VI, 147). It is Chisholm's observations which encouraged me to establish a link with Jung, for he notes: 'in the light of Valéry's "mythology", the serpent in particular becomes an appropriate symbol of thought; not so much the thought that is always at the level of consciousness, as the thought that lurks in hidden places of the mind. We might almost say it is the thought emanating from the body and counter-balancing the abstractions of pure intellect' (p. 27).

108. One of the most intriguing aspects of the genesis of the various manuscript versions of the poems of *Charmes* to emerge from de Lussy's study is precisely the all-pervasive and insinuating influence of the serpent at many levels.

109. 'Cette âme "hydre"' of *Ode secrète* 'c'est l'âme du dormeur sombrant dans les fantasmes du rêve' (de Lussy, *'Charmes'*, i. 143).

110. 'Or, ce que Valéry appelle "Le sentiment de *fécondité infinie*" (VI, 432) se définit pour lui par "une sorte de *sensation de possibilité* qui prend sa source dans la substance même de la connaissance" (XXVII, 275), sensation étroitement associée d'ailleurs au fameux "Ouroboros" qui se mord la queue' (Crow, 'Ebauche d'une ébauche... Voyage autour d'un titre valéryen', *BEV* 50–1 (1989), 35–44 at 39).

111. 'Une brève nomenclature que l'on peut dater avec une relative précision du mois de novembre 1918, met en parallèle "Eve" et *La Pythie*:

> 'Aurore
> Pythie
> Eve
> Palme'

(*Ch.* MS I, 9, in de Lussy, *'Charmes'*, i. 335).

112. Brian Stimpson reads *Ebauche d'un serpent* as expression of the subversion of confidence in the consistency of the Subject ('L'Espace parmi: une rhétorique de l'ambiguïté', *BEV* 50–1 (1989), 45–56). And a *Cahiers* remark (quoted in de Lussy, *'Charmes'*, i. 204), highlights further this sense of self-division: 'PPA. Greffe — auto-greffe — Je suis un être greffé. Je me suis fait à moi-même plusieurs greffes. Greffer des mathématiques sur la poésie, de la rigueur sur des images libres. Des "idées claires" sur un tronc "superstitieux"; du langage français sur un bois italien' (VII, 70).

113. De Lussy, *'Charmes'*, i. 335. Valéry, in relation to *Ebauche*, notes its value to him in referring to it as 'Etude d'une transformation' (*Ch.* MS I, 235, in de Lussy, i. 348).

114. De Lussy indicates, for example, the multiple origins of *La Pythie*, born, in part, from the same sonorous ocean as *Le Cimetière marin* (pp. 37, 79), in part from a rhythmic impulse demanding form (p. 133), and, equally, from the prosodic structure and theme of a strophe from Victor Hugo's *Lumière* (p. 164).

115. Evoking the birth of *La Jeune Parque* in Valéry's desire to follow the modulations of existence, de Lussy notes: 'Mais, à peine entrouverte, l'âme — "Pandore" — (deux des toutes premières versions de l'ouverture de *La Jeune Parque* portent ce titre) laisse apparaître un monstre qui se tord sous la figure symbolique du Serpent' (p. 14). Similarly, the link between feminine and serpentine is established in the following remark: '"Le songe que vient de faire la Jeune Parque lui apparaît à elle-même comme une *ébauche* du moi qu'elle ignorait", nous dit Duchesne-Guillemin, commentant ce fameux geste mythopoétique d'être vertigineux qui s'enlace' (Crow, 'Ebauche d'une ébauche', 40).

116. 'Le parallélisme établi entre "Eve" et *La Pythie* révèle que Valéry entend donner à "l'air" du Serpent un volume et une importance comparables à ceux de *La Pythie*' (de Lussy, p. 335). Eve is, in a sense, the Serpent, as the ambiguity of the narrative voice in *Ebauche*, strophe 27, ll. 1–4 suggests—'la fusion d'Eve et du Serpent dans une même expérience ambiguë de possession manquée et de joie déçue' (Killick, 'La Ligne et le cercle', 71–2).

117. De Lussy distinguishes valuably between the deep-seated level of poetic creativity and the final form which this receives in the published text: 'Rien n'évoque plus authentiquement l'essence même de la poésie que ce carrefour de poèmes, lieu

des métamorphoses et des possibles [. . .]. Il y a quelque fruit à opposer la poésie, qui est en perpétuelle mouvance et comme à la recherche d'elle-même, au poème, dont la forme "définitive" ne doit, le plus souvent, d'être fixée qu'à des contraintes toutes extérieures' (p. 240).

118. Several critics have explored the vital importance of the feminine element of Valéry's creative activity: in addition to Chisholm and Sewell, Charles Whiting's 'Femininity in Valéry's Early Poetry', *YFS* 9 (1965), 74–83 offers valuable insights. More recently, in Elisabeth Howe, *Stages of Self: The Dramatic Monologues of Laforgue, Valéry and Mallarmé* (Athens: Ohio University Press, 1990), the question of the serpent in relation to *La Jeune Parque* conceived as a spiritual autobiography receives attention, though little is said about the significance of the feminine gender of speakers of other monologues in Valéry's work.

119. Is it in this sense that one should understand his remark: 'Mélos. Comment définir ce trait divin — cette forme ou ligne d'univers que l'homme peut *engendrer* [. . .] mais qu'il ne peut *concevoir*' (X, 172)? [My italics.]

120. A *Cahiers* entry for *Air de Sémiramis* notes: 'Le prêtre tenant son ciboire, portant de bouche en bouche l'hostie / la mystérieuse nourriture, — semble un gros insecte d'or qui féconde infatigable des files de femelles —' (VII, 141, in de Lussy, p. 297).

121. De Lussy, revealing how certain unused strophes from *La Pythie* evoke other poems, notes: 'Face à l'évocation d'une Pythie mugissante et hors d'elle, Valéry dresse l'image contrastée d'une sagesse maîtresse de ses emportements, libre et "capable de tous les orgueils", préfigurant, par-delà la vision idéalisée du Moi, une reine Sémiramis qui envahira bientôt (en mai 1918) et pour longtemps, l'imaginaire valéryen' (pp. 168–9).

122. A further development of one of the strophes which, although originally part of *La Pythie*, ultimately shares more of the tonality of Sémiramis (de Lussy, p. 214). The emergence of Sémiramis from similar roots to those of *La Pythie* points to her connection with the serpent; Valéry was working on *Air de Sémiramis* alongside *La Pythie* and intended to contrast the two female figures (p. 256). See below, n. 125.

123. *AVA* MS, 165bis in de Lussy, p. 196.

124. *Cahiers* notes associate her with the fecundity of 'la reine des abeilles': 'Le Secret de la Reine — (des abeilles) Tout ce mystère de la création des reines — Quel sérail égyptien ou de Ninive' (VII, 141) in de Lussy, p. 297. One may perhaps read her presence as very explicitly associated with a feminine creativity essential to the poet's imagination.

125. In a note which relates and yet contrasts *La Pythie* and *Air de Sémiramis* it is the latter's quality as vocal energy which emerges:

> Chaque strophe de cette P[ythie]
> aurait dû être une face
> de la chose — et chaque strophe
> une attitude psychique et phys[ique]
>
> Sémiramis? autre —
> la puissance, la bêtise
> le jardin suspendu

aller rêver sur ces ponts de roses
abîmes.
                    énergie de la voix
(Cah. *Ch* IV, 5 in de Lussy, p. 256).

126. Highly revealing in this context of masculine and feminine components of the creative psyche is the interplay between the Pythia and Sémiramis as regards the birth of the voice which now occupies so important a position at the end of *La Pythie* (cf. Honneur des Hommes, Saint Langage). The genesis of this stanza, and the shifts from manuscript to manuscript which it undergoes, suggest an oscillation in Valéry's mind between masculine and feminine connotations of voice and language which are closely related to the foregoing discussion. Originally, and until a very late stage in its development towards its definitive state, *La Pythie* was meant to conclude as follows:

> Je suis la parole et la reine
> Simple en dépit de mes joyaux
> Pathétique et pourtant sereine
> Secrète et les regards loyaux;
> Divinement contradictoire
> Sous les ailes d'une victoire
> Gardant la pudeur et le deuil
> Libre, et de chaînes d'or baignée
> Mais de moi-même dédaignée
> Je jette l'ombre de l'orgueil.
> (Cah. *Ch* IV, 5 in de Lussy, p. 214)

It is worth noting the grammatical gender of the terms and images used here to evoke the power of language. Indeed, an earlier version of this same stanza stresses even more strongly the feminine connotations of the word as well as its power of mastery:

> O pure, ô non prostituée
> O sage, ô claire, ô chaste, ô plus
> Docile aux dieux qu'une nuée
> Qui cède aux souffles absolus,
> Leur esclave et qui soit maîtresse
> De tes maîtres, ô charmeresse
> Grande parole, chasseresse
> Des   de l'esprit
> (Cah. *Ch* II, 52ᵛ in de Lussy, p. 249)

In contrast the opening lines of the stanza which now concludes *La Pythie* ('Honneur des Hommes, Saint Language / Discours prophétique et paré') are significantly masculinized both in the grammatical gender and in the attributes of the linguistic power addressed, although the feminine as wisdom, anonymity, and voice is not entirely banished from the scene. In fact, these lines originally emerged from an early variant of *Aurore*, at that time entitled *Hymne*. De Lussy notes how, even at this stage, the stanza seemed 'étrangère à cette sphère d'inspiration' [*La Pythie*] (p. 149). Perhaps this deviant origin accounts for the sense of hiatus created at the end of *La Pythie*, for the strange impression of unfittingness, or alien quality of the discourse which is hailed as beneficent and whose origins were, in fact, in a feminine matrix (*Aurore, La Pythie, Sémiramis*).

127. In the Sufi tradition its presence permits a fully evolved state of consciousness to be achieved and, in Graeco-Roman mythology, it represents a mediating energy which connects heaven and earth. Llewellyn Vaughan-Lee, *The Lover and the Serpent: Dreamwork within a Sufi Tradition* (Shaftesbury: Element Books, 1990). James Lawler refers to the associations connecting serpent image and a desire for unity: '[Valéry] frequently used the image of the serpent to designate multiple facets of the mind that stretches out to know then waits for the body to join it' (*The Poet as Analyst: Essays on Paul Valéry* (Berkeley and Los Angeles: University of California Press, 1974), 256).

128. In this view, the serpent is an *imago* or archetypal image produced by the soul or creative spirit to enable it to experience itself fully; as the soul awakens to itself on the path of individuation it articulates its need for an absolutely individual expression of itself through symbols and tutelary figures or images, whose function is to ensure that it remains in contact with the deepest manifestations of its desire. James Hillman refers to the image in this role as '*psychopompos* or guide', suggesting that the psychic image is the shaman that human beings imitate (Shaun McNiff, *Art as Medicine* (London and Boston: Shambhala, 1992), 19). Very often these shamanic images adopt the guise of animals.

129. Valéry accords full recognition to the power of the image to resonate within the psyche on a virtually unconscious level when he refers, for example, to a process of 'imprégnation psychique d'une image' (XXIV, 803). Lawler points in the direction of unconscious processes in identifying an aspect of Valéry's compositional technique whereby the basic needs of the sensibility are satisfied in aesthetic form but in an implicit manner; the poet can communicate an image by formal treatment alone without expressing it explicitly (*The Poet as Analyst*, 258–60). In a similar vein Sewell, discussing the significance of *La Jeune Parque* in Valéry's creative biography, intriguingly suggests that it marks the self's assent to its own being, a 'forgiveness' of itself which is achieved through form (*Paul Valéry: The Mind in the Mirror*, 52–3).

130. Jung describes it as follows: 'The *coniunctio oppositorum*, [. . .] the royal brother–sister or mother–son pair, occupies such an important place in alchemy that sometimes the entire process takes the form of the *hierosgamos* and its mystic consequences' (*The Psychology of the Transference* (London: Routledge & Kegan Paul, 1983), 36). And, again: 'the real meaning of the *coniunctio* is that it brings to birth something that is one and united. It restores the vanished "man of light" who is identical with the Logos in Gnostic and Christian symbolism and who was there before the creation' (p. 86). 'The *coniunctio* [. . .] is an altogether transmundane event, a process occurring in the psychic non-ego [. . .] the *coniunctio* is a *hierosgamos* of the gods and not a mere love-affair between mortals' (p. 129).

131. Jung, too, evokes its significance as an expression of individuation in a discussion of a voice heard by one of his clients in a dream: 'Since the contents of our minds are only conscious and perceivable insofar as they are associated with an ego, the phenomenon of the voice, having a strongly personal character, may also issue from a centre—one, however, which is not identical with that of our conscious ego. Such reasoning is permissible if we conceive of the ego as being

subordinated to, or contained in, a superordinated self as a centre of the total, illimitable and indefinable psychic personality' (*Psychology and Religion*, 48).

132. The shadow is not coextensive with the unconscious personality but represents rather unknown or little-known attributes and qualities of the ego which may be denied in the self but seen in others. As Jung remarks: 'Wholeness is not so much perfection as completeness. Assimilation of the shadow gives a man body, so to speak; the animal sphere of instinct, as well as the primitive or archaic psyche, emerge into the zone of consciousness and can no longer be repressed by fictions and illusions' (*The Psychology of the Transference*, 77).

133. For the following discussion of the concept of *anima* see James Hillman, *Anima: An Anatomy of a Personified Notion* (Dallas: Spring Publications, 1987). The dangers of gender stereotyping are evident yet, personally, I value the imaginative potential of such hypotheses. Hillman's account constitutes a genuine attempt to explore the difficulties and subtleties of this problematic and precarious area in Jung's thought with balance and sensitivity.

134. Celeyrette-Pietri points suggestively in the same direction in her discussion of Agathe, yet another of Valéry's feminine *personae*: 'Agathe désigne peut-être aussi, devenue parlante, la "statue d'enfant nue et noire" qui s'est nommée Psyche et fut une sœur obscure et désincarnée de Narcisse' (*'Agathe' ou 'Le manuscrit trouvé dans une cervelle' de Valéry* (Archives Paul Valéry, 4; Paris: Minard, 1981), 63).

135. 'Since time immemorial man in his myths always manifested the idea of a coexistence of male and female in the same body. Such psychological intuitions were usually projected in the form of the divine syzygia, the divine pair, or of the idea of the hermaphroditic nature of the creator' (*Psychology and Religion*, 34).

136. 'Puis-je t'aimer, si je te contiens à titre d'être' ('Ulysse et la sirène', 119; all citations are from this article). Kurt Weinberg evokes Lust's role as that of 'the eternally feminine that leads us to the very centre of the self' (*The Figure of Faust in Valéry and Goethe* (Princeton: Princeton University Press, 1976), 38), and points to the richness of the integrative encounter of component parts of the personality: 'all of Faust's efforts to fool existence through the thinking act of the *cogito* are abolished, in the end, by the heart mirroring its tenderness in its own reflection, in Lust' (p. 37).

137. Bastet refers to the verbal technique at work in the manuscripts through which voice embraces voice as 'le procédé du "retournement" [. . .] cette reprise et cette explication par Faust de ce qui, chez Lust, se balbutie ou s'ignore encore' ('Ulysse et la sirène', 117).

138. Several contemporary interpretations attempt to penetrate the mysterious otherness of these texts. Close readings of specific texts are offered by Hélène Domon on 'Xiphos l'îlisible' (*BEV* 62 (1993), 15–27) and Anne Fontvielle on '*Acem*: une sortie de la Métaphysique' (*BEV* 64 (1993), 65–75) and 'Lecture de *Rachel* (*BEV* 68 (1995), 41–57). See also Jarrety, *Valéry devant la littérature*, 333–41 for an analysis of their textual function as subversion of representation, and Stimpson for a reading of these texts as redefining fiction in 'Counter-fiction', in Gifford and Stimpson (eds.), *Reading Paul Valéry*, 138–54.

139. 'Enfin, il arrive aussi que [. . .] je me mette à écrire ce qui s'était formé tout seul dans ma tête. [. . .] Il m'arrive de noter l'essentiel de ce qui m'est venu' (OII, 407).

140. Celeyrette-Pietri's analysis of *Agathe* follows a similar path in identifying the

proximity of internal discourse of consciousness with the voice of the unconscious; she discusses the significance of the feminine aspect in the context of the longstanding 'rêve synthétique' which informs Valéry's writing (*'Agathe' ou 'Le manuscrit trouvé dans une cervelle' de Valéry*).

141. 'Voici donc le recueil paradoxal de fragments' (OII, 408).

142. In Jung's conception, the nucleus of the psyche (the self) normally expresses itself in some kind of fourfold structure; the number four is also connected with the *anima*, because there are four stages in its development of which the fourth is symbolized by Sapientia, wisdom transcending even the most holy and the most pure (*Man and his Symbols*, 185). Jung also comments that, in Christian symbolism, the Trinity 'is of an exclusively masculine character. The unconscious mind, however, transforms it into a quaternity, being a unity at the same time, just as the three persons of the Trinity are one and the same God. The old philosophers of nature represented the Trinity [. . .] as water, air and fire. The fourth constituent on the other hand was [. . .] the earth or body. In this way they added the feminine element to their physical Trinity, producing thereby the *quaternity* or *circulus madratus*, the symbol of which was the hermaphroditic [. . .] *filius sapientiae*' (*Psychology and Religion*, 76). He notes elsewhere that the quaternity symbol of the squared circle may be shaped from the form of the serpent (p. 78).

143. '"Une porte ouverte, et une porte ouverte, Assem entre les deux, n'est-ce point une symbole du possible? Ou bien une sorte d'invitation à je ne sais quoi qui doit être d'entrer ici?... Après tout, que me font ces deux portes?"' (OII, 454).

CONCLUSION

The informing, mysterious presence of voice and of sound as accompaniments to consciousness throughout Valéry's writing life represents a nourishing 'enveloppe'. It serves as a kind of imaginary membrane, intuited, necessary, self-generated, surrounding and supporting the living, thinking being. It can be envisaged as a fragile, abstract casing or malleable form within whose parameters intellect and creative sensibility unfold. *Per sona*, etymon of personality, speaks of this sonorous ambience in which a subjectivity comes into existence, acquires definition; the 'sound which passes through' the complexity of the human organism lends it identity and, ultimately, style.[1]

Voice, for Valéry, is perhaps a form of imagination. It represents a space, presence, concept which allows free rein to the power of fantasy, liberating the subjectivity of desire into the realm of images and their fertilizing potential. Voice points beyond itself to the unknowable, to the unnameable, expressing an inherent yearning within the human being for a dimension of experience which cannot be delimited by language. Valéry's preoccupation with its immaterial enchantment suggests that his creative research may be situated within a dominant concern of twentieth-century art. Some of the most provocative and innovative statements of the modernist and post-modernist periods open up an alternative space for the a/theological imagination,[2] a space in which cultural expression, though no longer reflective of a theocentric awareness, retains a conviction that human creativity, however fragmented, evanescent, and incomplete its productions, possesses a spiritual significance. At a time, such as the present, when figuration—as form, shape, image, likeness, representation of either the material or the immaterial, theory—is necessarily called into question, disfigurement permits recognition of the failure to resolve issues in the framework of theory, suggests an inability to decipher or a lack of comprehension. Voice, within this context of a desacralized modernity, may be one manifestation of 'une fonction déchirée'; it is the trace of an effacement through which the impossibility of representing either presence or presentation is made apparent. Disfiguring gives fleeting form to the unfigurable.[3]

Valéry's pursuit of voice, the trace of a fragmented subjectivity which this study has explored, leads to precisely such a confrontation between consciousness and world as an encounter with dissolving structures and evanescent forms. The song of the serpent, elusive, simultaneously punctual and continuous in its vibration as form, embodies that intuition of the contemporary creative consciousness: the work of art—whether created object, theory, or reformulated self—hovers, provisionally, beyond the reach of language, at the limit between absence and presence. Words can do no more than frame their object, establishing it in a context or matrix from which it seeks to free itself. Language, of whose inadequacy Valéry was only too aware, and voice, whose complexity defies theorization, form a constellation in which each is necessary though not reducible to the other.

Notes to the Conclusion

1. P. Newham, *The Singing Cure: An Introduction to Voice Movement Therapy* (London: Rider, 1993), 37.
2. This is the term which Mark Taylor uses to describe the 'middle ground between classical theology and atheism', in his suggestive study of the interrelationship of art and religion: *Disfiguring: Art, Architecture, Religion* (Chicago: University of Chicago Press, 1992), 4.
3. Taylor, *Disfiguring*, 7–8.

BIBLIOGRAPHY

I Works by Valéry

Cahiers, 20 vols. (Paris: CNRS, 1957–61).
Cours de poétique, Yggdrasill, IX–XXIV, 25 déc. 1937–25 fév. 1939.
'Deux lettres inédites sur Stéphane Mallarmé' (1912), *Fontaine* 44 (1945), 556–61.
Lettres à quelques-uns, 1889–1943 (Paris: Gallimard, 1952).
Œuvres, ed. Jean Hytier, 2 vols. (Bibliothèque de la Pléiade, 1; Paris: Gallimard, vol. 1, 1975; vol. 2, 1970).
Paul Valéry – André Gide. Correspondance 1890–1940 (Paris: Gallimard, 1955).
Paul Valéry – Gustave Fourment. Correspondance 1887–1933 (Paris: Gallimard, 1957).
Pré-Teste, ed. F. Chapon (Paris: Bibliothèque Littéraire Jacques Doucet, 3–23 déc. 1966).
Vues (Paris: La Table Ronde, 1948).

II Secondary Literature

ABRAMS, M. H., *The Mirror and the Lamp: Romantic Theory and the Critical Tradition* (Oxford: Oxford University Press, 1979).
AIGRISSE, GILBERTE, *Psychanalyse de Paul Valéry* (Paris: Editions universitaires, 1964).
ANDERSON, KIRSTEEN, 'Valéry and Narcissus: Reflections on Auditive Consciousness', in K. Aspley, D. Bellos, P. Sharatt (eds.), *Myth and Legend in French Literature: Essays in honour of A. J. Steele* (Modern Humanities Research Association, 11; London: Modern Humanities Research Association, 1982), 184–209.
—— 'Valéry and the Feminine', in Gifford and Stimpson (eds.), *Reading Paul Valéry*, 251–61.
—— 'Valéry et la voix mystique: la rencontre du féminin', in *Paul Valéry: musique, mystique, mathématique*, ed. Gifford and Stimpson, 277–92.
—— 'Valéry et son éternel Narcisse: une alternative misosophique au problème de l'autobiographie', in *Colloque Paul Valéry*, ed. Ince, 139–53.
—— 'Valéry et Tomatis: étude sur la conscience auditive du poète', *BEV* 20 (1979), 27–44.

AUSTIN, L. J., 'Modulation and Movement in Valéry's Verse', *YFS* 44 (1970), 19–38.

—— 'Les Moyens du mystère chez Mallarmé et chez Valéry', *CAIEF* 15 (1963), 103–17.

—— 'The Negative Plane Tree', *L'Esprit créateur* 4 (1964), 3–10.

—— 'Paul Valéry: "Teste" ou "Faust"?', *CAIEF* 17 (1965), 245–56.

BACHELARD, GASTON, *L'Eau et les rêves: essai sur l'imagination de la matière* (Paris: José Corti, 1942).

—— *La Poétique de l'espace* (Paris: Presses Universitaires de France, 1957).

BARTHES, ROLAND, *Critique et vérité* (Paris: Seuil, 1966).

BASTET, NED, 'Faust et le cycle', *ENC* (1968), 115–28.

—— 'Genèse et affects: le Fragment II du *Narcise*', in Levaillant (ed.), *Ecriture*, ch. 3.

—— 'Langage et fracture chez Valéry', *PVC* (1974), 75–92.

—— *La Symbolique des images dans l'œuvre poétique de Valéry* (Aix-en-Provence: Publication des Annales de la Faculté des Lettres, 24; 1962).

—— 'Towards a Biography of the Mind', in Gifford and Stimpson (eds.), *Reading Paul Valéry*, 17–35.

—— 'Ulysse et la sirène: le quatrième acte de "Lust"', *Cahiers Paul Valéry*, 2 (Paris: Gallimard, 1977), 49–141.

—— *Valéry à l'extrême: les au-delà de la raison* (Paris: L'Harmattan, 1999).

—— 'Valéry et la clôture tragique', *AJFS* 8 (1971), 103–17.

—— 'Valéry et la voix poétique', *Annales de la Faculté des lettres et sciences humaines de Nice* 15 (1971), 41–50.

BATTERSBY, CHRISTINE, *Gender and Genius: Towards a Feminist Aesthetics* (London: Women's Press, 1989).

BEAUJOUR, MICHEL, *Miroirs d'encre: rhétorique de l'autoportrait* (Paris: Seuil, 1980).

BELLEMIN-NOËL, JEAN, *Les Critiques de notre temps et Valéry* (Paris, 1971).

—— 'En marge des premiers "Narcisse" de Valéry: l'en-jeu et le hors-jeu du texte', *RHLF* 70 (1970), 975–91.

BÉMOL, MAURICE, *La Parque et le Serpent, essais sur les formes et mythes* (Paris: Société d'Edition Les Belles Lettres, 1955).

BENVENUTO, BICE, and KENNEDY, ROGER, *The Works of Jacques Lacan: An Introduction* (London: Free Association Books, 1986).

BERGSON, HENRI, *Essai sur les données immédiates de la conscience* (Paris: Félix Alcan, 1909).

—— *Matière et mémoire: essai sur la relation du corps à l'esprit* (Paris: Félix Alcan, 1908).

BERSANI, LEO, *The Freudian Body: Sexuality and Art* (New York: Columbia University Press, 1986).

BLANCHOT, MAURICE, *L'Espace littéraire* (Paris: Gallimard, 1955).

BLÜHER, KARL A., 'L'Instant faustien — la quête du bonheur dans le mythe de Faust de Goethe à Valéry', *BEV* 11 (1976), 32–47.

—— and SCHMIDT-RADEFELDT, JÜRGEN (eds.), *Paul Valéry: le cycle de 'Mon Faust' devant la sémiotique théâtrale et l'analyse textuelle*. Colloque international de Kiel, 15–17 oct. 1987 (Tübingen, 1991).

BOA, PETER, 'Valéry's "Ego Poeta"—Towards a Biography of the Authorial Self', *Neophilologus* 62 (1978), 51–62.

BOURJEA, SERGE, 'L'Ennemi du tendre', *BEV* 24 (1980), 33–43.

—— 'La Fonction nocturne dans l'imaginaire valéryen', *BEV* 10 (1976), 32–49.

—— '"ou n'ose qu'à demi..." — l'invention de l'écriture', *BEV* 58 (1991), 57–87.

—— *Paul Valéry: le sujet de l'écriture* (Paris: L'Harmattan, 1997).

—— 'Sang et soleil de la Parque — "La Jeune Parque" et l'Eternel Retour', in *Paul Valéry 2: recherches sur 'La Jeune Parque'*, textes réunis par H. Laurenti (Paris: Minard, 1977), 123–46.

—— 'La Sensibilité dans les "Cahiers" de Paul Valéry', *BEV* 19 (1978), 37–58.

—— 'Soutenir', *BEV* 71 (1996), 5–22.

—— (ed.), *Mélange c'est l'esprit, volume d'hommages offert à Huguette Laurenti* (Paris: Minard, 1989).

BOWIE, MALCOLM, 'Dream and the Unconscious', in Gifford and Stimpson (eds.), *Reading Paul Valéry*, 262–79.

BRENNAN, TERESA (ed.), *Between Feminism and Psychoanalysis* (London: Routledge, 1989).

CAILLOIS, ROGER, *Approches de l'imaginaire* (Paris: Gallimard, N.R.F., 1974).

CAIN, LUCIENNE J., 'Métamorphoses de Narcisse', in *Paul Valéry, 1: Lectures de 'Charmes'*, textes réunis par H. Laurenti (Paris: Minard, 1974), 9–28.

CARDINAL, ROGER C. (ed.), *Sensibility and Creation: Studies in Twentieth-Century French Poetry* (London: Croom Helm, 1977).

CASEY, EDWARD, *Imagining: A Phenomenological Study* (Bloomington, IN: Indiana University Press, 1979).

CELEYRETTE-PIETRI, NICOLE, *'Agathe' ou 'Le manuscrit trouvé dans une cervelle' de Valéry* (Archives Paul Valéry, 4; Paris: Minard, 1981).

—— *Valéry et le moi: des Cahiers à l'œuvre* (Paris: Klincksieck, 1979).

—— (ed.), *Problèmes du langage chez Paul Valéry* (Archives Paul Valéry, 6; Paris: Minard, 1987).

CHASSEGUET-SMIRGEL, J., *Pour une psychanalyse de l'art et de la créativité* (Paris: Payot, 1971).

CHISHOLM, A. R., *An Approach to M. Valéry's Jeune Parque* (Melbourne: Melbourne University Press, 1938).

—— *Mallarmé's Grand œuvre* (Manchester: Manchester University Press, 1962).

—— '"La Pythie" and its Place in Valéry's Work', *MLR* 58 (1963), 21–8.

—— 'Victorious Eve (Ebauche d'un Serpent)', *AJFS* 8 (1971), 139–45.

COCTEAU, JEAN, *La Voix humaine* (Paris: Stock, 1930).

Colloque Paul Valéry: amitiés de jeunesse, influences, lectures, Université d'Edimbourg, nov. 1976: texte établi par Carl Barbier (Paris: Nizet, 1978).

Colloque Paul Valéry: Valéry et la littérature du passé, Université de Southampton, sept. 1982: texte établi par Walter Ince (London: Southampton University Department of French, 1984).

Corps et écriture: Actes du Colloque de Sète, *BEV* numéro spécial, 65–6 (1994).

CROW, CHRISTINE M., 'Ebauche d'une ébauche... Voyage autour d'un titre valéryen', *BEV* 50–1 (1989), 35–44.

—— '"Teste parle": The Question of a Potential Artist in Valéry's M. Teste', *YFS* 44 (1970), 157–68.

—— 'Paul Valéry and Maxwell's Demon: Natural Order and Human Possibility', *Occasional Papers in Modern Languages* No. 8 (Hull: University of Hull, 1972).

—— *Paul Valéry and the Poetry of Voice* (Cambridge: Cambridge University Press, 1982).

—— *Paul Valéry: Consciousness and Nature* (Cambridge: Cambridge University Press, 1972).

CULLER, JONATHAN, 'Jacques Derrida', in Sturrock (ed.), *Structuralism and Since*, 154–81.

—— *Structuralist Poetics: Structuralism, Linguistics and the Study of Poetry* (London: Routledge & Kegan Paul, 1975).

DALMOLIN, E., 'Du maternel au maternage poétique: Valéry et l'enfant', *BEV* 72–3 (1996), 233–45.

DÉCAUDIN, MICHEL, 'Narcisse: une sorte d'autobiographie poétique', *L'Information littéraire* 2 (1956), 45–55.

DERRIDA, JACQUES, *De la grammatologie* (Paris: Minuit, 1967).

—— *L'Ecriture et la différence* (Paris: Minuit, 1979).

—— 'La Forme et le vouloir-dire: note sur la phénoménologie du langage', *Revue internationale de philosophie* 21 (1967), 277–99.

—— 'Les Sources de Valéry qual quelle', *MLN* 87 (1972), 563–99.

—— *La Voix et le phénomène: introduction au problème du signe dans la phénoménologie de Husserl* (Paris: Presses Universitaires de France, 1967).

DOANE, MARY ANNE, 'The Voice in the Cinema: The Articulation of Body and Space', *YFS* 60 (1980), 33–50.

DOMON, HÉLÈNE, 'Xiphos l'îlisible', *BEV* 62 (1993), 15–25.

DUCHESNE-GUILLEMIN, JACQUES, *Etudes pour un Paul Valéry* (Neuchâtel: La Baconnière, 1964).

—— 'Valéry au miroir: les "Cahiers" et l'exégèse des grands poèmes', *FS* 20 (1966), 348–65.

EHRENZWEIG, ANTON, *The Psychoanalysis of Artistic Vision and Hearing* (New York: George Braziller, 1965).

ELIADE, MIRCEA, *Le Sacré et le profane* (Paris: Gallimard, Folio, 1965).

Entretiens sur Paul Valéry: Décades du Centre Culturel International de Cérisy-la-Salle, du 2 au 11 sept. 1965, sous la direction de E. Noulet-Carner (Paris: Mouton, 1968) (abbreviated *ENC*).

Entretiens sur Paul Valéry: Actes du colloque de Montpellier des 16 et 17 oct. 1971: textes recueillis par Daniel Moutote (Paris: Presses Universitaires de France, 1972) (abbreviated *EM*).

FAIVRE, J. L., *Paul Valéry et le thème de la lumière* (Thèmes et mythes, 13; Paris: Minard, 1975).

FEHR, A. J. A., *Les Dialogues antiques de Paul Valéry: essai d'analyse d'Eupalinos ou l'Architecte* (Leiden: Universitaire Pers, 1960).

FÓNAGY, I., 'Les Bases pulsionnelles de la phonation', *Revue française de psychanalyse* 34 (1970), 101–36 and 35 (1971), 543–91.

—— 'The Functions of Vocal Style', in S. Chatman (ed.), *Literary Style: a Symposium* (Oxford: Oxford University Press, 1971), 159–76.

FONTVIELLE, ANNE, '*Acem*: une sortie de la métaphysique', *BEV* 64 (1993), 65–75.

—— 'Lecture de *Rachel*', *BEV* 68 (1995), 41–57.

FREUD, SIGMUND, *Introductory Lectures on Psychoanalysis* (The Pelican Freud Library, 1, 14: *Art and Literature*; Harmondsworth: Penguin, 1976).

FROMILHAGUE, RENÉ, '"La Jeune Parque" et "l'autobiographie dans la forme"', *PVC* (1974), 209–35.

GAÈDE, EDOUARD, 'Le Continu et le discontinu dans les "Cahiers" de Valéry', *Revue de métaphysique et de morale* 70 (1965), 173–91.

GALAY, J. L., 'Problèmes de l'œuvre fragmentale: Valéry', *Poétique* 31 (1977), 337–67.

GALLOP, JANE, *Thinking through the Body* (New York: Columbia University Press, 1988).

GENETTE, GÉRARD, *Figures*, 3 vols. (Paris: Seuil, 1966, 1969, 1972).

—— 'Valéry and the Poetics of Language', in Harari (ed.), *Textual Strategies*, 359–73.

—— 'Valéry et la poétique du langage', *MLN* 87 (1972), 600–15.

GHEORGE, ION, *Les Images du poète et de la poésie dans l'œuvre de Valéry* (Langues et styles, 6; Paris: Minard, 1977).

GIAVERI, MARIA, 'La "voix ignorée" de *La Jeune Parque*', *BEV* 29 (1982), 45–61.

GIBSON, ROBERT (ed.), *Modern French Poets on Poetry* (Cambridge: Cambridge University Press, 1961).

GIDE, ANDRÉ, *Paul Valéry* (Paris: Domat, 1947).

GIFFORD, PAUL, *Paul Valéry: Charmes* (Introductory Guides to French Literature, 30; University of Glasgow French and German Publications; Glasgow, 1995).

—— *Paul Valéry: le dialogue des choses divines* (Paris: José Corti, 1989).

—— 'Self and Other: Valéry's "Lost object of desire"', in Gifford and Stimpson (eds.), *Reading Paul Valéry*, 280–96.

—— and STIMPSON, BRIAN (eds.), *Reading Paul Valéry: Universe in Mind* (Cambridge: Cambridge University Press, 1999).

GILMAN, MARGARET, *The Idea of Poetry in France, from Houdar de la Motte to Baudelaire* (Cambridge, MA: Harvard University Press, 1958).

GOMBRICH, E. H., *Meditations on a Hobby Horse or the Roots of Artistic Form* (London: Phaidon, 1965).

GORDON, ROSEMARY, *Dying and Creating: A Search for Meaning* (London: Society of Analytical Psychology, 1978).

GUERLAC, SUZANNE, 'Valéry: chronolyse', *BEV* 76–7 (1997), 13–27.

GUIRAUD, PIERRE, *Langage et versification d'après l'œuvre de Paul Valéry: étude sur la forme poétique dans ses rapports avec la langue* (Paris: Klincksieck, 1953).

HAMBURGER, MICHAEL, *The Truth of Poetry: Tensions in Modern Poetry from Baudelaire to the 1960s* (Harmondsworth: Penguin, 1972).

HARARI, JOSUÉ (ed.), *Textual Strategies: Perspectives in Post-Structuralist Criticism* (Ithaca, NY: Cornell University Press, 1979).

HAWKES, TERENCE, *Structuralism and Semiotics* (London: Methuen, New Accents, 1977).

HEIDEGGER, MARTIN, *On the Way to Language*, trans. P. Hertz (New York: Harper San Francisco, 1982).

HILLMAN, JAMES, *Anima: An Anatomy of a Personified Notion* (Dallas: Spring Publications, 1987).

HOWE, ELISABETH, 'Feminine and Masculine Time in Valéry's Androgynous Autobiographical Poem, *La Jeune Parque*', *French Forum* 17 (1992), 37–48.

—— *Stages of Self: The Dramatic Monologues of Laforgue, Valéry and Mallarmé* (Athens, OH: Ohio University Press, 1990).

HUSSERL, EDMUND, *The Idea of Phenomenology*, trans. W. P. Alston and G. Nakhnikian (The Hague: M. Nijhoff, 1964).

HYTIER, JEAN, *La Poétique de Valéry* (Paris: Armand Colin, 1953).

—— *Questions de Littérature: études valéryennes et autres*, présentées en hommage par Columbia University au Professeur Jean Hytier à l'occasion de sa retraite (New York: Columbia University Press, 1967), 3–173.

INCE, WALTER N., 'Etre, connaître et mysticisme du réel selon Valéry', *ENC* (1968), 203–22.

—— *The Poetic Theory of Paul Valéry: Inspiration and Technique* (Leicester: Leicester University Press, 1970).

—— 'Resonance in Valéry', *Essays in French Literature* 5 (1968), 38–57.

—— 'Transcendence or Inspiration by the Back Door', *MLN* 80 (1965), 373–8.

—— 'La Voix du maître, ou moi et style selon Valéry', *Revue des sciences humaines* 129 (1968), 29–39.

IRELAND, G. W., '"La Jeune Parque" — genèse et exégèse', *ENC* (1968), 85–101.

IRIGARAY, LUCE, *Ce Sexe qui n'en est pas un* (Paris: Minuit, 1977).
—— *Ethique de la différence sexuelle* (Paris: Minuit, 1984).
—— 'La Mystérique', in *Speculum. De l'autre femme* (Paris: Minuit, 1974).
JALLAT, JEANNINE, *Introduction aux formes valéryennes* (Pisa: Pacini, 1982).
—— 'Valéry et le langage mathématique de l'identité et de la différence', *AJFS* 8 (1971), 223–9.
JARRETY, MICHEL, *Valéry devant la littérature: mesure de la limite* (Paris: Presses Universitaires de France, 1991).
JULIEN, H., 'L'Orphée meurtrier des *Cahiers*', *BEV* 24:76–7 (1997), 87–101.
JUNG, CARL G., *Man and his Symbols* (London: Aldus Books, 1979).
—— *Memories, Dreams, Reflections* (London: Collins, Fontana, 1967).
—— *Psychology and Religion* (New Haven: Yale University Press, 1938; repr. 1976).
—— *The Psychology of the Transference* (London: Routledge & Kegan Paul, 1983).
KAO, SHUHSI, *Lire Valéry* (Paris: Corti, 1985).
KEARNEY, RICHARD, *The Wake of Imagination: Ideas of Creativity in Western Culture* (London: Hutchinson, 1988).
KILLICK, RACHEL, 'La Ligne et le cercle: structures d'un serpent', *BEV* 50–1 (1989), 67–76.
KLEIN, MELANIE, *The Selected Melanie Klein*, ed. Juliet Mitchell (Harmondsworth: Penguin, 1986).
KOESTLER, ARTHUR, *The Act of Creation* (London, 1964).
KÖHLER, HARTMUT, *Paul Valéry, poésie et connaissance: l'œuvre lyrique à la lumière des 'Cahiers'*, trans. Colette Kowalski (Paris: Klincksieck, 1985).
KOURIEH, J., 'Paul Valéry créateur par la forme', *BEV* 23:71 (1996), 53–79.
KOZEL, SUSAN, 'Athikté's Voice: Listening to the Voice of the Dancer in Paul Valéry's *L'Ame et la Danse*', *Dance Research Journal* 27 (1995), 16–24.
KRAVIS, JUDITH, *The Prose of Mallarmé: The Evolution of a Literary Language* (Cambridge: Cambridge University Press, 1976).
KRISTEVA, JULIA, *Polylogue* (Paris: Seuil, 1977).
—— *Pouvoirs de l'horreur: essai sur l'abjection* (Paris: Seuil, 1980).
—— *La Révolution du langage poétique: l'avant-garde à la fin du XIXe siècle. Lautréamont et Mallarmé* (Paris: Seuil, 1974).
—— *Séméiotiké: recherches pour une sémanalyse* (Paris: Seuil, 1969).
The Kristeva Reader, ed. Toril Moi (New York: Columbia University Press, 1986).
KURZVEIL, E., and PHILLIPS, W. (eds.), *Literature and Psychoanalysis* (New York: Columbia University Press, 1983).
LACAN, JACQUES, 'Dieu et la jouissance de *LA* femme', in *Le Séminaire, Livre XX, Encore* (Paris: Seuil, 1975).
—— 'Fonction et champ de la parole et du langage en psychanalyse' and 'Le stade du miroir comme formateur de la fonction du Je', in *Ecrits I* (Paris: Seuil, 1966).

LACEY, A. R., *Bergson* (London and New York: Routledge, 1989).

LANFRANCHI, GENEVIÈVE, *Paul Valéry et l'expérience du moi pur* (Paris: Bibliothèque des arts, 1993).

LANGER, SUZANNE, *Feeling and Form: A Theory of Art* (London: Routledge & Kegan Paul, 1979).

LAURENTI, HUGUETTE, *Paul Valéry et le théâtre* (Paris: Gallimard, 1973).

LAURETTE, PIERRE, *Le Thème de l'arbre chez Paul Valéry* (Paris: Klincksieck, 1967).

LAWLER, JAMES R., *Lecture de Valéry: une étude de 'Charmes'* (Paris: Presses Universitaires de France., 1963).

―― *Paul Valéry* (Paris: Champion-Slatkine, 1991).

―― *The Poet as Analyst: Essays on Paul Valéry* (Berkeley and Los Angeles: University of California Press, 1974).

―― 'The Serpent, the Tree and the Crystal', *L'Esprit créateur* 4 (1964), 34–40.

LAYTON, L., and SCHAPIRO, B. A. (eds.), *Narcissism and the Text: Studies in Literature and the Psychology of Self* (New York: New York University Press, 1986).

LAZARIDÈS, A., *Valéry: pour une poétique du dialogue* (Montréal: Les Presses de l'Université de Montréal, 1978).

LECHANTRE, MICHEL, 'L'hiéroglyphe intérieur', *MLN* 87 (1972), 630–42.

―― 'P(h)o(n)étique', in *Cahiers Paul Valéry 2* (Paris: Gallimard, 1977), 93–122.

LECHTE, JOHN, *Julia Kristeva* (London: Routledge, 1990).

Lecture plurielle d' 'Ebauche d'un serpent'. Hommage à Walter Ince, *BEV* numéro spécial, 50–1 (1989).

LEJEUNE, PHILIPPE, *L'Autobiographie en France* (Paris: Armand Colin, 1971).

―― *Je est un autre: l'autobiographie de la littérature aux médias* (Paris: Seuil, 1980).

―― *Le Pacte autobiographique* (Paris: Seuil, 1975).

LEMAIRE, ANIKA, *Jacques Lacan*, trans. David Macey (London: Routledge & Kegan Paul, 1977).

LEVAILLANT, JEAN, '"La Jeune Parque" en question', *PVC* (1974), 137–51.

―― (ed.), *Ecriture et génétique textuelle: Valéry à l'œuvre* (Lille: Presses Universitaires, 1982).

LIVNI, ABRAHAM, *La Recherche de Dieu chez Paul Valéry* (Paris: Klincksieck, 1978).

LUSSY, FLORENCE DE, *'Charmes', d'après les manuscrits de Paul Valéry: histoire d'une métamorphose*, 2 vols. (Lettres modernes; Paris: Minard, 1990, 1996).

―― *La Genèse de 'La Jeune Parque' de Paul Valéry: essai de chronologie* (Lettres Modernes, coll. Situation, 34; Paris: Minard, 1975).

―― 'Manuscript Steps: "Les Pas"', in Gifford and Stimpson (eds.), *Reading Paul Valéry*, 200–16.

MCNIFF, SHAUN, *Art as Medicine* (London and Boston: Shambhala, 1992).

MAIRESSE-LANDES, A., 'Valéry: le thématique, le biographique', *BEV* 23: 72–3 (1996), 331–40.

MAKA-DE SCHEPPER, MONIQUE, *Le Thème de la Pythie chez Paul Valéry* (Bibliothèque de la Faculté de Philosophie et Lettres de l'Université de Liège; Liège, 1969).

MALLARMÉ, STÉPHANE, *Propos sur la poésie*, recueillis et présentés par H. Mondor (Monaco: Editions du rocher, 1953).

MAMOON, S., 'Repousser aux forêts leur épaisseur panique: échos et renvois mallarméens dans les *Fragments du Narcisse*', *BEV* 24:76–7 (1997), 103–14.

MARTIN, GRAHAM D., *Language, Truth and Poetry* (Edinburgh: Edinburgh University Press, 1975) .

—— *Paul Valéry: 'Le Cimetière marin'* (Edinburgh: Edinburgh University Press, 1971).

MAULPOIX, JEAN-MICHEL, 'Major Poems: The Voice of the Subject', in Gifford and Stimpson (eds.), *Reading Paul Valéry*, 170–86.

MAURON, CHARLES, *Des métaphores obsédantes au mythe personnel: introduction à la psychocritique* (Paris: Corti, 1963).

MERLEAU-PONTY, MAURICE, *Phénoménologie de la perception* (Paris: Gallimard, N.R.F., 1945).

—— *Signes* (Paris: Gallimard, 1960).

METZ, CHRISTIAN, 'Aural Objects', *YFS* 60 (1980), 24–32.

MITCHELL, JULIET, and ROSE, JACQUELINE (eds.), *Jacques Lacan and the Ecole Freudienne: Feminine Sexuality* (London: Macmillan, 1983).

MOSSOP, D. J., *Pure Poetry: Studies in French Poetic Theory and Practice, 1746–1945* (Oxford: Clarendon Press, 1971).

MOUTOTE, DANIEL, 'Le Moi valéryen: contribution à l'étude de l'expérience intérieure chez Paul Valéry', *BEV* 1 (1974), 17–40.

NADAL, OCTAVE, *Abeille spirituelle: poème inconnu et art poétique de Paul Valéry* (Nîmes, 1968).

NASH, SUZANNE, *Paul Valéry's 'Album de vers anciens': A Past Transfigured* (Princeton: Princeton University Press, 1983).

NEWHAM, PAUL, *The Singing Cure: An Introduction to Voice Movement Therapy* (London: Rider, 1993).

NOULET, E., *Le Ton poétique: Mallarmé, Verlaine, Corbière, Rimbaud, Valéry, Saint-John Perse* (Paris: Corti, 1971).

OLNEY, JAMES (ed.), *Autobiography: Essays Theoretical and Critical* (Princeton: Princeton University Press, 1980).

PARENT, MONIQUE, *Cohérence et résonance dans le style de 'Charmes' de Paul Valéry* (Paris: Klincksieck, 1970).

Paul Valéry contemporain: colloque organisé en nov. 1971 par le Centre National de la Recherche Scientifique et le Centre de Philologie et de Littératures Romanes de l'Université des Sciences Humaines de

Strasbourg: textes rassemblés et présentés par Monique Parent et Jean Levaillant (Paris: Klincksieck, 1974) (abbreviated *PVC*).

Paul Valéry: musique, mystique, mathématique. Textes réunis et présentés par Paul Gifford et Brian Stimpson (Lille: Presses Universitaires de Lille, 1993).

PEETERS, BENOÎT, *Paul Valéry: une vie d'écrivain?* (Paris: Les Impressions nouvelles, 1989).

PHILIPPON, M., 'Valéry et les ténèbres de l'origine', *BEV* 71 (1996), 37–51.

PICKERING, ROBERT, '*Ebauche* et écriture de la présence d'absence', *BEV* 50–1 (1989), 57–66.

—— 'Energy and Integrated Poetic Experience in the Abstract Prose of Valéry's "Cahiers"', *AJFS* 16 (1979), 244–56.

—— 'Le Lyrisme mystique chez Valéry: "Eros", "Thêta" et la prose poétique des "Cahiers"', *BEV* 26 (1981), 41–56.

—— 'Paradigms of the Self: Valéry's Mythical Models', in Gifford and Stimpson (eds.), *Reading Paul Valéry*, 53–69.

—— *Paul Valéry, poète en prose: la prose lyrique abstraite des 'Cahiers'* (Archives Paul Valéry, 5; Paris: Minard, 1983).

—— 'Valéry et le cratylisme', in Pietra (ed.), *Valéry: la philosophie, les arts, le langage.*

—— (ed.), *Paul Valéry: Se faire ou se refaire. Lecture génétique d'un cahier (1943)* (Travaux de recherche menés par l'équipe Paul Valéry de critique génétique, Institut des Textes et Manuscrits Modernes, Paris; Université Blaise-Pascal Clermont-Ferrand II, Centre de Recherches sur les Littératures Modernes et Contemporaines, 1996).

PIETRA, RÉGINE (ed.), *Valéry: la philosophie, les arts, le langage*, Groupe de recherches sur la philosophie et le langage (Grenoble: Université des sciences sociales, 1989).

PILKINGTON, A. E, *Bergson and his Influence: A Reassessment* (Cambridge: Cambridge University Press, 1976).

POULET, GEORGES, 'La Conscience valéryenne du temps', in his *Etudes sur le temps humain*, 386–99.

—— *Etudes sur le temps humain* (Paris: Plon, 1972).

PRATT, BRUCE, *Le Chant du cygne* (Paris: Corti, 1978).

—— *Rompre le silence: les premiers états de La Jeune Parque* (Paris: Corti, 1976).

—— *Chant du Cygne: édition critique des premiers états de La Jeune Parque* (Paris: Corti, 1978).

RAYMOND, MARCEL, *De Baudelaire au surréalisme* (Paris: Corti, 1952).

—— *Paul Valéry et la tentation de l'esprit* (Paris: La Presse française et étrangère, 1946).

RICHARD, JEAN P., *Onze études sur la poésie moderne* (Paris: Seuil, 1964).

RINSLER, NORMA, 'The Defence of Self: Stillness and Movement in Valéry's Poetry', *Essays in French Literature* 6 (1969), 36–56.

—— 'Ebauche d'un serpent: portrait de l'artiste en six mouvements', BEV 50–1 (1989), 77–87.

ROBINSON, JUDITH, L'Analyse de l'esprit dans les cahiers de Valéry (Paris: Corti, 1963).

—— 'L'Architecture ouverte de "La Jeune Parque"', Poétique 37 (1979), 63–82.

—— 'Ecrire la mort: les langages des affects dans l'écriture manuscrite', BEV 62 (1993), 71–88.

—— 'Le Finale du Narcisse: genèse du texte et archéologie du sentiment', in Levaillant (ed.), Ecriture, ch. 4.

—— 'Valéry, the Anxious Intellectual', AJFS 8 (1971), 118–38.

—— 'Valéry's View of Mental Creativity', YFS 44 (1970), 3–18.

ROLAND, A. (ed.), Psychoanalysis, Creativity and Literature (New York: Columbia University Press, 1978).

ROMER, STEPHEN, 'Esprit, Attente pure, éternel suspens...: Valéry's Prose Poetry', in Gifford and Stimpson (eds.), Reading Paul Valéry, 121–37.

ROSOLATO, GUY, 'La voix: entre corps et langage', in La Relation d'inconnu (Paris: Gallimard, 1978).

ROTH-MASCAGNI, PAULINE, Musique et géométrie de trois poèmes valéryens (Brussels: André de Rache, 1979).

ROUGEMONT, DENIS DE, L'Amour et l'Occident (Paris: Plon, 1939).

SABBAGH, CÉLINE, 'Calypso, a Theme of Ambiguity, a Theme of Fascination', YFS 44 (1970), 106–18.

—— 'Les Disparitions de Narcisse', PVC (1974), 153–72.

—— 'Transformations textuelles: Le sourire funèbre', in Levaillant (ed.), Ecriture, 133–56.

SCARFE, FRANCIS, The Art of Paul Valéry: A Study in Dramatic Monologue (London: William Heinemann, Glasgow University Publications, 1954).

SCHMIDT-RADEFELDT, JÜRGEN, Paul Valéry linguiste dans les Cahiers (Paris: Klincksieck, 1970).

—— 'Valéry et les sciences du langage', Poétique 31 (1977), 368–85.

SCRUTON, ROGER, Art and Imagination (London: Methuen, 1974).

SEARLE, J. R. (ed.), The Philosophy of Language (London: Oxford University Press, 1971).

SEGAL, NAOMI, Narcissus and Echo: Women in the French Récit (Manchester: Manchester University Press, 1988).

SEWELL, ELIZABETH, Paul Valéry: The Mind in the Mirror (Cambridge: Bowes & Bowes, 1952).

SHERINGHAM, MICHAEL, French Autobiography: Devices and Desires; Rousseau to Perec (Oxford: Clarendon Press, 1993).

SILVERMAN, KAJA, The Acoustic Mirror: The Female Voice in Psychoanalysis and Cinema (Bloomington, IN: Indiana University Press, 1988).

SOLLERS, PHILIPPE, *L'Ecriture et l'expérience des limites* (Paris: Seuil, 1968).
STEEL, DAVID, 'Les Débuts de la psychanalyse dans les lettres françaises: 1914–1922', *RHLF* 1 (1979), 62–89.
STEINER, GEORGE, *Language and Silence: Essays, 1958–1966* (Harmondsworth: Penguin, 1969).
STIMPSON, BRIAN, 'An Aesthetics of the Subject: Music and the Visual Arts', in Gifford and Stimpson (eds.), *Reading Paul Valéry*, 219–35.
—— 'Counter-fiction', in Gifford and Stimpson (eds.), *Reading Paul Valéry*, 138–54.
—— 'L'Espace parmi: une rhétorique de l'ambiguité', *BEV* 50–1 (1989), 45–56.
—— *Paul Valéry and Music* (Cambridge: Cambridge University Press, 1984).
STORR, ANTHONY, *The Dynamics of Creation* (Harmondsworth: Penguin, 1976).
STURROCK, JOHN (ed.), *Structuralism and Since* (Oxford: Oxford University Press, 1979).
SUCKLING, NORMAN, *Paul Valéry and the Civilized Mind* (Oxford: Oxford University Press, 1954).
TAYLOR, MARK, *Disfiguring: Art, Architecture, Religion* (Chicago: University of Chicago Press, 1992).
TODOROV, TZVETAN, *Littérature et signification* (Paris: Larousse, 1967).
TOMATIS, ALFRED, *L'Oreille et le langage* (Paris: Seuil, 1978).
TSUKAMOTO, M., 'La Notion de l'"Implexe" dans le Cahier no. 240', in Pickering (ed.), *Paul Valéry: Se faire ou se refaire*, 97–107.
UBERSFELD, A., 'Lust ou la voix de l'autre', *Littérature* 56 (1984), 56–74.
ULLMANN, STEPHEN, *Language and Style: Collected Papers* (Oxford: Basil Blackwell, 1964).
Un nouveau regard sur Valéry: rencontres de Cérisy du 26 août au 5 sept. 1992. Textes réunis par Nicole Celeyrette-Pietri et Brian Stimpson (Lettres modernes; Paris: Minard, 1995).
UNDERHILL, EVELYN, *Mysticism: A Study in the Nature and Development of Man's Spiritual Consciousness* (London: Methuen & Co., 1911).
VAUGHAN-LEE, LLEWELLYN, *The Lover and the Serpent: Dreamwork within a Sufi Tradition* (Shaftesbury: Element Books, 1990).
VERNON, PAUL (ed.), *Creativity* (Penguin Modern Psychology Readings; Harmondsworth: Penguin, 1976).
WALZER, PIERRE O., 'Fragments d'esthésique', *AJFS* 8 (1971), 230–42.
—— 'Lettres closes: Paul Valéry à Catherine Pozzi', *RHLF* 90 (1990), 965–73.
—— 'Valéry: deux essais sur l'amour; Béatrice et Stratonice', *RHLF* 68 (1968), 66–86.
WARNOCK, MARY, *Imagination* (London: Faber and Faber, 1976).

WEINBERG, KURT, *The Figure of Faust in Valéry and Goethe* (Princeton: Princeton University Press, 1976).

WHITING, CHARLES, 'Femininity in Valéry's Early Poetry', *YFS* 9 (1965), 74–83.

—— 'Sexual Imagery in "La Jeune Parque" and "Charmes"', *Publications of the Modern Language Association of America* 86 (1971), 940–5.

YATES, FRANCES A., *The Art of Memory* (London: Routledge & Kegan Paul, 1966).

YESCHUA, SILVIO, *Valéry, le roman et l'œuvre à faire* (Lettres modernes; Paris: Minard, 1976).

INDEX